OWL

Environmental Problems: Nature, Economy and State

R.J. Johnston

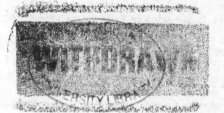

Belhaven Press
A division of Pinter Publishers
London and New York

For Rita

© R.J. Johnston 1989

First published in Great Britain in 1989 by
Belhaven Press (a division of Pinter Publishers),
25 Floral Street, London WC2E 9DS

British Library Cataloguing in Publication Data

A CIP catalogue record for this book is available from the
British Library

ISBN 1-85293-000-4   6008658034

Library of Congress Cataloging-in-Publication Data

A CIP catalog record for this book is available from the
Library of Congress

Filmset by Mayhew Typesetting, Bristol, England
Printed and bound by Biddles Ltd of Guildford and Kings Lynn

Contents

List of Figures

Preface

If many environmentalists are guilty of ignoring the importance of
political economy and the need to understand the role of state
institutions, it is equally evident that most post-industrial theorists
give little attention to environmental issues, let alone the political
economy of militarism and Third World exploitation. (Boris
Frankel, *The Post-Industrial Utopians*, 1987, p.145).

This book is not a normal study of environmental problems, because its
focus is neither the mechanisms of problem generation nor a series of case
studies on how such problems can be tackled. Rather it is an essay about
the production of such problems and the difficulties we face in tackling
them, individually and, especially, collectively. Its goal is to bring some of
the central material of social science about the ways in which economies
work and politics operate to the attention of students of environmental
problems, in a format that is relevant to their major concern.

Why write such a book? In 1979 I published the first edition of a book
entitled *Geography and Geographers: Anglo-American Human Geography since
1945*, in which I defended my decision to write about human geography
only as follows:

> I find the links between physical and human geography tenuous, as
> those disciplines are currently practised. The major link between
> them is a sharing of techniques and research procedures, but these are
> shared with other disciplines too, and are insufficient foundation for
> a unified discipline . . . . To a considerable extent . . . human and
> physical are separate, if not independent, disciplines. (Johnston
> 1979b, p.2).

This was attacked by some commentators, though not in published
reviews, and some even suggested that I did the discipline of geography a
political disservice by hinting that such a split existed. I defended that position in the second (1983, p.6) and third (1987) editions of the book,
however, and will continue to do so in the fourth (1990).

Some of the critics suggested that I was ignoring a large literature which
clearly demonstrated the human–physical symbiosis, especially in the fields
of resource and environmental management. I responded to this view in a
paper that, but for environmental circumstances (heavy snow), would have
been delivered at the Institute of British Geographers' annual conference at
Southampton in January 1982, and was published in *Progress in Physical
Geography* a year later, under the title 'Resource analysis, resource management and the integration of physical and human geography'. This made
two major points. Firstly, it demonstrated that neither group of

geographers working on issues of resource management – the so-called human:physical interface – took much account of the work of the other, and that indeed some of the human geographers whose work was frequently presented to me as indicative of the richness of that interface (Gilbert White and his co-workers, for example) referenced virtually no work that could be identified as physical geography. Secondly, I argued that human and physical geographers, in their search for accounts of what they observed and described, were increasingly using different conceptions of the nature of science whose epistemologies were mutually incompatible. Integration of the two was thus not feasible (as I had learned to my cost in an earlier published debate – Johnston, 1980b, 1982b; Eyles and Lee, 1982 – on the possibility of eclecticism within human geography). This was not intended as an attempt to separate human and physical geography institutionally, but merely to point out to physical geographers that the two parts of the discipline were philosophically distinct and thus could not be integrated and also that most of their writings at the interface failed to appreciate the nature of research in human geography. David Jones (1983, p.455) interpreted that as revealing 'such a depth of antipathy towards the "integration ethic", that it is quite possible that *collaborative* research will also be viewed as an unwelcome development'.

The debate continued, and was highlighted at another session at the annual conference of the Institute of British Geographers, at Reading in January 1986 (it snowed again). Four papers were presented in a session organised by Elspeth Graham and these were published, along with her commentary, in the Institute's *Transactions* later that year. In his contribution, Ian Douglas called on geographers to use their detailed research findings and methods to address the 'big issues' – of which he cited the nuclear winter controversy as an example – claiming that when they did 'the unity of geography is obvious' (1986, p.462; for a similar, more trenchantly stated view see Stoddart, 1987): that unity comes through, he said, 'in the complexity of the problems, the intricacy and ramifications of the interactions' (p.462). Alongside him, Andrew Goudie (1986b) identified five main arguments for the separation of human and physical geography: human geography is concerned with analysing spatial patterns of human activity and has little need to be concerned with the physical environment; the physical environment is becoming less important as a control on human activity; specialisation in science is necessary to rigorous development; geomorphologists would be better off in geoscience and human geography in social science; and physical geographers have failed to demonstrate the relevance of their work to human affairs because they have not been concerned with human processes. He argued against the fragmentation of the discipline. In my contribution (Johnston, 1986c) I suggested that the physical:human split debate was based on a semantic misunderstanding (an argument that Glick, 1987, at least found 'a revelation'). I suggested that the word geography has two major uses: a *vernacular* use which refers to the discipline's subject matter (so that to speak of physical geography is to speak of the physical environment); and an *academic* use which refers to activity within the discipline (so that physical geography is the study of the processes, and the forms that result from them, within the physical environment). Much writing confuses those usages. Many human geographers writing about physical geography use the latter term in its vernacular sense, for example, because they are not interested in the physical processes: as I put it 'the (human) academic geographer interested in population distributions is no more interested in the causes of the physical environment (such as the operation of jet streams) than in how a television works, and so is not interested in physical (academic) geography, only physical (vernacular) geography' (1986c, p.450). Each type of geographer needs the vernacular of the other in certain circumstances, I contended, but this does not produce an integration of the two academic concerns: if that point can be accepted, I concluded, 'I don't see the physical:human issue as important, therefore, and I am relatively content with the present accommodation' (1986c, p.450), and I do not for one moment dissent from Douglas, Goudie and Stoddart pointing us all to the 'big issues'.

I fear, however, that while the debate has not yet erupted again it has not gone away, and I also fear that my position remains misunderstood. Goudie (1986b, p.457), for example, noted that I 'criticized' (his term, not mine: see Johnston, 1983, pp. 134–5) 'some physical geographers for not taking sufficient cognizance of social factors and processes'. He responded to that by listing a large number of studies – 'an outpouring of material by physical geographers' – which explored the 'highly important interface area between man [sic] and nature'. True; but none of them deal with both academic human geography and academic physical geography – most incorporate vernacular human geography only. I do not criticise them for that. But I do argue that, as a collectivity, physical geographers have yet to come to terms with many of the epistemological issues that human geographers have been tackling in the last two decades. As a consequence, their treatment of why the 'big issues' are present – why we create environmental problems – and why we are apparently not doing very well at solving them, does not address the important issues of causation.

Hence this book, which is an attempt to bring to geographers and all others interested in the creation and potential removal of environmental problems the relevant understanding from human geography and related social sciences. Initially it was to have been written with a physical geographer but, not for the first time in my academic career, a potential co-author and I decided amicably to go our separate ways. (This resulted in the salutary experience of my having to read more contemporary physical geography than I otherwise would have done, which I found extremely stimulating.) Thus the focus here is on two basic questions: (1) why do we create so many environmental problems?; and (2) why, despite all our scientific knowledge and a great deal of pressure, are we not very good at solving them? The bulk of the book addresses these questions, the first through the medium of political economy (Chapters 3 and 4) and the second through the study of the state and collective action, at all scales (Chapters 5 and 6). First, however, the need for the approach is set in context by two introductory chapters, one dealing with the nature of the problems as they are currently perceived in vernacular debate and how they reflect the conventional wisdom about the interrelationships between peoples and environments, and the other with a very brief summary of the nature of scientific understanding of the environment, very necessary to an appreciation of the need for, and constraints on, collective action via the state.

The purpose of the book is thus to contribute to the literature on the 'big issues' by bringing together important material from the social sciences, as it relates to the study of environmental problems. It is not meant to present a scenario for the future, my solution to the problems, and so the final chapter, 'Alternative Futures', is relatively brief, setting out the major scenarios currently under discussion and putting them in the context of the material that has gone before. My general pessimism undoubtedly comes through, but I am not (yet) a fatalist.

Why add to the literature? In large part because I believe that the task as I conceived it has not been undertaken before. There are many excellent books that do part of the job, notably that of looking at environmental problems from the political economy standpoint, but none that cover both political economy and the state in the way that is done here. It is thus presented not as an innovative contribution but as a needed overview of some important issues.

This book was written in the first three months of 1989, when I was on study leave from the University of Sheffield, between laying down one large administrative burden and taking up another (potentially larger). I am grateful to the Department of Geography, the Faculty of Social Sciences, and the various university committees for that brief period of relative quiet, and in particular to Alan Hay for all that he did to try and ensure that it was as quiet as possible; at least it meant that I could learn the intricacies of word-processing at home in relative tranquillity. Many people stimulated me to write this book, in a variety of ways; I am especially grateful to Ron Cooke and Steve Trudgill, though they are totally absolved from responsibility for anything I have said, and to Peter Smithson who tried to ensure that I didn't misrepresent the work of physical geographers; he, too, is totally absolved. A particular expression of gratitude is to Iain Stevenson, who was a continual source of encouragement and helped me through more rough passages than probably either he or I care to remember.

This book is dedicated to Rita. That I have now written as many books as the years we have shared is a poor expression of thanks for so much contentment.

Acknowledgements

The publisher and author are grateful to the following for permission to reproduce copyright material:

Prof. R.J. Bennett for figure 2.1; Dr. S.T. Trudgill for figure 2.2; Prof. R.J. Chorley for figures 2.3, 2.4, and 2.7; Dr. R.J. Huggett and Blackwell Scientific for figure 2.5; Dr R.J. Huggett for figures 2.6 and 2.8; Prof. J.B. Thornes for figures 2.9, 2.11 and 2.13; Dr. J. Gleick for figure 2.10; Prof. A.G. Wilson for figure 2.12; Prof. A.S. Goudie and Prof. R.U. Cooke for figure 2.14; Prof. A.S. Goudie for figures 2.15 and 4.3; Prof. D. Harvey for figure 3.1; Prof. P.R. Gould for figure 4.1; Dr. P. Blaikie for figure 4.2; Prof. T. O'Riordan for figure 6.3.

Chapter 1
Introduction

The world is dying. What are you going to do about it? (*The Sunday Times Magazine*, cover, 26 February 1989)

Environmental problems moved rapidly to a high position on the British political agenda in late 1988 and early 1989, gaining a great deal of media attention – which undoubtedly stimulated interest as well as reported it. Thus, for example, of three magazines on the news-stands in the first week of March 1989, *The Listener* (9 March) carried HRH The Duke of Edinburgh's Dimbleby Lecture (delivered on BBC1 TV three days earlier) entitled 'Living off the land'; *Marxism Today* (March) had a major article on 'Green times'; and *Living Marxism* (March) followed up its lead article of the previous month, 'Can capitalism go green', with articles on both 'What's gone wrong with the German greens?' and 'An ozone-free zone?'.

The newspapers, too, carried an increasing volume of stories and articles addressing the general issues, with many carrying an implicit if not explicit message of impending ecological doom. In *The Independent* on 12 September 1988, for example, Lloyd Timberlake had an article entitled 'The greatest threat on earth' whose thesis was that 'ecological disaster will replace nuclear war as the biggest danger in the twenty-first century' (p.19). The *Guardian* for 7 February 1989 reported on 'The stripping of China's good earth', claiming that topsoil was being lost at the rate of 5 billion tonnes per annum (equivalent to losing a one-centimetre layer of all topsoil from the country's arable land since the revolution in 1949). This rate was believed to be twice that of the USSR and three times that of the USA; *The Observer* reported a week earlier, however, not only that India was losing 12 billion tons per annum but also that 'nearly half of Britain's arable topsoil is in danger of being blown and washed away by wind and rain' (p.31: 'Soil erosion sweeps shires'). And special features identified the culprits: *The Sunday Times* devoted two pages of its 26 February 1989 issue to an analysis of increased water pollution in Britain, under the title 'The water rats'; and a four-page special report in the *Guardian* for 24 February 1989, 'The darkening skies', presented the argument that atmospheric pollution 'may be inexorably altering the climate of the globe' (p.16).

The general tenor of all the articles conveys two main points: (1) the earth is facing an ecological crisis of unheralded proportions; and (2) governments must take action to stop that crisis coming about (as in *The Independent*'s story of 6 February 1989 that 'The Dutch think green for queen and country', reporting on the Queen's Christmas broadcast there which went into the ecological crisis and challenged the country's government to become 'green').

The goal of much that is written (and presented in the other media) is to scare, and the analysis is rarely deep. Thus the special issue of *The Sunday Times Magazine* (26 February 1989) describes the parameters of the crisis and blames humans for it, but fails to recognise why we are doing what we are doing to the earth. Thus:

> You damage the earth just by living on it. You burn fossil fuels – petrol, oil, coal – and huge amounts more are burnt by those who supply you with goods and services. You create waste, which has to be buried, burnt or discharged into the sea. You accept the profits of investments which are trading on Third World poverty and putting further strain on already over-stretched resources. You buy goods from farms and factories whose ill-effects from chemical wastes range all the way from dead fish to dead people. (p.20)

The blame, it seems, is on the individual, with the implication that individuals control situations, both through their own actions and through the political pressure they can bring to bear:

> For decades the health of the planet has been the obsessive concern of a highly vocal and occasionally irritating minority. Now it is at the top of the world's political agenda . . . . It is your world they are talking about. Your future that is in their hands. If you are concerned about your environment, you will want to know what you can do.

But is it all that easy?

This book was begun before the 'great leap forward' in public and political concern in Britain about environmental issues, but it was formulated to answer that selfsame question. Yet the stimulus to address the question came not from the media, but from an academic literature which, while not as provocative as the 'popular' presentations, nevertheless seemed to be just as naive, in general, as they are. In brief, much of the literature surveyed failed to provide any deep analysis of why we are generating the environmental problems that are becoming increasingly apparent, and why we don't seem to tackle them very effectively. That literature fails to draw on the social sciences, whose understanding of society provides the needed analysis. Thus this book is presented as an outline of the relevant understanding provided by social science that can contribute to an appreciation of how environmental problems are generated and what the political constraints to tackling them are.

People and Environment

At the heart of the set of issues that are faced here is the interrelationship of people and their environment. The nature of that interrelationship and its variations in time and space has produced a substantial scholarly literature (notably the seminal volume by Glacken, 1967). The present situation, and the growth of an environmental consciousness among the population of many countries, suggests a change in the interpretation of that relationship. The present chapter traces the foundations of that change, as an introduction to the rest of the book.

People, Environment and the 'Human Ascendancy'

At the beginning of his major work *Traces on the Rhodian Shore*, Clarence Glacken identifies three questions that have persistently been posed in human societies:

(1) Was the earth purposefully created for human habitation?
(2) Has the nature of the earth influenced the moulding of individual characteristics and of human cultures?
(3) In what manner have people changed the environment during their long tenure of the earth? (1967, p.vii)

The usual answers provided three ideas: that 'the planet is designed for man [sic] alone, as the highest being of the creation, or for the hierarchy of life with man at the apex'; that all life adapts itself to 'the purposefully created harmonious conditions'; and that 'man through his arts and inventions was . . . a partner of God, improving upon and cultivating an earth created for him' (p.viii). From these, Glacken argues that:

> in Western thought until the end of the eighteenth century, concepts of the relationship of human culture to the natural environment were dominated – but not exclusively so – by these three ideas, sometimes by only one of them, sometimes by two or even the three in combination . . . . This group of ideas and certain subsidiary ideas which gathered around them were part of the matrix from which in modern times the social sciences have emerged . . . . In Western civilization these three ideas have played an important role in the attempt to understand man, his culture, and the natural environment in which he lives . . . . (1967, p.viii)

The remainder of Glacken's book provides a rich series of illustrations and analyses of the changing relative importance of those ideas in Western thought. The treatment is largely chronological, and shows how over time the second and third ideas came to dominate, justifying the view of 'man as a controller of nature' and heralding the twentieth century in which 'man has attained a breathtaking anthropocentrism, based on his power over nature, unmatched by anything in the past' (p.494).

Western thought is dominantly Judaeo-Christian in its origins and content; in its early development, Glacken shows, much of it was concerned with linking the two creations – of humanity and of earth (p.151). The basic theme to emerge from that work was of a caring God – caring for the earth and all those who occupy it. Within that earth, 'man has a divine mission to control the whole creation. To achieve this, it is God's intention that mankind multiply itself, spread out over the earth, make its domination over the creation secure' (p.151). This was developed, and in medieval Christianity was formulated into the belief that 'man created in God's image has by God's grace dominion over all nature' (p.293).

The development of human civilisations was 'virtually synonymous with the conquest of nature' according to Thomas (1984, 25) – who illustrates the point by noting that the 30 copies of the Gutenberg Bible printed on vellum in 1456 used the skins of 5000 calves, thereby indicating the dependence of progress on the control of animal resources. That conquest was justified, Thomas argues, by the presentation of the human species as innately different from and superior to all others and, as Glacken had also shown, the justification was provided through particular readings of the Bible. But, as Thomas shows, acceptance of that view created dilemmas for some people during the eighteenth century, because the treatment of plants and, especially, animals offended their aesthetic and moral sensibilities:

> This was the human dilemma: how to reconcile the physical require-ments of civilization with the new feelings and values which that same civilization had generated . . . there had gradually emerged attitudes to the natural world which were essentially incompatible with the direc-tion in which English society was moving. The growth of towns had led to a new longing for the countryside. The progress of cultivation had fostered a taste for weeds, mountains and unsubdued nature. The new-found security from wild animals had generated an increasing concern to protect birds and preserve wild creatures in their natural state. Economic independence of animal power and urban isolation from animal farming had nourished emotional attitudes which were hard, if not impossible, to reconcile with the exploitation of animals by which most people lived. (1984, p.301)

This dilemma continued to develop through the nineteenth and twentieth centuries, until it was overtaken by another which questioned the role of 'man' in 'God's plan' and brought the idea of the 'conquest of nature' into sharp debating focus.

Conquest and Challenge

The nineteenth and twentieth centuries have produced massive changes in the relationships between human societies and the natural environment, with the dominant theme being the conquest of the latter by the former – despite some occasional set-backs. This has been sustained by an ideology in the West founded in the Christian doctrines enunciated above, and advanced through the belief that human creativity and ingenuity is such that it can surmount any difficulties that the environment might place in the way of its search for material advancement – after all, we have now conquered the moon, and will soon extend human sovereignty to other planets.

This outlook has been termed *technocentrism* by O'Riordan (1981a) and *technological environmentalism* by Pepper (1984). According to O'Riordan, technocentrism dominates capitalist ideology, and is identified by the values of rationality, managerial efficiency, optimism and faith:

faith in the ability of man [sic] to understand and control physical, biological, and social processes for the benefit of present and future generations. Progress, efficiency, rationality, and control – these form the ideology of technocentrism that downplays the sense of wonder, reverence, and moral obligation that are the hallmarks of the ecocentric mode. (1981a, p.11)

Central to this faith is the role of science, which provides the intelligence for the rational control of the environment – not only the physical science which provides the means of manipulating nature but also the social (especially economic) science which evaluates that manipulation in a common metric, money. Thus if, as some argue, manipulation of nature is creating problems and dilemmas, then this calls for greater investment in and application of science in order to advance human desires (Pepper, 1984).

The main opposition to this technocentric ideology until recent years has come from two strands of what Pepper calls ecological environmentalism. The first of these – what Pepper calls the 'non-scientific' strand – grew out of the 'moral and aesthetic sensibilities' to the 'conquest of nature' identified by Thomas. It contains within it a strong romantic element – defined by Pepper as rejecting materialism: 'Romantics noticed and hated the way that industrialisation made previously beautiful places ugly, and they rejected the vulgarity of those who made money in trade' (1984, p.76). To them, nature was independent of people, with its own integrity and ability to survive: respect for that integrity required human 'guardianship' of nature – 'man should be the steward even of those parts of nature for which he has no obvious use or need' (p.89).

Alongside this romantic ecological environmentalism – for which O'Riordan's term is ecocentrism – there is a scientific strand which has promoted, in a variety of ways, the view that there are limits to the capacity of the earth to cope with human demands upon it. Pepper identifies its origins with Malthus, traces its development in the concept of environmental systems (see Chapter 2) and the arguments for environmental conservation (of which George Perkins Marsh is frequently presented as an initiator: Lowenthal, 1965), and its culmination in the environmental models predicting ecological disaster, such as *The Limits to Growth* (Meadows et al., 1972). It is that culmination which is crucial here, since it provided the means of bringing together the two strands in a late twentieth-century ecological environmentalism.

Contemporary Ecological Environmentalism

The *ecocentric* mode of thinking, drawing on the romantic, non-scientific ecological environmentalism, has five major characteristics, according to

O'Riordan:

(1) It identifies a *natural morality*, a set of rules for human behaviour within the limits and constraints of natural ecosystems.
(2) It specifies the existence of *limits* to human activity, and hence to 'progress'.
(3) It promotes the protection of *options*, by maintaining the diversity and stability of ecosystems.
(4) It raises questions about *ends and means*, and thus about the political processes through which power is exercised and decisions about environmental use are promulgated.
(5) It preaches *self-reliance and self-sufficiency*, with anarchic communities that can respond flexibly to changing circumstances, avoiding the vulnerability of dependence on large corporations and trade. (1981a, pp.10–11)

The five are given different weight by different advocates, leading to a division of ecocentrics into two groups (O'Riordan, 1981b; Pepper, 1984). Both lack faith in technology, elite experts and centralised states as the source of solutions to environmental problems, and criticise materialist growth when pursued for its own sake. But whereas the *deep ecologists* promote the concept of a human society conforming to ecological laws the *self-reliance, soft technologists* focus more on the anarchist solution.

Against these two groups in contemporary society are ranged two types of technocentrist. The *environmental managers* (or accommodaters; O'Riordan, 1981a, p.376) believe that growth can continue if properly organised whereas the *cornucopians* (Cotgrove, 1982) are even more optimistic regarding human capabilities, have faith in scientific and technological expertise and believe that 'man can always find a way out of any difficulties whether political, scientific or technological . . . all impediments can be overcome given a will, ingenuity and sufficient resources arising out of growth' (Pepper, 1984, p.31).

The Contemporary Conflict

There has been conflict between ecocentric and technocentric environmentalists for at least the last hundred years, and both the early 'green politics' (Gould, 1988) and the development of town and country planning (Hall, 1988) owe much to the successes of the romantic ecocentrics. But recent decades have seen the escalation of the conflict to a central place on the political agenda of the so-called 'developed countries' of the world at least. The reason for this is somewhat paradoxical, for it is the findings of some scientists which have brought into question the foundations of the technocentric mode of thought, and especially its cornucopian strand. Science is revered in that strand as the source of human conquest of nature, and yet some scientists are now not only producing theories which put the notion of conquest into question but are also campaigning for changes within society that will slow, if not halt, the creation and exacerbation of environmental problems. Their concern is aided by enhanced public awareness of those problems, and is taken up by a range of others who, for their own reasons, wish to promote major social change.

Conflicts can be of two types. The first are those which are capable of solution – there is one right answer, and all the rest are wrong. The second are those which can be resolved – with an accommodation accepted by all the parties – but not solved, because there is no right answer. Most of the environmental problems that we face today are treated as in the second category. It may be that in the fullness of time they shift to the first, but at present there is much debate over the scientific findings – within the scientific community itself – and few fully verified theories of how the environment works (perhaps, as laid out in the next chapter, because of its great complexity, if not its inherent mystery). Thus before resolutions can be agreed upon, the existence of a problem has to be accepted. Increasingly, the latter is taking place, but not at sufficient speed according to many promoting the ecocentric view. Thus we have conflict over whether we are creating environmental problems and how serious they are, and only then over how we may solve (not resolve) them.

Academic contributions to the literature on these conflicts are of three types: those largely supporting the technocentric view, those favouring the ecocentric, and those which do not take a position but seek to analyse both. There are few in the last category, because most analysts, implicitly if not explicitly, are convinced by one of the others. Among them, the ecocentric dominates. Catton, for example, has written widely on the sociological implications of the carrying capacity of the earth being reached (e.g. Catton 1978, 1987), and has concluded that: 'Present human gratification is being achieved at the cost of environmental changes that ensure future human deprivation' (1983, p.298). He disputes the views of the technocentrics like Simon and Kahn, who believe that because of human ingenuity the term carrying capacity 'has by now no useful meaning' (1984, p.45). Catton contends that because of achievements in death control over the last century people received 'a magnificent blessing' but the resulting benefits 'helped us overshoot a permanent carrying capacity' (1985, p.83); it allowed *homo sapiens* to become translated into *homo colossus*, sustained by a 'myth of limitlessness' and leading us to 'rush toward a lemming-like fate without pausing to discern it' (p.84). We need a clearer definition of carrying capacity which is future-based rather than present-oriented: 'Carrying capacity means, for a given environment, the amount of use that can be exceeded only by impairing that environment's future suitability for that use' (Catton et al., 1986, p.180).

With that definition, and with the scientific evidence increasingly being made available, we would then conclude that the technocentric view is not sustainable and would promote an ecocentric future:

> ecologically realistic sociological analyses could sustain a measure of optimism by helping decision-makers understand the basic forces that shape societal systems, better anticipate impending problems, and more efficiently struggle to preserve and extend the resource base of our own

and other societies. (Catton et al., 1986, p.185)

From these premises, Catton seeks to build a new paradigm for his discipline, sociology; his arguments apply equally well to geography and other sciences and social sciences. The dominant paradigm in sociology at the present time, according to Catton and Dunlap (1980), is one of *human exceptionalism* which is based on the *dominant Western worldview*, which they characterise by four major assumptions:

(1) About the *nature of human beings* – people are fundamentally different from all other creatures on earth, over which they have dominion.
(2) About the *nature of social causation* – people can determine their own destinies, can choose their goals and learn whatever is necessary to achieve them.
(3) About the *context of human society* – the world is vast and provides unlimited opportunities for humans.
(4) About the *constraints on human society* – the history of human society is one of progress; there is a solution to every problem, and progress need never cease. (1980, p.34)

The human exceptionalism paradigm follows these dominant views entirely, by assuming that: both genetically and culturally humans are quite unlike all other animal species; social and cultural factors are the predominant determinants of human affairs; social and cultural environments provide the major contexts for human affairs, and the biophysical environment is largely irrelevant; and culture is cumulative, so that social and technological progress can continue indefinitely. They promote an opposing, new ecological paradigm, built on the following four assumptions (corresponding again to those of the dominant Western worldview):

(1) Humans have exceptional characteristics but remain one among many in an interdependent global ecosystem.
(2) Human affairs are influenced not only by social and cultural factors but also by the complex interactions in the web of nature, so that human actions can have many unintended consequences.
(3) Humans are dependent on a finite biophysical environment which sets physical and biological limits to human affairs.
(4) 'Although the inventiveness of humans and the power derived therefrom may seem for a while to extend carrying capacity limits, ecological laws cannot be repealed'. (Catton and Dunlap, 1980, p.34)

Similar cases have been made in other disciplines, not least in geography.

If we are convinced by, or at least feel some sympathy with, arguments such as Catton's regarding the carrying capacity of the earth, and are attracted to the ecocentric set of attitudes, then we need to understand why it is that we continue to press so hard against the carrying capacity constraints and why we don't promote actions which will relieve the strain – or more accurately, since clearly some actions are being taken, why it is that insufficient action has been taken to ensure that the ecological future of human society is being ensured. O'Riordan argues that there have been considerable advances since the nascent stage in the evolution of environmental strategies in the early 1970s but:

> Whether these reforms have actually altered the basic philosophies of the twentieth-century financial, corporate, trade-union, and political establishment is very much open to doubt, but at least innovations in procedure and analysis have occurred to the benefit of environmentally orientated decision-making. (1981a, p.372)

The media coverage of nearly a decade later reviewed at the start of this chapter suggests some wider appreciation of the issues since, but still indicates a need for deeper analysis of both the reasons for the problems that we have created and continue to create, and the ways forward that are available. With regard to the first of these issues, the argument of the present book is that an understanding of the origins of environmental problems must be found in the discipline of political economy, hence the concentration in Chapters 3 and 4 on modes of economic organisation. Regarding the second issue, most writers accept that individual desires are insufficient and that environmental problems must be tackled collectively – thus Fernie and Pitkethly write that:

> all resource problems – overpopulation, hunger, poverty, fuel shortages, deforestation – are fundamentally *institutional* problems which warrant institutional solutions. The success or failure of resource management is intrinsically tied up with institutional structures – the pattern of agencies, laws and policies which pertain to resource issues. (1985, p.vii)

Thus we need to appreciate the nature of collective action, the basis of those institutional structures; this is the focus of Chapters 5 and 6 of the present book.

The heart of this book, therefore, is not environmental problems but rather the conditions that lead to their production and the constraints on collective action in the search both to solve current problems and to ensure that new ones do not appear. Nevertheless, a clear introductory presentation of the environmental context is necessary, to establish the case for collective action, and this is provided in Chapter 2. Finally, although the book does not pretend to offer a blueprint for the future, Chapter 7 briefly reviews the major arguments about how political economy and collective action may be structured in the future, on the assumption that the case against the technocentric view is accepted.

Chapter 2
Environmental Systems

We live in a world that has been built by our ancestors, ancient and modern, and which is continuously maintained by all things alive today. Organisms are adapting in a world whose material state is determined by the activities of their neighbours ... (James Lovelock, *The Ages of Gaia*, 1988, p.33)

The physical environment of the earth has been the subject of a great deal of study by geographers and other environmental scientists. The details of their research findings are not of particular interest here, since this book is concerned not so much with examples of individual environments and how they work as with the generality of their findings. The focus here is on environmental systems (a concept which became increasingly popular with physical geographers from 1970 on: see Gregory, 1985), on the interdependence of all the myriad parts of the environment (its lithosphere, biosphere and atmosphere), on the changes in that interdependence, and on the role of human action in creating such changes. This then allows an appreciation of the nature of most (if not all) environmental issues and on the need for collective action if they are to be countered.

The Nature of Systems

Simply defined, a system is a set of linked components. The individual components need not all be linked directly to each other, but all are connected through indirect links. This can be illustrated by a simple example of an island ecosystem (Figure 2. 1; adapted from Bennett and Chorley, 1978, who derived it from Rykiel and Kuenzel, 1971). Initial focus is on the three system components in the central box of the diagram. In this, there is no direct link between the wolf population and the volume of plant biomass on the island, since wolves are carnivores and don't consume plant matter. However, the carnivorous wolves are dependent on the volume of biomass indirectly, since they are predatory on the moose population which is herbivorous. Thus the greater the amount of plant biomass, the greater

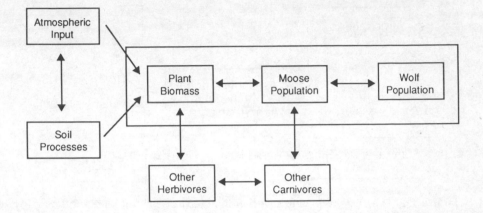

Figure 2.1 A simplified model of an ecosystem: Isle Royale (adapted from Bennett and Chorley, 1978, p.346)

the moose population that can be supported, and the larger the potential wolf population as a consequence.

This simple example not only illustrates the nature of indirect links but also can be used to indicate the complexity of the interrelationships within even a small ecosystem. Outside the two links isolated in the central box of Figure 2.1 is a large number of other links. The amount of plant biomass available to the moose population is a function both of the amount produced and of the competition with other herbivores. Atmospheric processes influence the production of biomass, both directly through the provision of energy and precipitation and indirectly through the provision of nutrients derived from the soil, whose constitution is partly a function of weathering processes on the local bedrock. Thus the size of the wolf population is indirectly linked to what goes on in both the atmospheric system and the soil system. It is also a function of the competition between the moose population and other herbivores for the available biomass – the more successful the moose in that competition the more wolves that can be supported – and also of its competition with other carnivores for moose – the more competitors there are, and the more successful they are, the smaller the wolf population.

Figure 2.1 has been used to provide a basic illustration of the nature of systems only. Most systems are much more complex than that, but the basic features are the same. It provides a foundation for the remainder of this chapter.

Types of System

In the search for the general principles of system structure and operation, much has been done to characterise systems and classify them. As indicated earlier, one way of classifying the systems is according to the part of the environment they occupy, and the basic division is between those in the

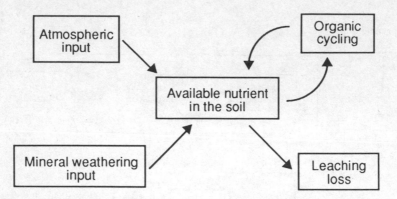

Figure 2.2 The system links involved in the study of soil nutrients (Source Trudgill, 1988)

atmosphere, the biosphere and the the lithosphere. This division would seem to match the basic division of physical geography into climatology, biogeography and geomorphology. But there are difficulties of definition here: where does the study of the soil fall – in geomorphology, in biogeography, or in both? The answer must be that the question is largely irrelevant because, as the structure of Trudgill's *Soil and Vegetation Systems* (1988) shows, they are all interrelated (Figure 2.2); if one's focus is on the available nutrients in the soil as the support of plant and animal life, one must realise that the volume of nutrients is a function not only of processes within the soil itself (the bottom right link) and between the soil and the vegetation that it supports (top right), but also between the atmosphere and the soil (top left) and the weathering processes that produce the raw materials of the soil (bottom left). Furthermore, those external systems are interlinked too; the atmospheric and weathering systems interact, both directly and indirectly, through the soil and the vegetation it supports (the richer the vegetation, for example, the less the direct erosional impact of atmospheric processes).

In brief, a classification of systems according to location within the environment is largely artificial, because all parts are linked to all others in some way. The analyst chooses a particular focus for a study, and defines the system that encompasses it accordingly. It may be confined to the atmosphere only, but it is quite likely that it will not.

A more valuable approach to system classification refers to the nature of the study being undertaken. There are several such classifications (as reviewed, for example, in Bennett and Chorley, 1978; Huggett, 1980; and Wilson, 1981a). One of the more popular among geographers is that proposed by Chorley and Kennedy, reproduced as Figure 2.3. The characteristics of the four types are as follows.

(1) *Morphological systems* show the relationships among the various components of a system, and are useful in the description of, for example, the interactions of different elements in a landscape, such as those comprising a slope system, a river channel system, and a drainage basin system.

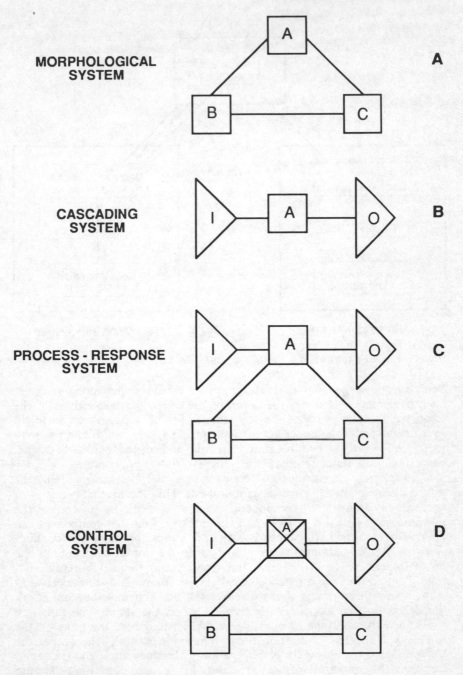

Figure 2.3 A typology of systems

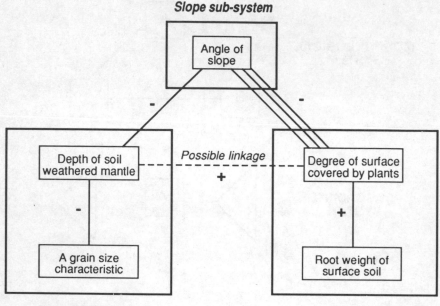

Figure 2.4 An example of a morphological system

With a slope system, for example, there are relationships among variables such as the angle of slope, the depth of the weathered material on it, the grain size characteristics of the soil, the acidity of the soil, and so forth; in a river channel the major components of the system are discharge, sediment load, velocity, bed roughness, nature of bed and banks, bedslope, vegetation, and water temperature (Huggett, 1980, pp.39–40).

By displaying the various components of a morphological system, the interrelatedness of the parts is emphasised. This means that when it is decided to study one component of the system, its place in the morphological structure is clear and the influences on that component can be readily identified; for applied work this means that once the relationships among the components are known, then the impact of change in one on the others can be identified. Thus Chorley and Kennedy's representation of an interfluve as a morphological system (Figure 2.4) shows relationships among three groups of characteristics of that system – the slope itself, the debris on that slope and the vegetation on the slope. The links are shown as either positive or negative, and the strength of the links by the thickness of the lines indicating them. Thus, for example, the deeper the soil weathered mantle on the slope, the lower the slope angle and (possibly) the larger the proportion of the area covered by plants (in part also because of a greater volume of moisture available to sustain growth). The steeper the slope, on the other hand, the smaller the proportion of its area covered by plants, which is the strongest relationship in the whole system. So removal of plant cover can lead to increased slope angles and a shallower soil mantle, with the consequence that an even smaller proportion of the area can be covered by plants.

A morphological system is largely a description of the relationships among the components, therefore, and as such is a useful indication of the complexity of the direct and indirect links. It does not account for the relationships, however, and as such must be supplemented by other types of system study if understanding of the environment is to be achieved.

(2) *Cascading systems.* These are linked components, through which energy or mass flows. Each component of the system receives inputs and produces outputs, which in turn become the inputs of other components; the inputs may be stored in the components, too, perhaps for a substantial period of time. As the mass or energy passes through a component of the system it may be altered in some way, or the component may store some of it. The flow of solar energy is thus a major example of a cascading system, from the sun itself into the earth's atmosphere, where some is reflected back and the remainder is passed through to the earth's surface, from whence it is returned, in an altered state, to the atmosphere and thence to outer space. The hydrological cycle is another example of a major cascading system. The atmosphere receives its water content through evaporation from the oceans (84 per cent) and evapotranspiration from the land surface (16 per cent). Of that moisture content, 77 per cent is returned as precipitation over the oceans and 23 per cent as precipitation on to the land surface; 7 per cent of the latter is transported to the oceans, prior to its return to the atmosphere. (The figures are from More, 1967.)

The study of cascading systems thus involves investigating movements of elements such as energy and water through the components of the environment, as against the description of structures which characterises the study of morphological systems. Again the main purpose of such study is description, but with the goal being to illustrate the workings of environmental systems. Ecosystems, such as that of Isle Royale quoted in Figure 2.1, are clearly cascading systems according to the definitions presented here. Huggett (1980, pp.119–20) uses Milner's (1972) model of the ecosystem of the island of Hirta, in the St Kilda group, to illustrate the flows that have to be measured. The island has only one large herbivore (sheep) which has no predators, and the system of which the sheep are at the centre is shown in Figure 2.5; the solar energy that enters the system is received by the vegetation and grazed by the sheep. As Huggett illustrates, this system (which is of course only a part of the total ecosystem of the island, since all of the flora are grouped together under the one category vegetation and none of the other fauna are included) can be translated into a computer model which predicts the sheep population of the island. The predicted and actual numbers are shown in Figure 2.6: Huggett argues that 'Agreement with actual fluctuations in population is good, though periods of heavy mortality are slightly out of phase, a deficiency in the model which could be corrected' (1980, p.122), which may be considered a somewhat optimistic conclusion. What the computer modelling does make clear, however, is that changes in one variable in the system only – the input

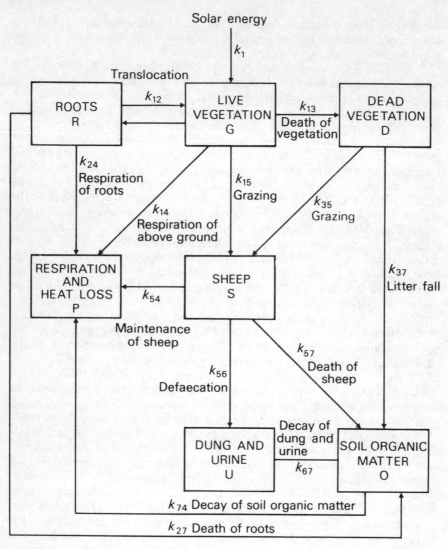

Figure 2.5 The ecosystem of the island of Hirta

variable, solar energy – can have substantial impacts on the populations within the ecosystem.

The island of Hirta is a very small ecosystem, and illustrates one of the main problems of much study of cascading systems – defining their boundaries. With an island this is relatively straightforward, and 'system closure' is readily achieved; perhaps that is why much pioneering work on ecosystems was done on islands. But with very many environmental systems, drawing boundaries around them for the purposes of investigation is somewhat artificial, and there is always the danger that important links

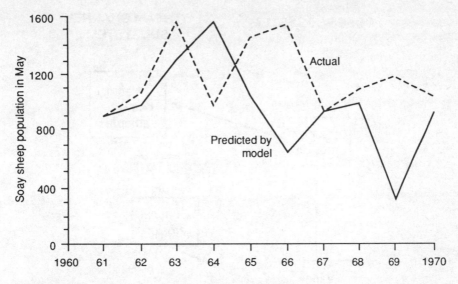

Figure 2.6 Sample output from the Hirta simulation

will be excluded from the study because one of the components involved is outside the system as defined.

Cascading systems such as ecosystems are very complex, with a large number of components and links. Even so, they are relatively simple compared with some of the models of the atmosphere that have been developed to study the flow of energy through space and time, in the three-dimensional spatial structure within which weather systems are generated. Those cascading models are usually represented as systems of differential equations, and some comprise several thousand such equations. They indicate just how complex the environment is, how much information has to be collected to calibrate the models and provide descriptions of the flows, and how difficult it is to provide detailed enough descriptions from which predictions are possible.

(3) *Process – response systems.* These are defined by Chorley and Kennedy as comprising intersections of morphological and cascading systems; the cascading systems provide the processes (i.e. the energy inputs) which produce the morphologies (the structural outputs). As the process input changes, therefore, so the morphological output alters; for example, the slope of a beach alters according to the power of the waves breaking upon it.

An illustration of a process – response system is given by Chorley and Kennedy's example of the relationships between the characteristics of a valley slope and those of the stream in its central channel (Figure 2.7). On the slope, the amount of erosion is a function of the slope angle: the steeper the slope, the greater the erosion. The output of that process is the weathered sediment that reaches the stream: the greater the amount of erosion, the larger the sediment production, and the greater the volume of

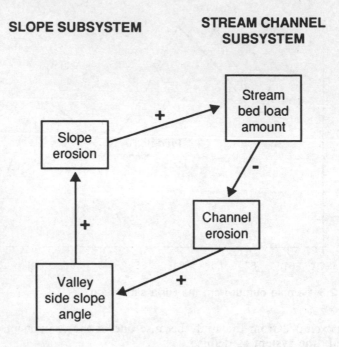

SLOPE SUBSYSTEM

STREAM CHANNEL SUBSYSTEM

Figure 2.7 Negative feedback in two morphological sub-systems

sediment entering the stream. Within the stream itself, the greater the sediment load carried the less the erosive power of the water. The erosion by the stream affects the slope: the greater the channel erosion, the steeper the valley slope. Thus we see the characteristics of the stream responding to those of the slope, and the characteristics of the slope reacting to those of the stream; each is a stimulus to a response by the other.

This interaction among the various components of a process–response system is known as *feedback*, and is a crucial feature of such systems. In the example just quoted, the consequence of the feedback is to 'damp down' the response. For example, if the sediment load of the stream is light, then there will be a high level of channel erosion. This will produce steeper valley slopes and stimulate greater slope erosion. A consequence of this will be greater sediment load for the stream, which will reduce the amount of channel erosion. Thus an indirect consequence of greater channel erosion is less channel erosion, because the output of the channel erosion generates slope erosion, which produces sediment that limits the channel erosion.

Such feedback mechanisms restore equilibrium to a system following some change to its structure, perhaps as a response to an outside influence (i.e. a process operating outside the system defined for investigation), or simply to a change which is inherent to the system itself. The latter can be illustrated by predator–prey models of ecosystems, such as the Isle Royale ecosystem of Figure 2.1. In this there is unlikely to be a precise

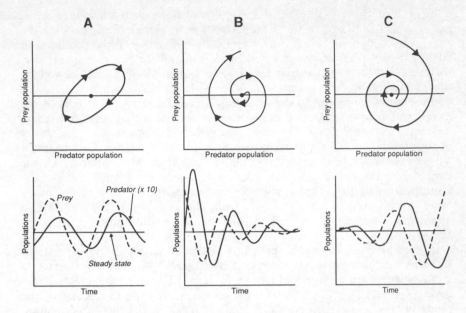

Figure 2.8 Predator–prey relationships in an ecosystem

balance between the numbers of predators (wolves) and prey (moose). At times the predator population will increase somewhat, thereby increasing its demands on the prey. More of the latter will be devoured, which will then mean less food for the predators. Competition among the wolves will lead to the survival of the fittest, and perhaps a fall in their numbers relative to those of the moose. There will then be an over-supply of prey available, which will encourage the expansion of the predator population. The result is a cyclically stable situation, as shown in Figure 2.8A, in which the variability in the number of prey (the moose) is greater than that of the predators (the wolves). The area within the ellipse of the left-hand graph is what Wilson (1981a, p.25) terms the phase space (or state space) of the system; it defines the limits of the two populations.

In the example of Figure 2.8A the relative size of the two populations is always changing; there is no equilibrium situation. This may not always be the case. Instead, there is a steady-state point to which the system will always return after some perturbation, as suggested by Figure 2.8B. Thus there may be a major increase in the size of the moose population, perhaps because of a good summer and a great deal of available biomass; few of the young die. This allows the predator population to increase, and the moose population consequently falls. There is then a consequential decline in the predator population, as fewer wolves can be sustained by the smaller moose population; the latter increases again, but not to its earlier levels, because the wolf population immediately increases again. The cycle continues, but every time the rise and subsequent fall in the populations are less, until the steady-state equilibrium is reached.

In both of these examples, there is equilibrium over the longer term, either with the return to the steady state (as in Figure 2.8B) or with the continued oscillations around the phase state. Of course, those equilibria in all but the simplest of systems will be defined not in two dimensions but in many. For example, in the Isle Royale system (Figure 2.1), as well as the moose and wolves in the central box there is also the biomass, whose volume varies according to the number of moose grazing. As it falls so the number of moose falls, with consequences for the wolf population; there are fewer wolves and fewer moose, greater biomass production, the ability to support more moose, greater possibilities for the predators, and so forth. The phase space has three dimensions. And then we can bring in the variables outside the narrowly defined system of Figure 2.1 – the atmosphere and the other herbivores and carnivores – to create a much more complicated phase space (or, from the example of Figure 2.8B, a much more complicated spiralling into the steady-state position in the n-dimensional space).

In each of these examples there is a return to an equilibrium position. But this need not be so, as suggested by Figure 2.8C. Here we start at a steady-state position from which there is a slight increase in the prey (moose) population. There is then a consequent increase in the size of the predator (wolf) population, which leads to a fall in the moose population greater than the original increase away from the steady-state. There is then a consequent fall in the wolf population, which not only allows the moose population to recover its steady-state size, it considerably exceeds it, and then encourages a similar increase in the wolf population. Every period of the cycle shows a greater amplification than the last, until eventually the prey population, which leads in each cycle, becomes extinct; the predator will soon follow, unless an alternative source of food can be found.

These three examples illustrate the two major types of feedback in a process-response system. The first, exemplified by Figure 2.8B, is termed *negative feedback*, because the consequence of its operation is to return the system to its original state. A system characterised by such feedback is known as *morphostatic*, because the morphological structure is maintained over the long term, even though there may be short-term deviations from it. The slope–channel systems (Figure 2.7) provide an example of such morphostasis; whenever a change from the equilibrium state is stimulated, a consequence of the response to that stimulus is that the system returns to its original state. Clearly the more complex the system, and the larger the number of components it contains, the longer is the likely time before it returns to equilibrium; this is known as the system's 'relaxation time'.

The other type of feedback, illustrated by Figure 2.8C, is *positive feedback* whereby the system does not return to its equilibrium but moves to a new one as a consequence of the new disposition of forces (in the example, that equilibrium involved the extinction of both species in the ecosystem). Such a system is known as *morphogenetic*, indicating that a change in its morphological structure is a consequence of the positive feedback processes. That morphogenesis may be continual in that no new equilibrium is attained; more likely, however, is a new equilibrium, which in an ecosystem may be a different floral composition and/or a different balance of the competing fauna from that which preceded it. The process of desertification is an excellent example of such morphogenesis; a system characterised by certain relationships between the vegetation, fauna and soil is altered – perhaps as a result of climatic change; perhaps because of increased human pressure on the fauna and flora – to one with different relationships, characterised by the lesser ability of the soil to sustain plant and animal life.

(4) *Control systems*. This final category is not distinct from the others in terms of its approach to describing and understanding systems; rather it is characterised by its focus on the practical application of systems under-standing to environmental control or engineering. As Chorley and Kennedy express it:

> When one examines the structure of physical process–response systems it becomes apparent that certain key variables or *valves* . . . are those wherein intelligence can conveniently intervene to produce operational changes in the distribution of energy and mass within cascading systems, and consequently to bring about changes in the equilibrium relationships involving the morphological variables linked with them in the process–response systems. (1971, p.9)

The importance of this 'instrumental' approach to the study of systems (as criticised, for example, in Gregory, 1980) is made clear in the subtitle of Bennett and Chorley's book, *Environmental Systems: Philosophy, Analysis and Control* (1978), in which the introductory chapter ends by stressing the 'dilemmas which confront man's [sic] intervention in natural systems which underlie his "living together with nature"' (p.22).

The need for an understanding of environmental systems so that societies can come to an accommodation with them is clear whatever the mode of production, so an instrumental approach does not necessarily imply the technocratic attitude described in the preceding chapter. It is as important for 'primitive' tribes to appreciate the way fertility declines in a soil, and thus know when to move on to new lands, as it is for advanced capitalist societies to appreciate the consequences of converting more and more forest to permanent pasture. The difference between the two is that the former recognise the limits of the environment and seek to live within them, whereas the latter, which many (though by no means all) systems analysts seek to serve, wish to alter the environment to serve their interests.

Chorley and Kennedy offer a defence of the need for the study of control valves in systems, and the application of the findings, in what they repre-sent as two vital differences between 'human and higher biological' systems and 'physical' systems. The first difference is that the former possess memories, which allow for control to be implemented (if you can't remember how a system reacted under certain circumstances it is not possi-ble either to seek to reproduce those circumstances – if the reaction was 'good' – or to prepare to ensure that the same reaction doesn't recur). The second is that 'the operation of physical systems is dominated by a tendency for negative feedback, whereas socio-economic systems possess strong positive-feedback loops which make change ongoing' (Chorley and Kennedy, 1971).

In other words, if left to itself the environment would sustain an equilibrium, but human 'interference', with its constant 'demands for more' which characterise growth, will harm that equilibrium. Thus they argue in favour of cybernetics, the science of control, with the study of 'man–environment systems' being seen as a special case of 'man–machine systems'; the environment is a machine to be understood and controlled.

Chorley and Kennedy illustrate their case with reference to atmospheric control systems, terrestrial control systems and ecosystems. Within the terrestrial category they deal separately with drainage basin hydrological system ('No spatial process–response system has proved so susceptible to human control as the basin hydrological system' 1971, p.317), erosional drainage basin systems, debris cascades, and ground-water systems. They illustrate the role of dams as control valves in drainage basins, regulating the flow of water so as to mitigate the impact of flooding.

Understanding Systems

Chorley and Kennedy's case for the study of control systems – that the environment is largely in equilibrium as a consequence of negative feedback mechanisms, but that human interference with those mechanisms may destroy the equilibrium – makes a compelling argument for the scientific study of such systems; it provides the information that societies can use to ensure that the changes they induce do not lead to a deterioration in the environment's capability to sustain human life. That information can take two forms. The first is typical of the technocentric view, and states that understanding will bring control which will allow continued demands to be placed on the environment: as long as we know how the environment works, then we can make sure it meets our demands without deteriorating. The other is a more pessimistic, ecocentric view which argues that what we know shows that we are making too many demands on the environment already; we are proving that it cannot cope, and should not increase our pressures on it. Bennett and Chorley present the latter view (apparently sympathetically), in the four-stage argument that if population growth continues, the pressure for control over environmental systems will increase so that 'Ways will therefore be found to subjugate the latter more rapidly, efficiently and completely . . .' (p.543); these ways will in turn make the environmental systems more vulnerable to forces 'as yet outside the control and prediction of society', resulting not only in more catastrophes of a Malthusian nature but also in conflicts that will make the practice of democracy increasingly difficult. This leads to the conclusion that:

environmental scientists would place population control at the centre of environmental planning strategies and would regard the present demographic explosion as the main impediment to the application of rational control strategies of systems modelling and control. (p.544)

(For an alternative view see Harvey, 1974.)

If the argument just summarised is a valid one, then it is necessary to produce the evidence to convince societies of the need for population control, at both the individual and the collective level; the products of environmental systems research must be used to educate people about the pressures on the environment that they are creating, and even more so about the (probably permanent) damage that could be caused if those pressures are not alleviated. So what is available to educate people with; what do we know about environmental systems and human impact on them?

Environmental system knowledge

At a general level, the adoption of a systems approach by an increasing proportion of the scientific community has provided substantial evidence of: the complexity of the systems that comprise the environment; the interlinking of all parts of the environment and of the fragility of the equilibria states of many of the systems and sub-systems identified and described.

With regard to *complexity*, the work undertaken by atmospheric scientists in their efforts to model the three-dimensional flow of energy through the atmosphere, involving many thousands of differential equations, illustrates the immensity of the task. And yet, as Gleick (1988) argues, even with such complex models they are still unable to forecast weather more than a few days ahead. As he put it, even with models containing as many as 500,000 separate equations, 'beyond two or three days the world's best forecasts were speculative, and beyond six or seven they were worthless' (p.20). The main reason for this is that, despite their size and complexity, the models are insufficiently detailed to capture reality (others would counter that the problem is not the models but the lack of sufficient computing power to make them work properly). In addition, Gleick's thesis is that the task is an impossibility, because the interactions that take place within the atmospheric system (and all other environmental systems too) cannot be predicted by sophisticated mathematical models. We return to this point later.

With regard to the *interlinking* of systems, the effects of events such as the 1986 release of massive amounts of radiation from the nuclear reactor at Chernobyl on health hazards many thousands of miles away illustrate how what happened at one place in one environmental system (the release of radiation into the atmosphere) affected other systems (local ecosystems) at other places, distant in both time and space, for the radiation once in an ecosystem may remain there for many years, if not decades. But the causal links are rarely easy to prove, and there is much scientific controversy – as, for example, over the claims that 'acid rain' in parts of Western Europe (such as Norway and Germany) is produced by British coal-burning power stations. And those links are relatively close in space as well as time. (Park details the debates over acid rain in Britain in recent years, and the position of the government and the Central Electricity Generating Board that 'there are still too many fundamental research questions as yet unasked or unanswered' to justify expensive programmes to reduce sulphur emissions from coal-burning power stations: 1987, Ch.10, p.242.) Possible links that are distant on one if not both of the parameters of space and time are even more contentious. For example, extreme weather events in the northern hemisphere during the winter of 1988–9, along with more local ones such as a wet summer in Australia, were linked by some observers to changes in the sea temperature in the south-east Pacific (*The Sunday Times*, 12 February 1989, p.A16). As many users of statistics point out, however, correlation should not be confused with causation; the latter can only be proven if the mechanisms underlying the links are understood, and there is much scientific work and debate proceeding with the aim of understanding those mechanisms.

Finally, with regard to the *fragility* of environmental systems, by which is meant the ease with which an equilibrium state can be disturbed, again there is much scientific evidence to show that small changes in one variable in a system can stimulate major alterations to the whole. Both hydrologists and geomorphologists have become aware of this in their attempts to understand why some rivers have single channels and others have braided channels; why one river may have a single channel in one reach and yet be braided in another; and why in one reach at some times the channel may be braided and at others not. This has promoted the realisation that a 'threshold' exists which when crossed leads to a major change in the morphological structure of the system. In the present context, the critical variables, as described by Thornes (1987, pp.30–1), are slope and discharge (Figure 2.9). In some situations, where the slope is shallow relative to the volume of discharge (for example at C in Figure 2.9), there is a single-channel meandering stream, whereas in others (for example D), where the slope is steep relative to the discharge, braiding occurs; in some circumstances (such as E) the stream is on the threshold between one state and another, and a slight change in one of the variables (probably the amount of discharge that it carries) will lead to a shift from one morphology to another. Identifying the existence of such thresholds, and modelling them successfully, is crucial for a proper representation of a system, and thus for designing control systems by river engineers. (Though, of course, the interlinking aspect of environmental systems means that control of one will almost certainly have a range of consequences for others, as shown by the effects on rivers both upstream and downstream of dams installed to control the flow of water.)

At the larger scale, the impacts of ecosystem changes again illustrate the fragility of the environment, especially when such changes are linked to other systems. In many parts of the world intensification of human occupation is accompanied by major changes in the vegetation cover. In the

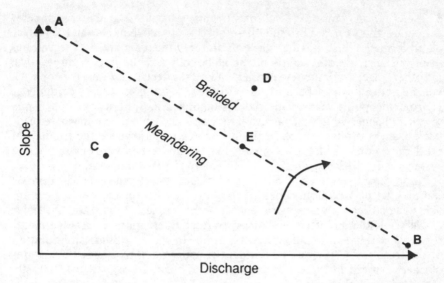

Figure 2.9 The threshold between braided and meandering river channels

Amazon basin in recent years, for example, over half of the tropical forest cover has been removed to make way for agriculture. The disappearance of the trees has, according to some, led to a substantial reduction in the amount of carbon dioxide returned to the atmosphere through transpiration, because of the loss of the store of carbon in the trees, with consequences for the composition of the atmosphere and its ability to absorb some of the incoming solar radiation, while the burning of the trees has accelerated what is known as the 'greenhouse effect' – less energy is leaving the earth's atmosphere because the heat is 'trapped' by the greater concentration of particles and of carbon dioxide in the atmosphere. The result is a process of global warming, it is claimed, which will lead not only to climatic changes but also to melting of glaciers, a consequent rise in sea levels, the drowning of many areas of land (including much that is now densely occupied by people) and adjustments to many morphological systems. A century earlier, the destruction of much of New Zealand's forest cover to convert the land to pasture led to rapid increases in the rate of soil erosion (Cumberland, 1947), a process assisted by the introduction of rabbits and other mammals which attacked plant roots.

The current debates about global warming and the greenhouse effect suggest that the composition of the atmosphere is being changed by greater burning of wood and fossil fuels, with consequences for climate and thence for other environmental systems. But the composition of the atmosphere can be altered by 'natural' events also, such as a major volcanic eruption. The eruption of Mt St Helens, Washington, USA in 1980 provided a graphic illustration of the amount of material that is placed in the atmosphere by one such event, and there have been many larger events in recorded history, notably that of Mt Krakatoa in the East Indies in 1783.

These eruptions emit large volumes of dust particles into the atmosphere, which are then carried around the globe by air movements, and so affect cloud formation and weather not only in the immediate area of the volcano itself but in many other parts of the globe too; and the impact on weather in other places stimulates further indirect effects. To most people, a volcanic eruption can be understood only as a random event; certainly it is from the point of view of those studying atmospheric systems. Thus weather change, which may precipitate climatic change if the negative feedback chain is broken and the equilibrium destroyed, can be the product of random events. This, of course, makes understanding environmental systems very difficult, and their prediction virtually impossible.

Leslie Curry proposed several decades ago that climatic change may be the product of a random series. He argued that within the earth there are two main stores of atmospheric energy – the tropical oceans and the polar glaciers – and then attempted 'to show that fluctuations in storage there, resulting purely from random events, can be of the magnitude and duration of the Ice Ages' (1962, p.24). Random year-to-year variation in the amount of energy stored in those two areas was sufficient, he argued, to stimulate major climatic changes.

Curry's argument preceded the mathematical work of Edward Lorenz (e.g. Lorenz, 1963) which provided an alternative case for climatic change as a consequence of small-scale, possibly random, fluctuations in critical variables and relationships. He produced a model of climatic systems, using what we would now know as a very primitive computer and representing the vast complexity of the atmosphere by a few equations only. He showed that if you started off his model at the same set of conditions each time, then you produced the same climatic series. But if the starting conditions varied only slightly (at the level of the fourth, fifth and sixth decimal points in the early experiments: one run started with a parameter at 0.506, and the other with only that parameter changed, to 0.506127) a very different series would develop. Figure 2.10 shows the two series diverging over time (the trace may be of average annual temperature, for example). The original difference was very small – 'A small numerical error was like a small puff of wind – surely the small puffs faded or cancelled each other out before they could change important large-scale features of the weather' (Gleick, 1987, pp.16–17) – but sufficient to produce very different weather systems, with presumed consequences for all other atmospheric systems. In Curry's terms, that small change could have been the result of a random event, like a volcanic eruption. The result illustrates the fragility of environmental equilibria, though the validity of the example is not accepted by all analysts.

These three general conclusions have been presented as summaries of what we know about environmental systems without any detailed descriptions, let alone assessment, of the current state of knowledge (which is given in the latest textbooks on the various environmental sciences and in up-to-date reviews such as those in the journal *Progress in Physical Geography*). What is important for the present book is to appreciate the nature of systems, their complexity, their interlinkedness, and their

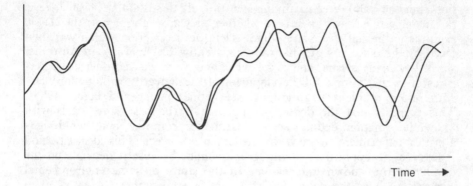

Time ⟶

Figure 2.10 Climatic sequences from slightly different starting configurations.

fragility, in order to develop the arguments regarding human 'interference' with those systems. But before turning to that, a brief excursion into how systems are studied is necessary.

Environmental systems analysis

How are systems studied, to obtain a full understanding of how they operate? As described earlier, a system can involve a morphology, with relationships between the links; it can be a set of flows through the component parts; or it can be a process–response mechanism, whereby one studies either a morphological change as a response to a particular stimulus or a flow change as a result of morphological alterations. In all of these, what is important is that the system operates as a whole, and its understanding requires an appreciation of that whole; to use a well-worn phrase developed by geographers some decades ago in another context, 'the whole is greater than the sum of the parts'.

There are two ways in which a system can be studied, the inductive and the deductive. In the former, empirical investigations are undertaken, which probably involve field measurements of the important parameters of the system (its salient morphological variables and/or flows), allowing a description to be drawn up. In the deductive approach, a model representation of the system is developed (usually though not necessarily mathematical; hardware and other analogue models may be of value in some circumstances). To be of value, this representation should conform to 'reality', and so should be tested in experimental conditions; if the model is a valid representation, then it should either reproduce an aspect of environment as it is/has been, or it should be able to predict accurately a future state. (A weather systems model, for example, should be able to take the conditions yesterday and simulate today accurately, and should be able to take today's situation and predict tomorrow accurately.)

There has been much debate among scientists, and philosophers of science, about the validity of the two approaches. The inductive is frequently criticised for its lack of critical experiments; it amasses information, but the validity of its findings is difficult to sustain because there is no unambiguous way of assessing whether they are right or not: the classic example is the 'all swans are white' scientific description which was then faced by the discovery of what were apparently 'black swans' in Australia; were they really swans, and if so, what now were the defining characteristics of swans? (For a full development of the 'poverty of induction' case with regard to physical geography, see Haines-Young and Petch, 1985). This suggests that the deductive approach is the best. One starts with known information, deduces some consequence from that, and then designs a critical experiment to see if the deduction is correct. This ideal situation is less easy to apply than might at first sound, because it depends on the quality of the known information. In the study of some environmental systems, such as the atmospheric, it can be argued that all you need to know are certain basic physical laws, then you apply the relevant mathematics, and produce the needed deductions. Those physical laws are well established, and provide an apparently unambiguous input to the calculations, but what physical laws can be used to model the flow of energy in the Isle Royale ecosystem (Figure 2.1)? There are no physical laws available to represent, for example, the efficiency of moose in grazing the available biomass, or the efficiency of the wolves in hunting the moose (at different densities); these aspects of the environment can only be portrayed through empirical enquiry. The same is true of most aspects of environmental systems; while the ultimate goal may be to develop a viable mathematical model, this can only be done by obtaining empirical field data (perhaps accompanied by laboratory data from experiments simulating environmental conditions) that can be used to calibrate the models.

The collection of field data is rarely straightforward, particularly as for much work long series of data are required in order to describe changing conditions; environmental scientists have displayed a great deal of ingenuity in designing equipment with which to capture the data they need. But apart from the actual data collection problems, there are other difficulties inherent in the empirical approach. The first is that, even if the whole system is appreciated and general models of it exist, it is very difficult to collect data for all of the links/flows in a single experiment. Thus any one piece of research will probably focus on a particular part of the system only. For example, Thornes provides a general model of a fluvial system (Figure 2.11). One study of that system may focus on the link in the bottom left-hand corner only, between discharge and channel slope, and attempt to describe the relationship between the two. This will probably involve measurement of the two variables at a range of sites, and regressing the one against the other to identify the relationship; the hope is that the relationship will be a strong one (i.e. a high correlation between the two variables, indicating that the channel slope value can be accurately estimated from the discharge variable). But channel slope is also affected directly by two other variables, according to the model. So where the value of the slope is not accurately estimated by the discharge variable, it could be concluded that this is because of the unmeasured impact of the other

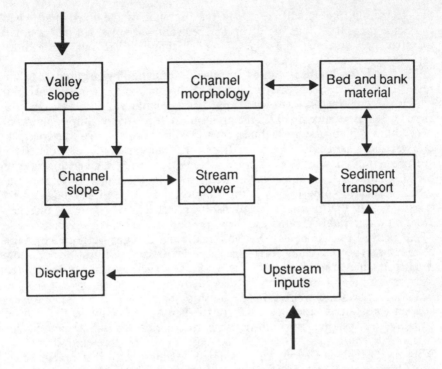

Figure 2.11 A model of the components and links in a fluvial system

variables. Thus the next stage of the work might be to measure those two, and produce a multiple regression equation which estimated channel slope as a function of the three variables. (Alternatively, an experiment might be designed in which the effects of two of the variables were 'held constant' by studying only streams with identical valley slope and channel morphology characteristics, for example; such an experiment is almost impossible in field conditions, though it may be possible in laboratories.)

Much scientific work is incremental, adding together the results of earlier findings to provide an overall description; thus workers may seek a synthesis of understanding of the fluvial system by taking the results of one study on one of the links and those of another on a second link, and so on, to produce a general model. But this piecemeal approach overlooks that basic characteristic of a system, that 'the whole is greater than the sum of the parts', in at least two ways. First, since it is virtually impossible to 'hold all other influences constant' in field situations, the results of a partial study are difficult to evaluate, since it is not known what the values of the other critical variables (some of which may be only indirectly linked to those being measured) are. This makes the calibrated parameter values in any model of dubious value. Secondly, the variables interact, and when they do so can operate differently than when they are acting in isolation. (This is why some chemical processes require the presence of a catalyst;

two chemicals interact differently in the presence of the third than when it is not present.) Thus if all of the relevant variables are not studied together the outcome may be a very incomplete, if not misleading, representation of the system.

The need for holistic studies is advanced further by arguing that the result of the interactions may well be a change in the 'dependent variable' which is not readily predicted by partial studies. A great deal of environmental science involves the application of relatively simple statistical procedures which assume a linear relationship between two variables; as one variable changes so the other does, in a constant ratio, so that if we are predicting channel slope from discharge, say, then a given increase in the discharge will produce the same change in the slope, whatever the initial discharge value. (This is the simple linear regression model.) This does not mean that nonlinear relationships are necessarily ignored, but they are almost invariably treated as linear, through some transformation of one if not both of the variables; thus, for example, it might be found that the change in slope is greater when discharge increases by x units from a low level than when it increases by x from a higher level, which can be handled by, for example, a logarithmic transformation of discharge.

Transformation of nonlinear relationships to a linear form is, however, still an oversimplification of many relationships, especially in the holistic situation of systems, as Thornes has made clear in his argument for 'dynamic systems theory' (1987). The mathematics is more complicated, as Wilson (1981b) has shown. In mathematics dealing with differential equations, the dependent variable is the change in one variable expressed as a ratio of the change in another; a simple example is population change over time, in which the dependent variable is

$$x = d_p/d_t$$

where d_p is the change in population, d_t is the change in time, and x is the differential ratio.

Such equations can be characterised by *bifurcation*, in which one of three things may happen at certain points in the trend (Figure 2.12). The first is simply a 'jump'; the slope of the trend remains the same (Figure 2.12a), but there is a discontinuity in it, as some threshold is crossed. The second is a switch from a steady trend to some periodicity (Figure 2.12b), whereas the third is a switch to what appear to be random oscillations, or chaos (Figure 2.12c).

The relevance of the first two of these shifts to the study of environmental systems has increasingly been appreciated in recent years. The existence of thresholds, as examples of 'jumps', has already been noted in the example of the switch of a river from a meandering to a braided state (p.24); what is of interest to the scientist in such circumstances, and perhaps even more to the engineer, is being able to predict when the 'jump' will occur, what combination of values of the relevant system variables produce this quantum shift. With regard to periodicities, the earlier discussion of predator–prey relationships in the context of Huggett's (1980) diagrams (Figure 2.8) has shown that what was formerly an equilibrium could be

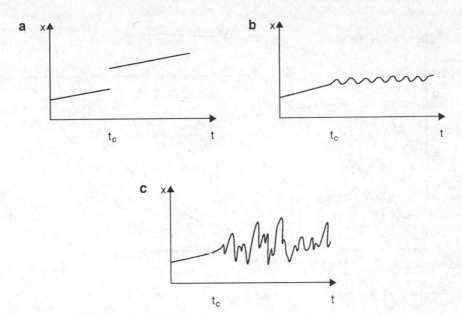

Figure 2.12 Types of bifurcation

transformed into a periodic relationship, as first the predators increase in numbers and the prey decline, followed by a decline in the predator population and a subsequent increase in the prey. Environmental scientists have also increasingly become interested in what are known mathematically as catastrophes, in which the relationship between two variables shows a complex form when a third is taken into account, because of the existence of bifurcations. Thornes gives an example of such a catastrophe (Figure 2.13) in which the basic relationship being studied is that between sediment load in a stream (Y) and the ratio of sorting to size of the sediment carried (X). When stream power is introduced as a third variable a cusp in the relationship between the other two is created, shown by the heavy shading, such that at certain values of X there is more than one possible value of Y – so no one answer is right. Outside the cusp there is only one value of Y corresponding to each value of X, but in that critical area Y cannot be predicted, which makes for difficulties both in modelling the rest of the system and in suggesting engineering solutions to environmental problems.

The relevance of the third type of bifurcation, apparently random oscillation, to environmental systems is illustrated by May's (1976) ecological experiments which provided early evidence of the existence of such oscillations (or chaos). He took a very simple equation in which the size of a population, a herbivore say, is expressed as a function of its previous size: in brief, the size this year is a function of the size last year, which does not seem to be an unreasonable assumption to make. The equation is

$$x_n = ax(1 - x)$$

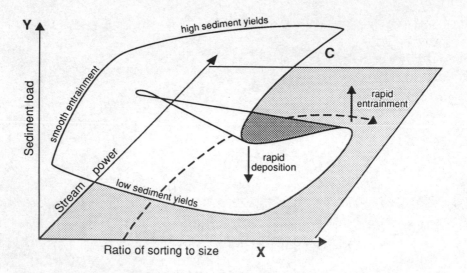

Figure 2.13 An example of a cusp catastrophe in three dimensions

where x is as the population at a given time, x_n is the next value of x, and a is the parameter of the equation which represents the rate of reproduction of the species concerned.

In May's mathematical experiment, x took on values between 0.0 and 1.0, on the argument that all environments have a certain carrying capacity only. (The equation is thus that widely known as the logistic.) If for the moment we take the value of a as 1.0, then the equation says that the next value of x is determined by the present value (which is the proportion of the carrying capacity) multiplied by 1 minus the present value, or the unused capacity. Thus if x is 0.4 (only 40 per cent of the carrying capacity has been attained) the next value will be 0.4 (0.6), or 0.24. The following year it will be 0.24 (0.76), or 0.18, and it will be 0.15, 0.13, and 0.11 in subsequent years. The species is slowly becoming extinct because it is not reproducing fast enough. If a is increased to 2.0, however, then if we start with x at 0.6, the next value is 2.0 multiplied by 0.6 multiplied by 0.4, or 0.48, followed by 0.4992, 0.50, and 0.50 thereafter. With a reproduction parameter of 2.0, the population stabilises at half of the carrying capacity; some shock to the system may take it up to 0.6 (a good summer with lots of grass perhaps) but it soon stabilises again at 0.5.

What May found, however, was that this stability only occurred with certain values of the parameter a. As that increased towards a value of 3.0, so the population remained stable; if a is 2.7, for example, the value of x stabilises at 0.6292. But with a value of 3.0 it alternates between 0.65 and 0.6825, and with a at 3.5 the value of x settles down to a four-year periodicity with values 0.3828, 0.8269, 0.5009 and 0.8750, which indicates very substantial annual variability from the same relationship which with lower a values produced stability. What May had shown was that at low reproduction rates a species would become extinct; at medium rates it remained stable relative to the carrying capacity of the land it occupied; and at higher rates its numbers varied substantially, because as it approached carrying capacity so its numbers were cut, and it then grew again. In some ways this is not unexpected, but what May found is that with even higher a values periodicity in the values of x disappeared, and the result was a chaos of values, with no apparent pattern to them (except that there may be brief periods of periodicity before chaos set in again).

The conclusions to be drawn from this finding (of which Thornes, 1987, pp.40–3, gives a further example) with regard to chaos are two, for the present purposes. The first is that the fragility of the environment already referred to is perhaps even greater than initially expected, because in certain situations rapid changes in variables can occur; in the predator–prey example the two populations could both fluctuate wildly, and in the stream discharge/channel slope relationship the result could be rapid and frequent alterations in channel slope if there were periodicity, if not chaos, in the change in discharge over time. (Clearly there are issues of scale here; local differences may occur within an overall pattern of stability – changes in channel form in various stretches of a river need not lead to changes in characteristics of the river basin itself.) The second conclusion is that, if chaos is general in the environment, and Gleick (1988) argues that the accumulation of evidence suggests that it is, then not only do we have a fragile environment but we also have a very unpredictable one. Such a conclusion has clear implications for human interrelationships with the environment.

One final aspect of environmental systems related to the basic concepts already introduced is that of evolution, which is applied to geomorphological systems and to ecosystems, if not to atmospheric systems. Within geomorphology, for example, the concept of the 'normal cycle of erosion' associated with the work of William Morris Davis (see Chorley et al., 1973) is well known for its central argument that landscapes evolve from a youthful to an old-age stage, with characteristic forms at each, whereas in the study of ecology the concept of a climax vegetation, that most suited to a particular set of other environmental conditions, is also well known. Many people now consider such concepts untenable and not in line with the empirical evidence. They do not deny that landscapes and ecosystems change, however. In the latter, for example, the floral and faunal composition of areas changes as some species become more prolific and others move towards extinction, while species change in their characteristics as they adapt successfully to changed situations. But those changes may not be a part of a teleological sequence towards a predetermined end, but rather consequences of the need to respond to new stimuli in the environment which call for new structures. Thus the jump bifurcations in particular, which may be brought about by random events, such as volcanic eruptions or three good summers in a row, are the equivalent of evolution and suggest how aspects of the environment may change.

Human 'Interference' in the Environment

Chorley and his co-authors (Bennett and Kennedy) argue that human societies, represented as systems, should be considered separately from systems in the physical environment because of two distinct characteristics: the ability of humans to remember; and the positive feedback that is common in human systems compared to the negative feedback they see as typical of environmental systems. Because of the former characteristic, humans are able collectively to learn much more about their physical environment than are other forms of animal life, and the advances in intellect that have been built on that characteristic have enabled humans to alter the environment, both intentionally and unintentionally, to a much greater extent than any other species. (It is for this reason that human activity is often considered 'interference' with the environment, rather than just activity within it; it is sometimes considered outside the 'natural' aspect of an environment, with the implication that human 'interference' is 'unnatural'. The distinction is really one of scale; all human activities are natural, but have far greater potential impact – *vide* the nuclear weapon – than those of any other species.) The second characteristic suggests that human societies have a tendency to grow *ad infinitum*, which is not a characteristic of other species. In strict biological terms this is probably not so, and there is no reason to believe that humans *per se* have a higher a value in May's equation (p.31) than other species. But what is undoubtedly the case is that combining the natural growth tendencies with the first characteristic – mental power – means that human growth has more impact on the environment than that of other species; the way in which that growth is organised is the particular concern of the next two chapters. The growth can be sustained to a greater extent because humans have developed an ability (limited, but we don't know how or to what extent) to extend the earth's carrying capacity, which other species do not have.

What is entirely clear is that human societies have 'interfered' with 'natural' systems in a great variety of ways, and are apparently increasing their 'interference' very substantially at the present time. The extent of the human impact on the environment has been fully documented by Goudie, who argues that 'the complexity, frequency and magnitude of impacts is increasing, partly because of steeply rising population levels and partly because of a general increase in *per capita* consumption [of food and energy]' (1986a, p.285).

It is not the purpose of this book to provide detailed illustrations of that interference; nevertheless, a brief outline of its nature in a range of environmental systems indicates the salient features of human activity within the environment that are central to the arguments in the rest of this book.

Goudie's (1986a) material is organised to show the nature of human impact in six different types of system. The first two relate directly to ecosystems. With regard to *vegetation*, he shows that a great deal of the earth's natural vegetation cover has been removed, particularly to extend agriculture, as with the massive deforestation that continues to occur

(Williams, 1989). One of the most contentious issues regarding vegetation change at present is that of the spread of desert conditions, especially in the Sahel area of Africa, a consequence according to Goudie of 'a combination of human activities . . . with occasional series of dry years' (1986, p.49). Important outcomes of these human-induced vegetation changes have included the 'opening-up' of soils to weathering and erosive forces, and a reduction in the diversity of plant species; new species have been developed, but many of these prove only weakly resistant to plant pests. By changing the floral environments, human activity is also imperilling the survival of many fauna, and Goudie identifies five major impacts on *animal* populations: domestication, dispersal, extinction, expansion and contraction (p.70). Some of these changes, especially extinction and contraction, are due to deliberate policies of reducing numbers, if not eliminating certain species, but many more are the indirect impacts of, for example, changing habitats through the extension of agriculture, pollution of habitats (as with water bodies), and the methods of clearing land (such as the impact of fire); there has also been the deliberate attack on micro-organisms in attempts to control diseases of humans and other species, but these fall outside Goudie's coverage.

From ecosystems within the biosphere, Goudie turns to human impacts on the *soil*, which is 'one of the thinnest and most vulnerable human resources and is one upon which, both deliberately and inadvertently, humans have had a very major impact' (p.109). The nature of the soil in any place is a function of the interaction of five factors – parent material, topography, climate, organisms within the soil, and time. Human activity can affect each of the first four directly and indirectly, and thereby influence the time in which a soil has to develop. The chemistry of many soils has been affected by such activity, and the amount of anthropo-genetically induced soil erosion has increased very substantially in recent centuries, with clear consequences for the ability of the soil to sustain plant, and thus human, life.

Fresh and salt *waters* are also affected directly and indirectly by a range of human activities. They have been major receptacles of waste materials, for example, both as deliberate policies (as with the continued dumping of human sewage into rivers, lakes and seas and the current policies of depositing nuclear waste in certain ocean deeps), and as the reservoirs into which polluted rivers flow and polluted air is deposited through precipitation. They have also been modified in many ways, as is clear in the management of river channels (to control flooding and to extract water for other uses). In urban areas especially, the extraction of water from rivers and ground-water sources has major direct and indirect impacts, and the alterations in the nature of the ground cover have significant consequences in the movement of water through the hydrological system from atmosphere to oceans; flood peaks increase, for example, with less infiltration and more rapid run-off.

Human activity is a major *geomorphological* agent, stimulating the various processes of weathering, erosion and deposition involved in the creation of land-forms, at all scales. This is clearly illustrated in Cooke and Reeves's

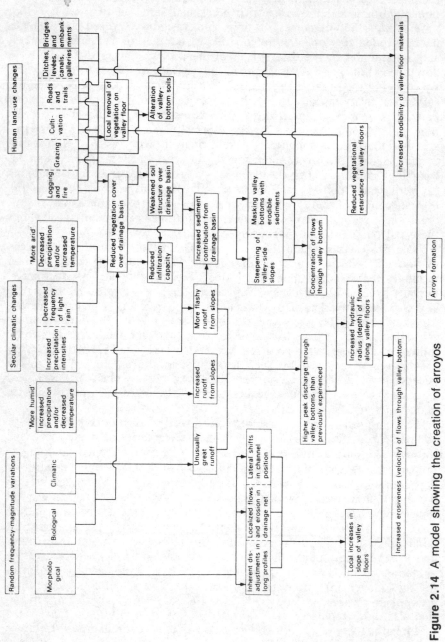

Figure 2.14 A model showing the creation of arroyos

model of the development of arroyos – deep gullies incised within broad valley bottoms and plains – in the south-western United States (Figure 2.14). They show that six types of land-use change, reflecting increased intensity of human occupance of the area, have led to alterations to both vegetation cover and soil structure, which have both increased the erodibility of valley-bottom soils. Together with other factors related to both the nature of the local climate and short-term climatic change (themselves also possibly linked to human activity in the area and neighbouring districts) human activity has also increased the erosive force of the water flowing through the valleys.

Arroyo formation is an example of largely unintended interference with geomorphological processes, but, as with other aspects of environmental systems, there has also been much intentional interference too. This is because many aspects of geomorphological systems, especially those involving flows, are considered as 'hazardous' for human occupance of areas. Coasts provide excellent examples of this, where the rapid changes in, for example, beach form as a result of short-term changes in erosive and depositional forces threaten human investments and lives. They have been countered by a great range of coastal protection works, which themselves have had secondary impacts on other aspects of coastal erosion and deposition.

Finally, Goudie looks at impacts on *atmosphere and climate*, emphasising the impact of human activity in three ways – through the production of heat, alterations in atmospheric quality, and changes in the albedo of land masses and oceans (Figure 2.15). The role of the first two is relatively well known, even if not fully understood. The production of heat is well documented with regard to the creation of 'urban climates', in the areas where that production is concentrated, and the nature of atmospheric pollution, with its consequences for the ratio of incoming to outgoing radiation, the creation of clouds, and the transfer of pollutants through precipitation (as with acid rain) is also widely discussed. With regard to the third impact, the albedo of a surface is its ability to reflect radiation; in general, the denser the vegetation cover, the lower the albedo, and the greater the proportion of the incoming radiation that is retained at the earth's surface. Basically, the higher the albedo, the greater the surface cooling, and the lower the convective activity in the lower atmosphere; with the removal of tropical forest, therefore, it is argued that climatic change (lower rainfall there, compensated by higher rainfall in the temperate zones but less in the Arctic latitudes) is a major consequence. Interestingly, this surface cooling in the tropics as a result of forest clearance is occurring at the same time as warming of the atmosphere there, as some argue, because of the greater concentration of CO_2 – the so-called greenhouse effect. Furthermore, a decrease in convective activity over the former area of tropical forest should lead to less cloud and less rainfall there; there will then be more direct heating and less evapotranspiration so the area could become warmer. It is such complexity in the feedback mechanisms of environmental systems that makes the prediction of the consequences of action so difficult, and underpins the lively debates among environmental scientists.

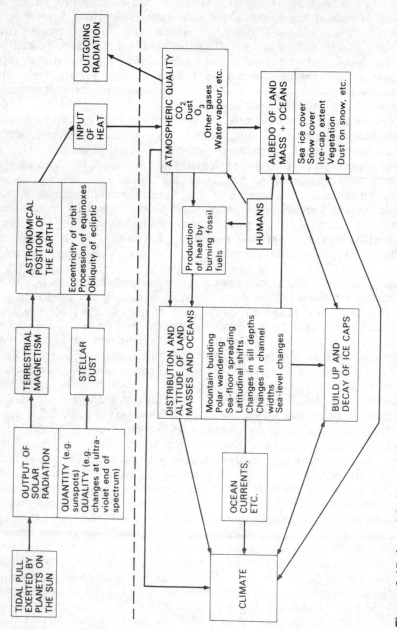

Figure 2.15 A model showing human contributions to the generation of climatic change

Goudie's classification, supported by a very large number of examples and assessments of the extent of the impacts, makes clear not only that human 'interference' affects all components of the environmental system and is increasing in its quantity, but also that the consequences are widespread in both space and time. An activity in one place does not simply have direct impacts on the environment there; it has knock-on effects for other aspects of the local environment as energy and mass are moved through systems and call forth responses in the morphological structure of most, if not all. Further, those knock-on effects are not limited to the local environment but are transmitted, rapidly in some cases, slowly in others, to other places, because of the interlinking of systems. The movement of air through the atmosphere and of water through the hydrological cycle are the main transport agents, and since no part of the earth is isolated from all others none is immune from the potential consequences of human 'interference' elsewhere; even the remotest island can receive pollutants carried in the wind and/or rain and deposited there, and can receive others carried on and in the sea waters or by plants and/or animals which serendipitously arrive there.

As a final point with regard to the nature of these changes, they should be classified into those which are reversible and those which are not; the latter are clearly the most worrying, especially if they are increasing in magnitude, since they involve changes to environmental systems that cannot be recovered. In one sense of course, no impact, however slight, is reversible because once it has happened it has triggered other responses that may not be reversible; once a small piece of land has been destroyed, it can never be replaced in exactly the same condition. But there are cases of reversibility, especially with regard to flow resources which are naturally renewed; if certain types of air pollution cease then the air will be cleaner, increasingly so as the remnants of earlier pollution are deposited – though, of course, it may be more difficult to reverse the impacts of earlier deposition. There are other impacts which could be reversed, though the process may be very slow; soil deterioration could be countered by returning the ecosystem to its 'original' state (whatever that might be?) and allowing the slow process of soil creation to operate, which is the way in which some argue desertisation should be countered. Those which are not reversible include the extinction of plant and animal species, and also those which produce weathering and erosion; once a slope has been eroded it cannot be returned to its original condition.

It may well be that certain changes in environmental systems are reversible, as the work of conservationists has increasingly shown over the last century, though the costs of many of the reversals are great and it would be much preferable if the need for reversal didn't arise. Goudie lists nine arguments for restricting impacts. The *ethical* argument is that all species have rights and that nature is there for humans to share, not to dominate and alter for utilitarian ends. The *scientific* case is that we understand so little about environmental systems that we should preserve them for future study, while the *aesthetic* case is that ecosystems and landscapes should be retained to enrich human life and values (in part for the *recreational* value);

these four are linked in a *future generations* case that we only have a 'leasehold' on the earth, and should sustain it for those who will follow. Linked to the future is the *genetic diversity* case, that once species are extinct they cannot be recreated, with potential problems for the future – similarly, once landscapes are destroyed they cannot be replaced – which is associated with the *environmental stability* argument that the more diversity there is, especially in ecosystems, the 'more checks and balances there are to maintain stability' (Goudie, 1986a, p.291). *Economic* arguments suggest that because of our scientific ignorance we are as yet unaware of much of the wealth of the earth that could be exploited to sustain human societies. Finally, the *unintended impacts* case is, as argued here, that the nature of environmental systems is such that a change in one component of one can have substantial, unexpected, effects on another, somewhere else in time and/or space.

For the present we are concerned here neither with detailing the amount of human interference nor with the arguments for its limitation, though both are central to much of the rest of the book. The sole purpose of this brief section is to highlight that human societies are able, wittingly or unwittingly, to affect environmental systems in myriad ways, with consequences that can be very large. If, as the evidence accumulated by Goudie (1986a) and others suggests, those consequences generally are deleterious to the contemporary environment, and they are increasing, then the conclusion must be that action should be taken to limit them. We need to understand what type of action, and we need to understand why those consequences are being produced in any case. That is the purpose of the rest of this book.

In Summary

The major purpose of this chapter has been to illustrate the nature of environmental systems and their interrelationships with human societies, thereby raising two questions that are central to the rest of the book. With regard to the systems themselves, the chapter has illustrated the complex holism of the earth's environment, which can be disaggregated into separate parts for analysis and illustration but which in effect comprises one single interacting whole, with all parts affected, ultimately, by what happens in all others. To the extent that there are environmental issues and problems, therefore, they are global in scope, though they probably vary locally in their impact and extent.

Despite a great deal of scientific effort, much about these systems remains unknown, in large part because of their immense complexity and the complicated nature of the interactions that occur. Study has suggested that many environmental systems are characterised by negative feedback, and so tend to maintain themselves in a steady state, although that may be interrupted by events in other parts of the system, or in what (for analytical ease at least) are other systems. But this steady-state, or equilibrium, is in general very fragile, and can easily be disturbed, with potentially major consequences not only locally and regionally but also globally. Human activity can be a major interruption to the equilibria and there is a growing body of evidence to show not only how that activity has had substantial impacts but also that the quantity and quality of the impacts is increasing. Because of the complexity of the interactions within environmental systems, assessing the full nature of those impacts, and the likely consequences of further impacts, is extremely difficult; the evidence is, however, that it is likely to be deleterious (though not all agree with this conclusion: see the alternative views of Council on Environmental Quality, 1982; and Simon and Kahn, 1984).

All human activity affects the operation of environmental systems to some extent. So what is important in evaluating the nature of the impacts is the degree to which it is either reversible or limitable, since it cannot be avoided. This issue raises many unknowns, because imperfect appreciation of how environmental systems work (indeed, if the arguments regarding chaos are valid, it may be that we can never fully appreciate this) means that we cannot be sure what we should not do, what we may do, at least to some extent, and what it is relatively safe to do.

Hence we come to the main questions that are the focus of the rest of the book. The first concerns the production of these impacts: why do we need to make increasing demands on the environment? What is it in our societies that has impelled that development in recent centuries? Unless we can answer that question we cannot tackle environmental problems fully, since we won't know why we are producing them in the first place. The second question is how do we tackle them. If it is accepted that human activity is having an increasing, and largely deleterious, impact on the earth's environmental systems, how can societies be mobilised to modify their activity in order to reduce, if not end, that impact? Since the environment is a whole, this implies that society must respond as a whole too, so how can collective action against environmental despoliation be undertaken?

Chapter 3
Modes of Production

In the social production which men carry on they enter into definite relations that are indispensable and independent of their will . . . . The sum total of these relations of production constitutes the economic structure of society – the real foundation on which rise legal and political superstructures and to which correspond definite forms of social consciousness. The mode of production in material life determines the general character of the social, political and spiritual processes of life. (Karl Marx, Preface to *A Contribution to the Critique of Political Economy*)

The previous chapter has introduced the importance of appreciating that the earth is a complex of interdependent systems, the operation of which can be substantially affected by human activities. In order to appreciate why it is that the systems' operation is so frequently and substantially influenced by human activity, we need to understand the features of human societies that lead them to interfere with natural environmental systems to such an extent that they threaten their continued existence, if not indeed the existence of the earth itself. Only when that appreciation is available can we turn to an analysis of how the environment might be protected from the undesirable consequences of human use. Thus this chapter looks briefly at the basic nature of human societies, to the extent that this assists in understanding their interrelationships with their environments.

The Bases of Social Organisation

The fundamental goal of all individuals is survival. In certain circumstances it is possible for individuals to survive entirely independent of any others, to care for themselves without even any contact with others. But they cannot survive biologically for ever, and when they die there is no inter-generational reproduction. Survival of the species involves collective action. It is possible for two individuals to ensure this, with little or no contact with others, and for their successors to do likewise, but the nature of human genetics makes this unlikely as a continuing process over several generations, for two reasons: first, it is possible that a couple either are unable to produce children, or can only produce them of a certain gender, thus halting the reproduction process; or, secondly, continual inbreeding tends to weaken the genetic stock, with possible extinction as a consequence. So wider interaction is necessary to ensure continued inter-generational reproduction. Species survival requires a social organisation.

If survival is a social issue, then societies must be organised towards that end. (See, for example, Dalton's introduction to Polanyi, 1971.) Survival need not be the only reason for social organisation, and much of what is undertaken collectively is not necessary to that end. But survival is fundamental – if a society cannot ensure its reproduction, both day-to-day and inter-generational, then all else will ultimately fail. The crucial element of a society's rationale cannot be left to chance, to pragmatic decision-making; the fundamental organising principles of a society must address the issue of survival, which of course means a focus on obtaining and then allocating sufficient food and water and, where relevant, raw materials for creating shelters from environmental resources.

Means of organising societies to ensure their survival have evolved over many millennia, in many different places and a myriad ways. Differences between them reflect the environmental conditions in which the societies are located, but also the responses of individuals and groups to those societies and how they have learned to respond to the stimuli set. There is no implied environmental determinism, requiring a particular response to a certain type of environment. Some environments may be so hostile to human occupance that no societies have found a way of surviving in them over a long period, and others may be very constraining so that societies of very similar type have evolved in them independently. But most environments offer a range of opportunities. These may not all be perceived by their inhabitants, who have to choose which opportunity to take up from those they have identified. But for a variety of reasons, of which chance may be one of the most important, different people in similar but isolated situations may identify different opportunities in their environments, and build societies accordingly. Those societies are cultural organisations, and the result is a complex cultural mosaic.

In detail, as much anthropological research has shown, that cultural mosaic comprises a very wide range of types of social organisation. But for the present purposes it is possible to simplify them to only three, using a typology introduced by Karl Polanyi (1971, p.149) to represent the main forms of economic integration. These were seen by Polanyi as 'ideal types' (as Dalton stresses: Polanyi, 1971, p.153), and many economic systems contain elements of two, if not all three.

Reciprocity

The characteristic feature of a society based on reciprocity as its fundamental organising principle is collective rather than private ownership of property, especially the means of reproduction – notably land. The society's resources are held communally, and they are organised collectively

– usually by groups tied together in kinship obligations – to ensure that sufficient food and other materials is obtained for all. There will be some division of labour, notably according to age and gender, and some individuals may have more influence than others on decision-making within the society, either because they impose themselves on the society or because the society recognises their wisdom and is prepared to defer to them. Within the society, no group or individual will receive a disproportionate share of the products, the allocation of which is decided collectively and is thus considered equitable. It need not be equal, for the society may decide that certain individuals or groups should get more than their proportionate share, perhaps because of the nature of the work that they do within the society, which is more physically demanding, perhaps as a small reward for some above-average contribution, or perhaps because of agreed rules drawn up to ensure survival. It may be, for example, that children are fed more than adults at certain times, such as those of relative food scarcity, as a recognition of their importance to the society's future. On the other hand, too many children may be seen as a threat to the future, because they consume much more than they contribute, leading to policies for sacrifice of some to promote the general good.

Over the full span of human history, societies based on reciprocity have almost all existed at relatively low levels of subsistence, and can best be described as *primitive communist* in their structure (although, as Polanyi stressed, reciprocity is not necessarily confined to small, primitive communities and can be a characteristic of a large and wealthy empire too). Nevertheless, reciprocity was probably the only mode of production for many millennia, predating any more complicated organisational structures. The great majority of such societies almost certainly had precarious existences, subject to the vicissitudes of the environment. In resource-poor milieux, the chance of societies being decimated as a consequence of inability to support themselves, and even of being eliminated, was undoubtedly large; the quality of life was almost certainly low for most of the time, with very poor life expectancy. Many such societies became extinct, and have left few if any signs of their presence. In richer environments the potential for a better quality of life was present, but societies frequently bred to the limits of their environment so that in years when the environment was inclement, and especially in sequences of such years, there was societal hardship. Responses to this may have varied, including the voluntary or forced decision of some members to move away and find a new unoccupied environment where they could found a new society.

Such primitive communist societies lived in relative equilibrium with their environments, since they lacked the environmental appreciation, and even more so the technology, with which to tackle the environmental vicissitudes. The degree to which they could control the environment and make it do what they wanted was extremely limited. In most cases that equilibrium would not have been a particularly pleasant one. Means of surviving in and with the environment permanently were evolved, as with slash-and-burn agriculture, but they allowed relatively little comfort or leisure, and life expectancy was short. It is not possible from the outside to evaluate the degree of contentment felt, of course, for there was little if any opportunity for developing feelings of relative deprivation. What is crucial here is to note that the relationship between a society and its environment was one in which the latter dominated, in the long term if not the short.

Societies based on reciprocity are not necessarily primitive communist, and a very substantial proportion of the world population today lives in societies based, in stated principle if not entirely in practice, on reciprocity – 'to each according to his needs; from each according to his abilities'. Such societies differ from the primitive communist in two main ways. The first is their scale: whereas virtually all primitive communist societies have been very small, involving populations counted in hundreds only, modern communist societies are extremely large with one, the Chinese, being the largest in the world with more than one billion members. This difference in scale is very much a consequence of the second difference, in level of technological ability, and hence relationship with the environment. Because of that, and because of their importance in the world scene, modern communist societies are discussed below: primitive communist societies will get only passing mention from here on.

Rank redistribution

Rank redistribution societies differ from those based on reciprocity in that some of their members hold more power than others do without representing the consensus view of the society as a whole; these individuals and groups impose themselves upon the others, although they may use ideological and other means to try and legitimate that usurpation of power and their own positions as either or both natural and necessary. Quoting Aristotle, Polanyi (1971, p.93) notes that the 'three prizes of fortune' are: honour and prestige; security of life and limb; and wealth. Those with power in a redistribution-based society can dictate to those without it, not necessarily with regard to all aspects of their lives but sufficiently so that the powerful, who are almost certainly a minority, and probably a small one, are able to enjoy the three prizes of fortune based on work done by others at their command. In most rank redistribution societies the power of the elite group does not extend far into the lives of the others, but it penetrates those important areas concerned with meeting the elite's needs, well beyond what is necessary for subsistence and reproduction.

The origins of power in such societies are obscure. Archaeological evidence suggests that in most it was linked to either religious or military characteristics (and probably both: see, for example, Wheatley, 1971, on the origins of urbanisation). Individuals and groups were able to claim power over others by recourse to some magical or metaphysical source. Their power base was ideological, in that it was created by them and supported by the myth that they created and sustained inter-generationally. In brief, they claimed some kind of divine right to rule, a right sustained by a priestly cohort linked to those with power (if the priesthood were not the power-holders themselves) and with occasional recourse to divine intervention – notably in the environment – to illustrate that power.

Although the ideology may have been necessary to secure the power of the elite, it was rarely sufficient to sustain control over the majority of the population, who may have been both resentful of the exercise of the power and sceptical of its claimed origin. So the ideology had to be supported by some form of coercive force involving a military presence. The military was used to ensure that the directives of the power elite were followed, and its demands met. Thus the military had to be sustained alongside the elite (and the priesthood), so that the powerless had to deliver sufficient resources (food, raw materials for shelter, clothes, weapons, means of movement and so forth) not only for the elite but also for the groups employed to support the elite and who were unable (rather than unwilling, as in the case of the elite) to provide for themselves. So there was a marked division of labour in the society at two levels: between the producers and non-producers; and, within the latter, between the elite and its functionaries.

Fundamental to rank redistribution societies is the unequal distribution of power, with a hierarchical social structure. The basis of that unequal distribution varied extremely widely between those societies, as did the means of expressing and implementing the claimed superiority. The goal was the same: to enable the reproduction of the elite through the work of others. Slavery is a clear example of this, in which the individuals concerned – the slaves – were commodities owned by others, subject to their power and lacking control over their personal labour and reproduction; imperial Rome is an excellent example of such a society, in which the affluence of the elite was founded on their ownership of large amounts of slave labour. But, as Finley has argued, although slaves have been ubiquitous throughout human history in all modes of production, slavery has been the 'dominant labour force only in the west in a few periods and regions' (1983, p.441).

Of the many different types of rank redistribution society, that most relevant to the European experience is *feudalism*, in which the twin bases of elite power were land ownership and the institution of serfdom. Land, or at least some of it, and probably the most fertile, was not held in common by the society as a whole, but was owned by individuals, who determined how it would be worked. The work was done by a class of serfs, peasants who were obliged to work for part of their time for the landlord, to provide the means of self-reproduction for the elite, and worked for the remainder on land which they had been allocated; they obtained the means of their own reproduction from the latter, which they did not own but merely held as part of their relationship with the landlord. The situation of these 'unfree' peasants was defined in law, and they were entirely subject to the lord's jurisdiction on all matters, being bound to the lord and unable to move to another estate.

In relatively primitive feudal societies there was a simple division between landowner and others, but in the more developed, larger in scale and spatial extent (reflecting the ability of military technology to control larger areas effectively), there was a hierarchy of landownership. In a threefold division of society, for example, there may be an overall landowner, a monarch perhaps, who allocated much of the land under her or his control to a class of lords, who could use the land as they wished in return for loyalty to the monarch, the payment of certain dues (to sustain the monarch's standard of living), and the provision of certain services, such as an army when required. Those subsidiary lords would then use their land either by requiring the resident population to work on it, providing them with food and shelter in return, or by allocating land to them and requiring certain payments (in kind or in money) in return for the land, from which the population could also obtain an existence. Most feudal lords combined the two, keeping some land to themselves on which their tenants were required to work but also allocating land among their tenants and making demands on them as well.

Although the 'unfree' peasants were a mainstay of the feudal mode of production they were rarely in a majority, for alongside them were the 'free' peasants, who were tenants of the landlords but owed them no labour. Their contribution to the elite's existence was not through the provision of feudal labour – working on the landlord's demesne – but through the payment of taxes of various forms which the landlord was empowered to exact from all tenants and also through the ability of the landlord to require them to work (in mills and craft industries, for example), at a rate of recompense determined by the employer. In addition, the 'free' peasants were subject to a range of fines and rents, which required them to sell part of their produce in order to raise the needed money.

Feudalism did not comprise self-contained, self-sufficient societies, therefore, and although most of what was produced did not get traded on open markets (either being consumed in the peasant households or being transferred from the peasants – in kind or in labour – to the elite) there was some buying and selling. According to Hilton, the pressures to market farm produce were twofold. First, there was what he termed the 'social division of labour between cultivation, manufacture, ruling and waging war' (1983, p.168) which required the labour of the cultivators to support the full-time or part-time activities of the others; although some of that support could be demanded from the peasants, the latter became aware that if they produced a surplus to their own and their landlord's requirements it could probably be sold on the market, to their own benefit, thereby providing a motivation to greater production. Secondly, there were what Hilton termed 'the special needs of the ruling class' (p.169), whose consumption habits reflected much more than needs in a subsistence sense:

> What was consumed was only partly a matter of enjoyment: it was also a matter of display and reward – in other words it had a political func-tion. The consumption goods . . . were relatively small in bulk and high in price, and . . . they were produced a long way from the place of con-sumption – the Middle and Far East in particular. These goods were the commodities of international trade which in a stable feudal society could not be obtained, or at any rate only sporadically, by means of warfare and

plunder. The feudal ruling class needed money to buy them, money which was obtained through rent and jurisdictional profits, and which peasants obtained by selling their surplus product on the local markets. (p.169)

Thus within feudalism there were powerful growth impulses, by which the landlords demanded increased production from their serfs and greater rents and other payments from their peasantry, in order to promote their consumption habits and status. At the same time the peasantry was strongly pressured to increase its production in order to obtain the money needed to pay rents and fines, and also to purchase items of consumption for themselves. So feudalism was strongly tied to a system of markets and trade and to the growth of a network of market centres.

The details of the feudal mode of production vary widely, as historical evidence indicates. Bloch, for example, argues that feudalism developed in much of Europe as a response to the inadequacies of ties of kinship as a source of security in troubled times. In all places, it had two features that 'appear to have been indispensable' (1961, p.187) – the monopoly over the raising of armies held by the vassal lords, and the tie of vassalage (the obligations of the serf, who was 'the man of another man') as the predominant form of government. But given those two characteristics, different detailed forms of feudalism evolved: as Bloch remarks of England, it was 'a society of Germanic structure which . . . pursued an almost completely spontaneous course of evolution' (p.181).

Whereas most primitive communist societies were in relative equilibrium with their physical environment, albeit a dynamic and brittle one, most rank redistribution societies have not been so, because of the tendency of the elite to increase the pressure on the powerless to produce more, either directly (by making greater demands on the labour of serfs) or indirectly (through market mechanisms, as described earlier). This pressure may have resulted simply from increased human requirements, as a consequence of population growth, or it may result from acquisitiveness and greed. In the former case, for example, if a society is well organised and substantial supplies are provided for the elite, this could well lead to a high survival rate for its children, and hence a geometric growth rate in the elite population. The demands for resources will increase, and the powerless will be expected to produce more, with consequences for the environment. In order to ensure that more is produced and delivered, a larger military and/or priestly group may be needed, which in itself means an even greater increase in the demands on the powerless and the land that they occupy.

If the powerless are unable to respond by producing the needed extra resources, the elite class must reduce its demands. Over time, it may learn the limits that the local environment poses to its expansion – either in numbers or in its demand for goods – and may limit its size in some way. The result will be an equilibrium relationship with the environment. But such an equilibrium is less likely in feudal societies than in those based on primitive communism. It is likely that those with power will want to improve their lot, either in terms of the necessities of existence – a better diet, for example, or better housing – or in terms of 'luxuries', which would include ways of displaying their power through conspicuous consumption and permanent status symbols. These desires will be transmitted to those who provide for them; if they are unable to respond, then the elite may seek to extend their control, occupying more land and bringing more people into a subservient relationship to them, perhaps through military conquest: Hilton suggests that warfare was 'the favourite occupation of the [feudal] ruling class' (1983, p.170). Whatever they do, in the long term the demands on the environment increase, to meet the direct and indirect demands of the elite. In part those demands were imposed as demands on the peasantry, and were the cause of conflict within feudal societies as the peasants tried to resist the increased requirements they were forced to meet.

Markets

The fundamental principle in this third method of organising society is the market, in which goods and services are traded between buyers and sellers – capitalist societies are integrated through the market-place, rather than through the obligations of kinship and other social relations that characterise the other two, though not all interactions in capitalist societies are market transactions (as with social relationships within households, for example: see also Pahl, 1985). Within the general principle there are many variants, depending on the way in which markets are operated, the relative power of the buyers and sellers, and so forth. One of those variants, capitalism, has attained a dominant position in the contemporary world, having grown out of the previous modes, notably feudalism, and developed in a way in which the fundamental resource traded is labour power. Since an appreciation of capitalism is central to the arguments developed in this book, it will be given a more extended treatment than that alloonted to modes of production based on rank redistribution and reciprocity.

The Capitalist Mode of Production

The capitalist mode of production involves the use of two naturally given resources, land and labour, along with a third, capital (which is a human creation), to produce the goods and services that people consume in order to ensure their self-reproduction and desired quality of life, and also to ensure societal inter-generational reproduction. Its dynamo is the accumulation of wealth, which is derived from the profits of production. It is a mode of production which cannot be static, and as a consequence cannot sustain an equilibrium with its environment. Appreciation of that point is fundamental to much of the remainder of this book.

Capitalism is sometimes equated with industrialisation, and at others with the operation of markets for goods and services, but while both are significant features of capitalism, they are not defining characteristics of the mode of production. According to Desai (1983, pp.65–6), capitalism has six major characterising features:

(1) Production takes place for sale rather than for consumption by the producer.

(2) Labour power is bought and sold in markets, with the buyers agreeing contracts with the sellers over rates of payment (either for items of work or for periods of work) and the conditions, including the length of employment, of work.

(3) Exchange is almost universally through the medium of money, which is the most flexible way of redeploying the rewards of production. The importance of money gives financial intermediaries a particularly significant role in the operation of capitalism.

(4) The capitalist (or a managerial agent acting on behalf of a capitalist or a consortium of them – e.g. the shareholders in a company) who purchases the labour power of others also controls the process of production, determining how products are made and sold, and in what quantities.

(5) The capitalists and their agents also control financial decisions, which include those to borrow in order to invest, what to invest in, and where, and so forth. The sellers of labour power (the proletariat) have no control over those decisions, but their livelihoods are determined by them.

(6) There is competition between segments of capital, for labour, materials on which labour works, and markets. This competition is subject to laws of value which force the capitalist to adopt new techniques and practices which will cut costs, and to accumulate to make possible the provision of improved machinery. This constant revolution in value is an important feature of the dynamics of capitalism. (1983, p.65)

Capitalism originated in a transition from feudalism in the parts of Europe where accumulated wealth was available to be invested in new ways, and where the nature of social relationships enabled this to be successful (Hechter and Brustein, 1980). Substantial new wealth was accumulated through, for example, the investment of capital in trade involving slaves, agricultural production, precious metals and simple manufactured commodities. It then evolved into its industrial phase, with substantial investment in routine production of commodities in factories through the employment of large, disciplined labour forces, and then into its later stages (variously termed 'finance capitalism', 'monopoly capitalism', 'post-industrial capitalism', and so forth) in which relatively small numbers were involved in the actual processes of production and many more in both its facilitation and the organisation of distribution and exchange.

Means of production

Capitalism operates through the mobilisation of the three means of production – land, labour and capital; to some there is a fourth means, enterprise, but in the argument developed here enterprise refers to the way in which capitalism is operated and is not a separate resource on which the mode of production draws. Each of the means of production is privately owned, and this is fundamental both to the operation of capitalism and to its ideology.

Labour is the power to work, and is clearly a personal attribute, even though much work involves collaboration with others. In some types of society, such as those based on slavery, the individual's labour power is owned by another. This is not the case in capitalism; the individual is free to sell his or her labour power to anybody who wants to buy it – or not to sell it at all, in which case the individual must have an alternative means of support. Labour power has two components; the physical power to work, and the mental ability to undertake tasks. The former is genetically derived, though it can be either enhanced or reduced; the latter is a genetic endowment that can be enhanced through training and experience. The genetic endowments and the degree to which they have been enhanced comprise the commodity which individuals take to the labour market. They sell that commodity in order to be able to obtain their needs and demands; because they lack the ability to meet those themselves, they must obtain the means to purchase them – i.e. to buy the products of other people's labour.

Land provides the resources on which people work, and is fundamental to all production, even though not all people deal either directly with the land or work on its products; the majority of people who work in most capitalist societies are involved neither with primary (production from the land) nor secondary (manufacture of products from the raw materials yielded by the land) occupations, but rather with the tertiary and quaternary occupations involved in the organisation of production and the distribution of the outcomes. Land also comprises two main components: the raw materials which can either be consumed or transformed; and the environment within which other raw materials (such as foodstuffs) can be developed. It too is privately owned, and just as the owners of labour can determine how they will use that resource, so the owners of land are free to determine how they will use that means of production.

Capital differs from the other two means of production in that it is not a naturally occurring phenomenon but a human creation. Yet it plays a central role in the mode of production: without capital, land and labour cannot be employed. It is in effect a collective term for a variety of phenomena used in production, distribution and exchange; it includes the buildings within which work takes place, the machinery therein, and the money invested in those fixed assets, and is also used as a term to define the stock of wealth held by an individual or group. Capital is fundamental because unless money is invested in the work process, for example in building factories, installing machinery and fuelling it, purchasing raw materials, employing labour, and selling the resulting products, no goods are created, nothing is available for people to buy and survive on, no jobs are available for people to earn money with which to obtain the means of reproduction, and so forth. So how does it come about, and why is it invested?

Capital is the result of labour, specifically the surplus derived from employing labour. That surplus is created because the income from the sale of the products of the purchased labour is more than the costs of employing it, and the land resources on which it worked. The surplus value of any product is the difference between the cost of producing it and the price received when it is sold (the production costs include the selling expenses, such as marketing and advertising). It accrues to the person or group who invested in the production process, and is generally known as the profit. (The technical definition of profit in this labour theory of value is given in Harvey, 1982, Chapter 2.) That profit is added to the person's or group's stock of wealth, and can be used by them either to purchase goods and services or to invest in further production, and hence further profit-making. If profits are not made, the investors have no returns on which to sustain themselves. More importantly for the mode of production as a whole, they have no available money that can be used as capital to invest in further rounds of production, and hence in providing employment for labour. The dynamic of capitalism requires both that profits be made and that capital be invested in making more profits.

The difference between capital and land and labour, therefore, is that the one is the product of the other two. This raises important questions about the origins of the initial capital. Answering them lies outside the main arguments of this book. All that is important here is to note that capitalism developed as a mode of production in areas of feudal societies, where the wealth of the elite was directed, through a sequence of stages and much trial and error, into the creation of the capitalist mode of production. It emerged in societies where most individuals possessed only their labour power and were dependent on the owners of land for their livelihoods. Those powerful owners of land used some of their amassed wealth either directly in the employment of labour or indirectly by investing in those who intended to. Capitalism grew out of societies based on inequality, and developed that inequality.

Employing labour and making profits

The motive force of capitalism is the accumulation of wealth derived from profits. If people don't want to amass wealth, then they don't want to make profits, and if they don't invest in making profits, nothing gets made, people don't have work, and reproduction becomes impossible. Thus the desire to accumulate wealth from profits had to be accepted as the 'natural' way of organising society, and that ideology had to be promoted by those who already believed in such a method of organising society. The success of that ideological experiment can be assessed by the contemporary role of capitalism.

How did the mode of production develop? Early capitalism involved both direct and indirect purchase of labour power by those with available capital. The direct route involved employing people either in agriculture or, increasingly, in manufacture. Investment in manufacturing began in many places by people investing not in factories, in which they set employees to work, but in raw materials on which they employed people to work in their own homes; profits were made by paying those people less than what the goods produced could be sold for. The indirect methods involved not employing people directly, but rather buying goods from them, which were then sold elsewhere, at a profit; again the investor had to have available money to bridge the gap between the purchase from the producer and the sale to the consumer, and any costs involved in getting from one to the other. In every case, the investors' decisions were determined by their interpretation of the market-place: they would not invest in a commodity if they thought they could not sell it, and they would not pay more for it than a percentage (less than 100) of the price they expected to obtain. Markets determined what was produced; if there was no likely sale there would be no investment, since if the product could not be sold profits would not be made, and the investors' stock of wealth would be reduced rather than enhanced. This principle remains central to the operation of capitalism.

At this early stage, then, we can identify three groups within the population. The largest by far was that comprising individuals whose only available resource was labour power; in order to survive they had to sell it. The others were those who in addition to their labour power also possessed other means of production. There were those with land, who employed labour in order to produce saleable commodities from the land; in addition to the land, they needed some capital to cover the costs of employing the labour in the period before the products were sold. Finally there were those with capital, obtained in a variety of ways (inheritance, borrowing, gifts and so on). They invested this either directly in production or indirectly in facilitating production through trade. Those with labour power only depended on the other groups for their existence, and thus were relatively powerless; those with land and/or capital were much more powerful and it was their investment decisions that formed the direction of the society's development. For a long period those investors with available capital operated as individuals, and so the major distinction within society was between those with capital – the capitalists – and those without – the labourers. Over time that distinction was replaced by another. As capitalism expanded, the capital investment requirements were increasingly greater than those that individuals could meet from their amassed wealth (or were prepared to 'gamble' on a single venture). It was necessary for them both to combine and to borrow from others to obtain the necessary sums. Thus the precise distinction between capitalists and labourers disappeared, and was replaced by that between the labourers and those who employed them, who benefited in part from the outcomes (their incomes were conditional on successful profit-making) but who were accountable to a wide range of other investors (i.e. the capitalists' agents, to use Desai's term; see p.50). Increasingly the difference within capitalism is between the managers of capital and the workers, which is not to deny the existence of many individuals and families with great wealth based on their investment in labour.

A mode of production based on the trading of agricultural products and the outputs of relatively unsophisticated manufacturing processes requires an infrastructure, which has two components. The first is the built environment, comprising the transport networks and the vehicles that traverse them, the buildings in which trade is to be conducted, and so on. The second is a facilitating environment, providing in particular the services on which trade is based. These too called for investment, by people who perceived that capital used in that way would produce a return – i.e. would be profitable. New sectors of the economy emerged to facilitate the basic processes of producing, distributing and exchanging: all were subject to the same basic principles – only invest if profit will ensue.

Competing and selling

In the 'ideal' capitalist economy there is a very large number of sellers plus an equally large, probably much larger, number of buyers. As a consequence, no one buyer or group of buyers and no one seller or group of sellers can determine the price of a commodity with little or no reference to the others; the price is a function of demand and supply. In such a market buyers are seeking the cheapest items, at a given quality, or at least within a certain quality range, and in order to sell to them the producers of the goods must meet the buyers' criteria. Success in the market therefore involves producing goods at a price and quality acceptable to the buyers. To a large extent price and quality are relative rather than absolute criteria. Clearly there are price limits beyond which consumers will not go – because they cannot afford to, given the many other demands on their available resources – and there are quality limits below which they will not buy. But in most situations the alternative goods on display offer an equivalent return, and customers are seeking the 'best buy'; this usually means they are looking for the most competitive price.

Producers are well aware of this, of course, and their decision whether to produce a certain commodity reflects their evaluation of the market. But having entered it, they face competition, and competition that will change as others enter and some withdraw. To succeed they must compete successfully. In the market for any commodity the successful competitors are those whose production costs are lowest. If the price is fixed they make the largest profits, but if they are prepared to lower their price they may reduce the profit on each individual item but, by increasing their sales volume, increase their profitability overall, and relative to their labour costs (even though they may employ more workers). How, then, do they ensure that they succeed in such ways?

If the largest profits accrue to those with the lowest production costs, there must be differences between producers in the costs that they incur. These can come about in a variety of ways; one producer may have access to a cheaper raw material source than another, for example. But raw materials are the product of labour power, indirectly if not directly, and ultimately virtually all variations between producers depend on the relative costs of their labour – relative, that is, to what they produce. The more productive a unit of labour, measured perhaps as the amount produced for every pound spent on that person (both directly, in wages, and indirectly, in the materials provided and the machinery used) the greater the profit from the expenditure. If a commodity can be sold for £20, the investor who produces it for a £10 investment will make more than the person who pays £12. Greater productivity means greater profits.

Productivity is of fundamental importance, then; the more that workers produce, relative to what they are paid and is spent on them, the more profits they generate for their employers. Thus the differences between producers' relative success in the market-place reflect differentials in their workers' productivity. Those differentials may reflect different capacities of the workers – they are fitter, or more able – but are usually the product of investment (in training, for example). In other cases they may reflect the resources used – one farmer has more fertile soils than another, for example. But in the majority of cases they reflect the amount and efficiency of work; the more efficient the work process, the greater the return on the wages paid.

Greater work could simply involve greater expenditure of effort; one employer's staff works harder for the same amount of money than does another's. But it is more likely to be differences in the effectiveness of work that produce the greater profits, because one group has better tools to work with than another. Increased productivity is usually achieved by replacing labour by machines. This is sometimes called replacing 'live labour' by 'dead labour', since machines are themselves the product of labour. The machines may be expensive to install, but are so much cheaper to run (fuel and maintenance are less expensive than labour) that the investment promises to repay the initial outlay with interest and so can be afforded; the cost of buying and running the machine is less than the cost of producing by using 'live labour'. Some operations are more readily performed by machines than others, and no production process is as yet entirely automated – and, of course, machines can't invent and maintain machines, so labour is needed somewhere. But where labour can be replaced by more efficient machines – which frequently means that a skilled operative is replaced by a semi-skilled or unskilled machine-minder – the potential competitive advantage in the market-place from the investment in the replacement of labour will probably be realised.

The drive to increase productivity and thus profits is ever-present, because it means greater wealth acquisition. It is particularly pressing when competition is intense, perhaps because the market is more or less saturated, and even more so when it is in decline. In the latter situation, producers are competing for a declining market; in order to maintain their profitability they must increase their market share. To do this they must be competitive; the winners are the producers with the lowest costs and/or the best products, because they can outbid their competitors. In particular, those with the lowest production costs can undercut the prices of the less efficient, and force the latter out of the market. In periods of buoyant demand the relatively inefficient may be able to survive, but as competition becomes tougher it is the fittest who survive.

So far, the discussion of increasing productivity in order to compete successfully has been presented in terms of the production of goods. But it applies equally to many of the service industries, which depend on labour for the distribution and exchange procedures, and for facilitating the operation of the whole system. The retailing industry has been subject to drives to increase productivity in a variety of ways in recent years; supermarkets replace labour by space in giving customers access to the goods, for example, and high technology at the checkouts increases the number of customers that an employee can handle in a given period, for a certain wage. (And this book is being written on a word-processor, which is quicker than longhand and removes the necessity for a secretary–typist.)

There are three probable consequences of increased productivity. The first is that the process of survival of the fittest means that the relatively inefficient producers are eliminated from the competition. Eventually, the number of producers still active is sufficiently small for them to collude if they wished to fix the price, and so to some extent protect themselves from possibly losing in the continued competition. The ultimate expression of this is the creation of a monopoly in which a single producer gains control of the market for a product – either by causing all the competitors to fail or by buying them out. A monopolist is less subject to the constraints of the market than is the case when there are many competitors, though the degree to which monopolists are released from the rigours of the marketplace depends on the elasticity of demand for their products. Monopoly situations can lead to a range of consequences considered undesirable both for consumers and for the future of the capitalist system: monopolists are less likely to invest in further improvements if their profits are ensured, which could initiate a downward spiral of production and consumption.

The second consequence is also a result of success. The market for most products is not ever-expanding, particularly if the product cannot easily be transported several thousand miles. Thus as productivity increases, so the ability to produce more than the market can consume comes ever closer. The technological advances that allow productivity increases result in the production of more goods than can be sold, and so in the end the drive to increase profits leads to the situation in which the making of profits becomes more difficult, even for the more successful, efficient producers. The only answers to this on behalf of the producers are either to seek new markets or to switch their investment into other product lines where the market is more buoyant and the promise of profitability brighter.

Linked to this problem in certain circumstances is the situation in which increased productivity itself reduces the demand for goods. Products are bought by people using their wages. But if they are made redundant by the productivity increases – fewer people are needed to produce the same volume of goods, and those who are still employed are paid less because they are less skilled – then fewer people have wages to spend and those who have, have less to spend. (The workforce becomes increasingly polarised, between the well-paid skilled workers who design and maintain the machinery that increases productivity, and the poorly paid, unskilled operatives.) Competition in the market leads to the market being destroyed. This tendency is countered if capital is invested in new lines of production, creating new jobs. This may involve bringing into the capitalist system the production of goods and especially services that was formerly outside it. The growth of leisure-based industries in recent years is an example;

increasingly people purchase leisure (television programmes, for example) from producers, rather than creating their own entertainment. This is the process of commodification whereby, as a consequence of its very success, the capitalist system has to invade more aspects of life in order to survive.

The third consequence of increases in productivity is that they may lead to increased conflict between employers and their employees over two main issues: wages and the conditions of work, and job security. On the first, employers are concerned to hold wages as low as possible relative to prices, in order to sustain profitability levels. They may be prepared to make some additional payment as a reward for productivity increases, but not so great as to wipe out the benefits to their profits of the investment in greater productivity. Employees, on the other hand, are concerned to increase their wages in order at least to maintain if not to increase their spending power and level of living. Alongside these debates over wages (over the proportion of the selling price that should go in wages relative to the proportion that goes into surplus value) may be others over the conditions at work. Employees may claim that they are being asked to work harder, or in more dangerous conditions, and seek recompense accordingly, either directly – in higher wages – or indirectly – through a shorter working week, for example, or longer holidays, or other fringe benefits. These disputes become more contentious, and the power of the employees in them increased, if the employees act collectively through a trade union or similar body. By negotiating in strength, and with the ultimate sanction of withdrawing their labour, which will of course hurt them but will also have immediate impact on the profitability of the organisation, the workers are better placed to win concessions from their employers than are individual employees.

This conflict between employers and employees is fundamental to the operations of capitalism, since all changes introduced by employers to enhance their profitability have consequences for their employees In the short term it is the employees who have most to lose, since they haven't the cushion of accumulated wealth to sustain them during a period when they are not earning. If they are prepared to hurt themselves, however, they may win concessions from their employers whose potential profits are rapidly being eroded by the loss of production and income. But this success merely writes the script for the next act of the conflict; having made concessions, the employer will then want further productivity increases in order to survive in the competitive market.

Longer-term competitive consequences

In this brief description of how capitalism works, the earlier statement that it is necessarily a dynamic mode of production has been clearly illustrated. People's survival is dependent on them being able to find work, so that they can buy the goods that they need for personal and societal reproduction. They can only find work if others with capital available are prepared to invest it in making things for sale, and they will only do that if they believe that there is a market for the products in which they can compete successfully and make profits. Having determined that they can, and so entered the market, they then find that to survive in it they must continually act to increase the productivity of their operations, without which they will fail, their workers will be wageless again and there will be no profits to invest in creating further jobs, products, and the means of survival. Capitalism is a competitive activity in which continued improved performance is a necessity, and if people don't succeed, many others lose.

One of the consequences of this system, already alluded to, is that it contains within itself the seeds of its own destruction; success can be the cause of failure. Increasing productivity can mean that the ability to produce goods far outstrips the ability to consume, for reasons already described. The result is a crisis, alternatively termed a crisis of overproduction or of underconsumption, depending on the point of view. Whichever term is used, the result is the same; too much is produced, and profitability suffers. Whenever profitability suffers, investment slows, jobs are at risk, and with them people's life chances.

The actors within the capitalist system are aware of these issues, of course, and are continually seeking ways of countering them. In the short term their response is to try and increase profitability by the traditional routes: cheaper raw materials, perhaps from another supplier whose labour is cheaper; more efficient production using fewer (and preferably cheaper) workers and better machines; more effective advertising and marketing, expanding the demand for the product either by convincing those who formerly didn't buy it to do so or by convincing those who did to replace their existing purchases more frequently. As will be detailed later, these may involve geographical strategies, searching the world for cheaper materials, cheaper labour and more markets.

But there are limits to these strategies. Sooner or later the market will become saturated and sales cannot be increased, and the limits to increased productivity will be approached. Profitability will be eroded, and only the fittest will survive. The only solution then for most competitors in that sector of the system will be to withdraw, and to find alternative uses for their capital: fixed capital (buildings, machines, raw materials, even land itself) may be put to alternative uses that can yield profits, as also may labour. This may be painful; many people may find themselves unemployed, temporarily at least, as the transition occurs, and they may need to be retrained to participate in the new activities. But if those activities can be identified, and then developed, the problems should be short-lived.

What happens, however, when such a need to restructure occurs not just in one sector of the economy, or even in a few firms, but in very large segments of it, affecting the jobs of very many people and the capital investments of large numbers too? And are such major events likely? The evidence of the history of capitalism, and certainly of the last 200 years or so, is that indeed there is a major slump affecting many parts of the economy at the same time, about once every fifty years. Profitability declines in a number of important sectors concurrently, with the result that the possibilities for alternative uses of capital are limited: buildings cannot be transferred to other uses, there are no new tasks for which labour can be retrained, and so on. Eventually each of these slumps has been followed by a new period of prosperity, built on a new generation of industries – the outcome of investment in research and development – creating and then meeting a new set of demands and, it seems, drawing more of the world into their sphere of influence. But the restructuring is often painful, as capital is withdrawn very substantially from certain activities, which almost certainly means certain places, and is eventually placed elsewhere. In the interim, it may be that the capital-holders perceive no worthwhile investments and prefer not to commit themselves to ventures unlikely to increase their stock of wealth, and which may even erode it. In such situations they may prefer to use their money in ways that are much less likely to create jobs for others, for example by investing it in commodities like land, precious metals, jewellery and works of art, whose exchange value they believe will increase in the long term.

Such 'unproductive' use of capital cannot go on for long, since it will lead to a decline in the store of wealth and also to a crisis in the system as a whole, since insufficient investment in production means not only fewer goods and services produced for consumption but also fewer workers with incomes to spend on those goods and services. The dynamo will wind down, unless capital is directed towards potentially profitable investments. Harvey has illustrated this with his representation of three circuits of capital (Figure 3.1). The primary circuit involves investment in the production of goods and services, from which surplus value will be extracted and profits made, with consequent wealth accumulation. But during periods of underconsumption capital is moved into the secondary and tertiary circuits. The former involves investments in fixed capital, such as the built environment, including, for example, buildings in the expectation of profits from this investment, either in rents from the use value or in enhanced exchange value. The tertiary circuit involves investment in science and technology, in the expectation of advances in production methods that will enhance future wealth accumulation strategies, or in improving human labour, as with education. In both cases much of this investment is made collectively, through the institutions of the state, because individual capitalists are unlikely to make investments in the potential long-term advantages. This provides part of the argument for the necessity of the state in capitalist societies, as developed further in later chapters; at this stage we note that the long-term survival of capitalism requires institutions which ensure investment in the infrastructure (both physical and mental) necessary to the continued operation of the dynamo of wealth accumulation.

Capitalism and place

This brief description of some of the elements of the capitalist mode of production carries with it a number of major geographical implications, since the prosperity of people is intimately tied up with the prosperity of the places in which they live. But the geography of capitalism is not simply

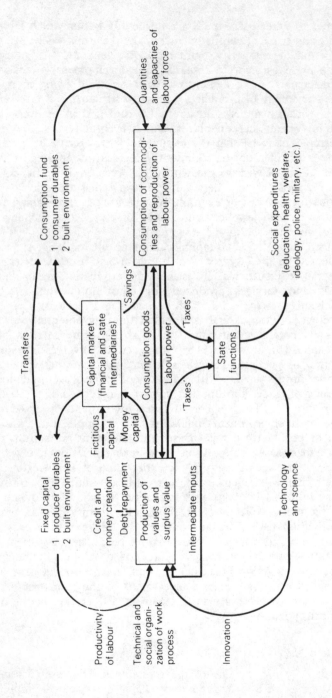

Figure 3.1 The circuits of capital

an outcome of the operation of non-geographical processes; the continual restructuring of geography is an integral part of the continual restructuring of capitalism. Capitalism makes, destroys, and remakes places, as will be illustrated here.

The basic process of creating and changing geographies (or places) is well portrayed in a model developed by Ann Markusen (1985). This represents the life of an industry as a profit cycle, comprising four stages. In the first stage, a new product is being developed and profitability has yet to begin: investment in research has been forthcoming because potential profitability has been perceived, because a market is thought either to exist or to be creatable. At the second stage, the market is being opened up, returns on the initial investment in research and development are being obtained, and profitability begins. The initial developers who invested in the product may reap a rich reward at this time if the market does develop as predicted, because of their near-monopolistic position. Eventually, however, their success attracts competitors, who are able to enter the market without the expensive research and development investment. Competition increases and profit levels decline overall, but vary between competitors depending on the degree to which they increase productivity-enhancing investment – which will depend on their perception of the future market trends. By the fourth stage market saturation has been reached, and the crisis of over-production (or underconsumption) of the product has set in. As the level of profitability declines, many of the competitors will choose to disinvest from the sector, seeking alternative outlets for their money and expertise, and those remaining will be less inclined to invest in further profitability increases. The market for the product may entirely disappear. More likely, however, is the continued existence of a relatively static level of demand, and some producers remain to serve this, probably those able to survive because of relatively low costs.

The geography of this profit cycle reflects the differences between the stages; increasingly that geography is being written and rewritten globally rather than nationally, let alone regionally or locally. At the first and second stages the development is contingent on the availability of both capital and skilled labour; it is most likely to be found in places where those are relatively abundant (on the geography of venture capital see Thompson, 1989). With the move into the second stage factories are established which are likely to need skilled labour, because of the newness of the product and the processes involved; the workers in them may be relatively highly paid, not only because of their skills but also because their relative monopoly allows the employers to meet the wage and other demands (which they are immediately able to add to the price of the good or service), in order to ensure continued production and high profits. This may be to those workers' disadvantage at the third stage, when the production process becomes much more routinised, because they will probably be highly paid relative to those of firms who have entered the industry at the routine stage and established their factories in places where labour is relatively cheap. The initial manufacturers may find it necessary to shift to such locations as well, which means that the original incubation areas for the industry lose out in the mature stages of its development. At the final stage, it will be the factories with the most productive workers who remain in production, which could well be in regions where skills are few; their prosperity is based on providing cheap, relatively amenable workers for routine production – profits are not great but are relatively assured by employing them.

To some commentators, the spatial dispersion of production activities envisaged in the profit cycle model is a characteristic of a form of capitalism that is increasingly becoming obsolete. In the 'Fordism' era the mass production of commodities took place in large factories with production line organisation and mainly semi-skilled labour; but 'Fordism' is now being replaced, it seems, by what is variously termed 'post-Fordism', a 'regime of flexible accumulation', and 'disorganised capitalism' (Lash and Urry, 1987), characterised by much smaller production units and a greater integration of factories and workshops into production complexes comprising interdependent units most of which survive on subcontracted work (Thrift, 1989). Thus while 'Fordism' allowed great spatial flexibility to producers, and apparently led to a decline in large cities as investors sought cheap production locations (a process widely known as 'counterurbanisation'), 'flexible accumulation' requires spatial proximity of linked production units, and is restimulating the growth of major cities (Scott, 1988).

A major feature of this profit cycle is that the pace of operations has increased substantially in recent decades; the length of the period of 'excess profits' in the second stage is now much shorter than it was only a few years ago, and the competitive years of the third stage are both fewer and fiercer. Restructuring takes place more frequently, so geographies change more often.

This process of restructuring involves a geographical process of 'uneven development, whereby the fortunes of places change rapidly, but within a well recognised overall structure. Basic to the geographical structuring is a division of the capitalist world into two main zones – a core and a periphery. Within the core are concentrations of two main types of activity; the financial institutions which facilitate the operation of the global capitalist system, and the research and development clusters. The core is where the innovations develop, and where the factories of the 'excess profits' second stage are located. It is where the investors live. The periphery lacks skilled labour and capital in large quantities, but has resources and cheap labour to offer. It is where factories are opened in the third stage, and where those that survive in the fourth are likely to be found. But many of them are owned by organisations located in the core, and the profits from peripheral activities are thus likely to be destined for the core (where the financial institutions will reallocate them, perhaps to other areas of the periphery).

Places in the periphery therefore have a fragile economy relative to those of the core. A few may be able to rise up into the core, via a semi-peripheral stage, as the result of exploiting local advantages – as with Japan in the present century – but for most peripheral areas escaping that status seems a remote possibility. Within the core, different areas compete for power. In each of the major boom periods of the world economy in the last three centuries, one core area has dominated, but the strains of success usually lead to its replacement in the next. (These strains are related to the politics of core status also, which sees the state in which the core area is located becoming overstretched geopolitically and therefore unable to assist the core in the restructuring process of the switch from one period of the cycle to the next.) Thus the major concentration of political power has migrated around the core, but the relative position of core and periphery has remained substantially unchanged for long periods.

It is common to associate the core–periphery division of the capitalist world economy with the geography of the nation–states of the contemporary world political map. This is a substantial generalisation, because the processes creating cores and peripheries are really class processes. Thus while it is proper to see the division of that map into cores and peripheries, as a consequence of colonial and imperial processes, it must also be recognised that individual countries (in both the core and the periphery on a global scale) contain their own cores and peripheries, as indeed do individual cities (see, for example, Hechter, 1975). Thus the processes of uneven development operate at a variety of spatial scales, producing complex maps of economic power and complex movements of investments and profits.

Capitalism in summary

Capitalism is clearly an extremely complex mode of production, and this introduction has only been able to sketch some of its features which are fundamental to understanding the genesis and possible approaches to solving environmental problems. In brief, the survival of capitalism depends on the continued circulation of capital, by which capital is invested in the production of commodities (goods and services) in order to create surplus value and thus increase the stock of capital. It is difficult to improve upon David Harvey's (1985b) summary of the basic features that underpin the circulation of capital, in the following ten points.

(1) The production of an ever-increasing stock of capital depends on continual expansion of the value of commodities produced. Growth is necessary to capitalism, so that it must be sustained and legitimated through a pro-growth ideology.
(2) Growth can only be achieved through the profitable sale of the products of human labour.
(3) Profits are obtained through the exploitation of labour, from the surplus value which is the difference between the costs of production and the selling price of commodities.
(4) Since the success of capitalism depends on the buying and selling of labour power, then there is a class separation between those who sell labour power and those who buy it; without that separation, and the social relations that it implies, capitalism could not operate.
(5) The relationship between the classes implies antagonism and conflict,

over wages and working conditions.
(6) The competition that underlies capitalism requires continued technological and organisational advances, so that some investors can increase their competitive advantage over others.
(7) Technological and organisational development require investment, in advance of profit-making; the survival of capitalism requires ensuring that continued investment.
(8) Capitalism is crisis-prone, because growth and technological progress are antagonistic; this will occasionally result in major crises of capitalism with disruption of the circulation process.
(9) The usual manifestation of crisis is that of overproduction, in which the surplus capital yielded by profits cannot be absorbed by further rounds of investment.
(10) In order to surmount the crisis of overproduction, it is necessary to devalue the surpluses by writing off capital investments.

Harvey's analysis thus focuses on the importance of crises in the operation of capitalism. As will be argued in the next chapter, those crises, and the growth dynamics from which they emerge, including the increased value of commodities in circulation and the need for continued investment in technological and organisational improvements, produce responses that are likely to have particularly severe consequences for the physical environment.

Advanced Communism/Socialism

These two linked modes of social organisation differ from capitalism in the relative importance of the basic components of an economic system – production, distribution and exchange. Under capitalism, it is production and exchange which are dominant and together they provide the dynamo which keeps a system in operation. Furthermore, growth in the volume of production, and hence also of exchange, is a necessary element of capitalism's health; as described earlier, continued accumulation drives the capitalist mode of production, and if it fails to occur, decay is the consequence – stagnation, over more than a short period, is inconsistent with the capitalist mode. Under advanced communism/socialism, on the other hand, the major focus is on distribution, on the allocation of the fruits of production among the members of society, through mechanisms which may not involve exchange as it is understood in the capitalist system. Thus the two types have very different ideologies promoting their acceptance; the capitalist ideology focuses on the creation of wealth within society, and argues that the operation of markets is the best means of assuring that this privately produced wealth is widely distributed through society, whereas the communist/socialist ideology focuses on the collective production of wealth and its equitable allocation by mechanisms other than markets which, it is argued, are rarely equitable in the distribution of power between buyers and sellers.

Therefore capitalism and advanced communism/socialism differ in their apparent need for central co-ordination and control. Under capitalism, it would seem, there is little need for a powerful state, or similar institution, since markets can operate independently; the decisions on what to produce and what to purchase are made by individuals according to perceptions of markets and needs. (In fact, as described in a later chapter, capitalism does need a strong state, but in a very different form from that required under advanced communism/socialism.) On the other hand, if decisions on production and distribution are to be made collectively, it is necessary to have an institution within which those collective decisions can be made; such an institution would need the acceptance of the population it serves. This is clearly a case for a state, or some institution similar to that which we term the state, that can draw individuals together in a collectivity, determine their goals, and develop means of attaining them.

Although the origins of advanced communism/socialism can be found in many sources, the ideology gathered momentum during the nineteenth century, particularly under the stimulus of the work of Karl Marx. As he and his followers developed it, the ideology saw the communist mode of production as a successor to capitalism, with socialism as an intermediate stage. Indeed, communism was seen as the logical outcome of capitalism which contains within itself the seeds of its own destruction; the in-built antagonisms between capitalists and workers would eventually lead to the latter overthrowing the former and taking over the economic and political organisation to promote their own collective ends.

Communism is a mode of production and social organisation in which the means of production, distribution and exchange are collectively rather than individually owned and in which there are no class distinctions based on the buying and selling of labour power. It is created out of the successes of capitalism, but because of its failures. The successes of capitalism are its ability to solve the problems of production; the inventiveness of individuals in the creation of ways of making products that contribute to a high material quality of life. The failures include its inability to ensure that the high material quality of life is available to all; under capitalism, according to Marxian arguments, there must always be major disparities in levels of living, because the success of the mode of economic organisation depends on keeping down the costs of labour and thus ensuring that all people have sufficient income to attain high material standards. This failure will increasingly become apparent to those who suffer from it, who can be politically mobilised to create a new form of social organisation, a new mode of production, in which such disparities disappear. Under capitalism, goods and services are produced if they can be sold; under the new mode of production they would be produced if the population wanted them, and would be equally available to all.

This new mode of production – which is termed advanced communism here to distinguish it from the primitive communism described earlier – would be achieved by the appropriation of the privately owned means of production by the state, on behalf of the population at large. This could occur in one step, through what would be a revolution, or it could be a steady process of the continued advance of public ownership and the decline of public property. State ownership of the means of production, distribution and exchange would ensure that decisions about what should be produced, for whom, and how it should be allocated would be made by the population at large (through a representative body which had their popular support) rather than by a small number of owners of large wealth whose decisions were determined by profit-making potential rather than 'real needs'. It should be noted, however, that not all those who accepted the analysis of the successes and failures of capitalism subscribed also to the prescriptions of communism. For example in *The Future of Socialism* (1956), an important book that influenced Labour party thinking in Britain for a generation, C.A.R. Crosland argued that equality could be achieved through planning involving co-operation between the state and the capitalist organisations, without major nationalisation and public ownership; he promoted instead a system of 'competitive public enterprise' in which

ownership is thoroughly mixed-up – a society with a diverse, diffused, pluralist, and heterogeneous pattern of ownership, with the State, the nationalised industries, the Cooperatives, the Unions, Government financial institutions, pensions funds, foundations, and millions of private families all participating.

and concluded that

State ownership of all industrial capital is not now a condition of creating a socialist society, establishing social equality, increasing social welfare, or eliminating class distinctions. What is unjust in our present arrangements is the distribution of private wealth; and that can be cured in a pluralist as in a wholly State-owned economy, with much better results for social contentment and the fragmentation of power. (1956, p.340)

According to those who accepted the communist prescription, as socialism spread through a society so private ownership would be diminished and collective control over the economy would replace it. Once this was achieved the transition to communism would be complete and, according to some, the need for a central state would disappear. *Anarchism* would replace it, using that term in its original sense and not as a synonym for chaos; society would be organised through myriad small communities, in each of which all were equal and each of whom had equal negotiating rights in determining the priorities and programmes of larger collectivities. Central direction through a state would be unnecessary, and individual freedom would be maximised (thus removing one of the fears of Crosland and some other interpreters of communist societies, that economic equality could only be achieved at the expense of individual liberty).

According to this set of views, communism builds on the prosperity created by the successes of capitalism, and transforms the way in which that prosperity is enjoyed; it is fundamentally a global mode of production, promoting the interests of all. Thus socialism should develop, as the precursor of communism, in areas of greatest capitalist success. In general terms, this has not been the case. Whereas some countries in which capitalism has been successful have seen socialist experiments (in Britain and parts of Western Europe in particular, but certainly not in the United States) these have not moved far towards the goals of collective ownership promoting equality. In several of those experiments, the collectively owned enterprises have been very similar to privately owned capitalist enterprises in their mode of operation – expected to make profits, for example, and to react to market signals. In recent years there have been major shifts away from the socialist experiments, as the capitalist ideology has gained renewed support among the population at large, as reflected in the politics of the parties elected to run their societies. (Some parties with socialist roots, and still to some extent promoting socialist ideas, are clear y now not socialist in what they do when in power; New Zealand's Labour Party in the mid-1980s provides a clear example of this.)

Where it has been introduced, notably in the countries of Eastern Europe and East Asia, communism took over from modes of social organisation where capitalist success had not been achieved; the societies were either in an early stage of capitalist penetration, and with low material living standards for the great majority of their populations, or had not yet attained even that level. Thus there were few successful capitalist operations to be taken over in a socialist revolution, which could make a wide range of goods and thereby ensure high overall levels of material prosperity for all, if the products were equitably distributed. Instead, the development of a very strong state has been necessary in those countries, a state which would plan the achievement of such high levels by a programme of industrialisation which would achieve what had been attained in Western Europe and North America by the very largely unplanned operation of capitalism. The level of direction necessary and the control imposed on the population is seen by many as totally contradictory to the ideology of communism, with its emphasis on freeing the individual from the control of others. Apologists for totalitarian regimes argue that they represent a necessary transitional period because the communist revolutions occurred away from the areas of capitalist success (and have not been assisted by the capitalists); only when high material levels have been achieved – and this is happening, as life expectancy figures show (see Johnston, 1989) – could the promised liberation be allowed. Thus instead of being achieved out of capitalist success, communism is being achieved without it. Whether the achievement will eventually be celebrated is an issue of much debate; recent evidence from the communist countries suggests that it cannot, that central state direction cannot attain the high material standards that decentralised capitalism did, and that only by allowing some privatisation of the means of production, distribution and exchange (i.e. a shift to socialism, if not to capitalism) will major improvements be attained.

Within communist societies it is clear that the goal is to attain levels of material welfare equivalent to those of capitalist societies, without of course the excesses 'enjoyed' by small proportions of the population in capitalist societies, where consumption levels (in, for example, house size) far exceed what can really be described as 'needs'. In large part, this is because residents of the communist societies are aware of those levels, and wish to emulate them; in the long term, if the communist society fails to deliver such standards, it will be deemed to have failed. Only in a few cases, as in Tanzania, has there been much explicit promotion of levels of consumption well below those attained elsewhere, on the grounds that such standards are neither necessary nor sustainable. In general, the communist ideology is that the material standards achieved in the capitalist world can similarly be achieved in the communist, through a different mechanism. Thus the production goals in the two are very similar in terms of what is wanted, and this is important to later discussions of relationship with the environment.

Sphere of Production, Civil Society and the State

The discussion so far in this chapter has focused exclusively on the economic base of a mode of social organisation, hence the term 'mode of production'. That economic base is fundamental; if a society cannot organise its survival then other aspects of its members' lives are irrelevant. The foundation of any mode of social organisation, therefore, must be the way in which production is organised to ensure societal reproduction.

But although the economic base of a society is fundamental to its existence, it is not to be implied that the organisation of production is the only distinguishing feature. Indeed, even casual observation of contemporary capitalist societies will show that although they share that economic base they differ in many other ways. Profit-making and wealth accumulation are central features of all of those societies, and they all experience the crises associated with overproduction. But they differ in many other aspects of their social and political organisation, differences that are often summarised as cultural.

The origins of these cultural differences often lie in the pre-capitalist societies, which in turn reflected local responses to their physical environments. Those cultural practices became part of the capitalist heritage, and were allowed to remain in place so long as they didn't prevent the operation of the capitalist system. And as capitalism developed, so new cultural practices emerged that were unique to particular societies. Thus, for example, the political development in many capitalist countries of Western Europe saw the emergence of an electoral cleavage between the employer and employee occupational classes. But such a cleavage was not necessary; capitalism didn't require it, and it failed to appear in some countries, such as the Republic of Ireland (as well as the United States). The politics of capitalism does not necessarily involve the two economic classes in opposition in the electoral arena. (On electoral cleavages, see Taylor and Johnston, 1979; Harrop and Miller, 1987.)

One model of the entire structure of capitalist societies sees them divided into three major sectors – the sphere of production, the sphere of reproduction, and the state (Urry, 1981). Discussion in the present chapter has focused on the sphere of production, on the organisation of the means of survival. With this, although the fundamental organising principles are common – the making of profits through the surplus value accruing from the employment of labour within capitalism, for example – there are many variations from place to place in how that is done, both on an international scale (as documented in detail in Lash and Urry, 1987) and locally within individual countries (as exemplified for the British coal-mining industry in Griffiths and Johnston, 1990). Thus one can have a geography of the operations of capitalism.

The sphere of reproduction, also referred to as the sphere of consumption and as civil society, refers to the organisation of social life outside the workplace. Clearly, social life must be organised in ways that are not contrary to the economic goals of a society, but the limits are apparently very broad. Modern capitalist societies, for example, differ very widely in the nature of the relationships between the sexes, in the nature of education and religion, in the dominant sports and recreation activities, and so forth. All these are part of the local culture, and add to the richness of the geography of capitalist (and other) societies.

An illustration of this cultural richness, and of its links to the geography of modes of production in the contemporary world, is given by Todd's work on family structures. He identifies seven different types of structure, each of which is characteristic of certain areas of the world, producing a set of anthropological regions. The value systems inherent in those different family types provide what he terms the infrastructure of society: 'it determines the temperament and ideological system of the statistical masses which make up sedentary human societies' (1985, p.196).

Importantly, according to Todd, the geography of that infrastructure is not in itself determined, but rather is 'incoherent':

it is completely independent of its economic and ecological environments. Most family systems exist simultaneously in areas whose climate, relief, geology and economy are completely different. It is impossible to perceive any global coincidence at all between ecological or economic factors and family types. (pp.196–7)

Nevertheless, different family types do promote different types of social development, which are linked to economic structures, as he argues in a later book which links his anthropological model to the processes of 'development' (Todd, 1987).

Variations in cultural values are also relevant to an understanding of environmental use, since (as detailed in the previous chapter) environmental attitudes also vary between societies. Blaikie (1985) illustrates this in quoting examples of societies where cattle are kept not just as food sources but also as status symbols; cattle are 'a store of wealth' as well as a 'source of income', and status is positively related to the number of cattle owned. The acquisition of greater status can thus have deleterious effects on the environment, through over-grazing, and agricultural advisers believed that they could reduce that problem if higher-yielding cattle were made available; stocking densities could be reduced but the same level of output achieved. This failed to take account of the status symbol importance of cattle; the result of the activity was that cattle densities increased, not decreased.

This brief example is just one illustration of the importance of appreciating cultural values in developing a full understanding of societies and their relationships with their environments; as many attempts to alter agricultural practices have shown, people are influenced by a wide range of factors other than those involved with the economics of survival. So in attempting to alter land use practices it is necessary to appreciate that economic arguments may be insufficient to promote change. In this book, however, the main concern is with the economics and politics, and the cultural variations receive little attention; the aim is not to provide a complete guide to the understanding of the origins and solution of environmental problems, but simply to stress the need to appreciate both their economic origins and the political limits to action.

Those political limits are defined in the third sphere of society, the state. As will be argued in more detail in Chapter 5, modern analysis suggests that the state is necessary to the capitalist mode of production, in ways that are not relevant to pre-capitalist modes (see Johnston, 1982a). The state must be there to do certain things, otherwise capitalism will fail. But there are many ways in which those roles can be performed, many ways in which the script can be interpreted by the actors. And the state is not constrained only to actions linked to its necessary roles. The state is the focus of non-economic power in society, and can be used by those who win control of it to promote goals other than those related to the accumulation of wealth. Again, we can see that those goals very considerably between states, and over time within the same state; certain states, such as the Irish, are much more influenced by religious goals than are others, such as the Swedish, for example.

There are, then, three main sectors in modern societies, but the sphere of production is the foundation for the other two. Each requires the other; the sphere of production requires a state and a civil society, and neither of the latter pair could exist without a successful method of organising production. But the mode of production does not require a particular form of its civil society or of its state; these vary considerably from place to place, and can have significant impacts on the relationships between society and environment. Here and in the next chapter the focus is on the sphere of production, and in the following two it is on the state.

Chapter 4

Resources, Land and Environmental Use

Capitalist production . . . develops technology and the combining together of various processes into a social whole, only by sapping the original sources of all wealth – the soil and the labourer. (Karl Marx, *Capital*, 1977, p.475)

All life on earth is dependent for existence on that earth, indeed for most forms of life that dependence involves a reliance on other forms of life. Thus sustaining life is only possible if other life forms are present – which for humans means many different plant species and a smaller number of animal species. (Some people survive, to a greater or lesser extent, without dependence on animal species; none do so without dependence on plant species.) Most humans differ from other forms of animal life in that their continued existence has been organised so that it depends on other materials from the earth as well. This is not because of 'natural', or genetic, differences between human and other species, but rather because of the way that the human species has evolved to its present condition of ecological dominance, if not predominance. That evolution began with the use of inanimate materials as tools, and has been extended to the contemporary situation in which an extremely large range of products is created by transforming animate and inanimate materials obtained from the earth into commodities that are defined by human societies as 'useful'.

The earth is thus the resource base on which human societies rely. The nature of that resource base is fixed, by the processes through which the earth has evolved, but the identification of aspects of the environment as resources is not 'natural' in most cases (Spoehr, 1956). Resources are defined by humans themselves, and the process of resource definition is one of continual change, as new uses for earth materials are identified, and previously unused materials are translated into resources by the discovery of ways in which they can be made of use. (The exceptions are air and water; humans are genetically created to identify these as resources necessary to their individual reproduction.) Thus even with foodstuffs, whether or not a given plant or animal provides desirable food is a human determination, and groups differ in what they identify as desirable; what is acceptable to some, according to their cultural norms, is not acceptable to others. Part of the cultural geography of the world comprises different interpretations of the natural environment and whether its various components are usable resources.

We saw in the previous chapter how the most dynamic of modes of production, capitalism, is based on forever extending the range of goods and services offered to people for sale. It is thus dependent on a parallel extension of appreciation of what can be done with the raw materials of the earth (not just its surface and other inhabitants of that surface, but also its core and its atmosphere). Thus capitalism requires an ever-expanding resource base (and, according to the argument of the preceding chapter, so does advanced communism/socialism, because one of its major goals appears to be mimicking capitalism in the range of material goods produced and distributed). Resources are 'made' by humans, through their relationships with the earth. But there are limits to that 'manufacturing' process provided by the nature of the earth itself, and so we need to start this chapter on the interrelationships between humans and their environment by identifying the nature of the resource base.

The Nature of Resources

A number of classifications of resources have been proposed, many of which are based on the distinction between renewable and non-renewable, or stock and flow, resources (see, for example, Rees, 1985). This forms the basis of our discussion here.

Stock resources

Stock resources are inanimate components of the earth, and are therefore fixed in quantity. As such, human use of them is limited; once the stock has been exhausted, it is no longer available. Thus reliance on stock resources for the production of goods and services means that societies must be prepared to change their demands when the stock runs out – or when it is no longer possible to make use of the remaining stock (as in capitalist societies where the costs of obtaining the resource are greater than the return that can be obtained from the products made with it). Stock resources are a stimulus to human inventiveness, therefore, in that at some stage they will have to be replaced; either an alternative material for the same product must be identified or a new product to replace it must be invented.

A basic distinction within stock resources is between those which can be consumed only once and those which can, theoretically at least, be consumed many times. Fossil fuels provide a very good example of the former category: once they have been burned they have been destroyed. Most minerals are examples of the second category. These can be transformed into a great variety of commodities, but the technology is available – in most cases at a substantial price – to regain the original mineral resource from the discarded product: the extent to which this is done depends upon the 'need' for the mineral relative to the costs of winning more supplies from the ground and of developing alternatives. With some, it is possible, again theoretically at least, to recycle them so that there is no loss of stock at all.

A crucial feature of the use of these stock resources, especially those that are consumed only once, is that having been consumed they do not simply disappear but are transformed into other states. With fossil fuels, the output of burning involves the creation of what we know as 'waste products' or 'pollutants' which are emitted into the atmosphere and, through the operation of the hydrological cycle, are distributed through most ecosystems; from some, such as coal, there is also a residual mineral. These latter 'wastes' may be redefined as resources, if uses can be found for them, in which case they become another stock resource. For others, however, further uses have not as yet been found, and their disposition (as with the wastes from the generation of nuclear power) may cause considerable problems for the producers.

Flow resources

Flow resources make up the great majority of those used by human societies; they differ from stock resources in that they are constantly renewed by processes external to their use by humans. In effect most stock resources are renewed too; for example the processes by which oil is created continue alongside the consumption of oil. The real difference is in the time involved. The production of new stock resources is a very slow process, taking millennia in some cases, and so is much slower than the rate of human use. Flow resources are constantly reproduced, at rates which may equal those of their use.

The critical feature of the use of flow resources is thus the rate at which they are replenished relative to the rate at which they are used. At the extreme, the resource can be exhausted, in one of two ways. First, exhaustion can result because no more of the resource is available. It is not destroyed but it is limited in quantity, as with the amount of solar energy entering the earth's atmosphere each day. (It is appreciated that human activity can alter that amount, as recent debates concerning the greenhouse effect suggest.) Similarly, the amount of water passing a point on a river in any one time period is ultimately fixed so that the amount of power that can be generated from its passage is limited, and once that amount has been achieved the resource is exhausted. (River control measures can seek to regulate the flow but not increase its amount, except where water from other sources is introduced, with consequential losses there.)

According to this first definition of an exhaustible resource, the amount available is fixed, but is always there to be used. According to the second definition, the resource can be destroyed and made no longer available. These are what Rees terms 'critical zone resources', to distinguish them from the non-critical zone resources described in the previous paragraph. In the critical category, the rate at which the resource is used is crucial. If it exceeds the rate at which the resource is reproduced naturally, the resource will be depleted, eventually reaching a stage at which reproduction ceases and the resource is exhausted. All plant and animal species fall into this category, and many have become extinct because of human exploitation – either directly, because the species has been used by humans, or indirectly, because the species consumed by humans is no longer available to the others dependent on it in the ecological web of life.

A resource that falls somewhere between the stock and flow categories, but is probably best identified with the latter, is soil. This naturally renews itself, more slowly than most plant and animal species but much more rapidly than the minerals identified as typical of the stock resource category. If used in certain ways, its fertility and ability to support plant life can be sustained and its natural processes of regeneration supported. But if the fertility is removed rapidly, in a variety of ways, then in effect it is being 'mined' in the same way that a mineral is mined; its ability to support plant life is diminished, and eventually it can no longer do so. (As an intermediate stage it may be able to support some plant life, but not the sorts of plants that are perceived as a resource by the human occupants.)

Some, if not all, flow resources can be enhanced by human activity – either intentional or otherwise. For example, pastoral practices can increase the number of animals in certain species. But such an increase has a cost, in the long term if not in the short term. If we accept that the total resource base of the earth is fixed by the amount of solar energy entering the atmosphere each day, then there are limits to the earth's carrying capacity. It may be that those limits are nowhere near being reached at present, as human ingenuity discovers yet more ways of increasing the flow resources (through multiple cropping, for example) without destroying the base of stock resources. Yet use of the earth will ultimately be exhausted (using the term in the first of the two meanings introduced here) so that increasing the volume of some flow resources can only be achieved by decreasing the volume of others. The management of the earth's resources involves determining the most effective way of approaching that level of exhaustion.

Resource limits

The categorisation of resources outlined above indicates that there are clear limits to human activity provided by the environment. Just what those limits are, and how soon they will be reached, is the cause of much debate. Optimists argue that we are at present so far from the limits that to all intents and purposes we can assume that they do not exist. The carrying capacity of the earth may not be infinite, but it is so much greater than it is currently being called upon to sustain that there is no need for concern. The pessimists, on the other hand, argue that the limits are near, and that the problems induced by approaching them are being exacerbated by the nature of human use (misuse/abuse?) of the environment.

An example of the debate between the optimists and the pessimists concerns the availability of oil as a major fossil fuel. According to the pessimists, the likelihood of discovering further major as yet untapped reserves, and particularly reserves that can be recovered at acceptable financial costs, is remote. According to the optimists, there are many areas where as yet search has been very limited and the experience of earlier decades of prospecting must be that the chances of major finds are high. And with regard to exploiting difficult reserves, the optimists argue that only a few decades ago it would have been impossible to exploit the oilfields beneath the North Sea. This is now being done on a large scale, and if that problem can be solved so too, it is argued, could the problem of exploiting reserves found, say, under the Antarctic ice-cap. (On this general issue see Odell, 1989.)

Also relevant to a discussion of resource limits is the issue of food supply and hunger. Is the earth reaching its carrying capacity in terms of human numbers, particularly given the rapid growth of population in recent decades? There are two aspects to this. The first concerns population growth: pessimists argue that it is out of control and that a catastrophe will soon occur because the earth cannot feed the extra millions; optimists argue that the recent rate of growth is but a small blip in a long-term trend of much less rapid expansion of numbers (see, for example, Woods, 1989). The second aspect concerns not so much the ability of the earth to produce the needed food but the ability of human societies to organise food production and distribution to ensure that all are adequately fed. In this part of the debate, the optimists point to the current overproduction of food in much of the core of the world economy, which is leading governments to pay farmers not to produce, or at least to reduce the intensity of production. If that is possible, then surely a different way of organising the means of production, distribution and exchange would ensure adequate food for the many millions who are now starving, or virtually so, and on whom the pessimists focus their attention.

Much of the debate about the carrying capacity of the earth focuses on the physical constraints, but there are others who direct their attention to the social, economic and political limits. Those favouring the latter recognise both that there are ultimate limits and that these may be either reached more quickly or reduced by environmental practices; those favouring the former accept that social, economic and political change is important in ensuring effective winning of resources from the earth. What is crucial for both to appreciate is the extent to which environmental practices, and hence the approach to the limits, are largely determined by economic forces – by the mode of production – and also that the extent to which those practices can be altered requires an appreciation of the nature of the political forces that operate. Advancing such appreciation is a major goal of this book, since without it the creation of a self-sustaining interrelationship of society and environment will not be possible. The remainder of this chapter looks at the relationship between mode of production and environment, and the next chapters turn to the state and political forces.

Primitive Communism, Feudalism and Environmental Use

In looking at the relationships between various modes of production and the environment, most attention will be paid to capitalism. This brief, introductory section looks at primitive communism, as an example of a mode of production based on reciprocity, and on feudalism in Britain as an example of one based on rank redistribution.

Primitive communist societies are those which have had the most intimate relationships with their environments, because in many senses they have been most dominated by them. Their level of technological development has been such that they have been able to 'control' the environment to a limited extent only. Instead they have had to develop a pragmatic alliance with the environment, living in ecological balance with it. The nature of that alliance has varied very substantially indeed, from society to society. This reflects in part the variability of the environment; different physical circumstances call forth different responses. But it also reflects different sequences of human learning in different places. Most environments offer a range of possibilities to humans seeking means of survival within them – which fruits to gather, which animals to capture, how to prepare foods, and so forth; for a variety of reasons, many of them closely linked to chance, those possibilities have been appreciated and acted upon differentially. The nature of the relationship with the environment created becomes part of the society's culture, part of the inter-generational inheritance of practices which allow survival in the environment. Those practices will change over time; change may be 'forced' because of an environmental event – a drought, for example, may perhaps result in the search for an alternative source for part of the diet – or it may come about pragmatically as the result of a 'chance' discovery (eating a previously ignored fruit, perhaps). The result is a complex mosaic of people–environment relationships, which is the foundation of the current cultural geography of the earth.

Although the environment offers many possibilities in most situations, it is likely that in many cases where the range of possibilities is virtually the same similar practices will have evolved, for one or both of two reasons. The first is that some possibilities offer better life chances than others, and it is likely either that eventually separate societies will discover these and adopt them (perhaps with some differences of detail), or that societies that don't will eventually perish and only those that find the most appropriate survive. Secondly, similar environments are usually adjacent, and so it is likely that there will be contact between separate societies and a sharing of expertise; again, the likely outcome is similarity in the general nature of the practices adopted, even if there are differences in detail.

An example of this similarity in general but differences in detail is provided by the patterns of land tenure within the Pacific prior to the penetration of those island chains by capitalist agriculture and land-holding conventions. Crocombe illustrates this by noting that:

Within the Pacific area people often emphasize the great diversity of tenure systems . . . . But in world perspective, all the tenure systems in the Pacific had much in common, both in the environment and in the cultures of the peoples, and these factors set the boundaries within which each tenure system evolved and operated. (1972, p.219)

Thus inheritance was the standard way of obtaining land, for example, and there was no market for its sale. In New Guinea and Polynesia, however, inheritance was mainly patrilineal; in Micronesia it was matrilineal; and in Melanesia (apart from New Guinea) 'there are both patrilineal and matrilineal systems, as well as ambilineal and bilineal' (p.227).

In these primitive communist societies the Malthusian spectre is always present: either they will breed beyond the carrying capacity of their environment, or change in their environment (even a relatively minor one such as a drought for two years) means that they can no longer sustain their numbers. Over time, they may learn ways of changing the balance, either by improving the carrying capacity in some way or by developing means of surviving periods of relative famine. But their general situation is one of a dynamic equilibrium with the environment of the type described in the discussions of predator–prey models in Chapter 2. Their level of technological development is such that they cannot alter that equilibrium substantially, at least in the short term. Over long periods of time they may destroy the environment by their overconsumption of the flow resources, in a small area; their only hope for survival then is to find another environment nearby that will support them, while the one they have deserted can be rehabilitated if they haven't totally destroyed the major flow resource – the soil – and this can be regenerated naturally, as fauna and flora recolonise the areas abandoned by humans. (For detailed data on the practice of swidden and other types of agriculture in such societies, see Bayliss-Smith and Feachem, 1977.)

Not all primitive communist societies fail to degrade their environments, however, as Allen and Crittenden (1987) illustrate with the example of the Kakoli people of the Highlands of New Guinea. They had three types of land use practice. On the valley floors and flood plains there were permanent open fields where sweet potatoes (introduced about 400 years ago) were cultivated; and on gully-sides there were swiddens, where crops were grown for a few years, followed by a 10–15-year fallow period while the land recovered: in both cases, equilibrium was maintained. But on the upper slopes, at the forest–grassland boundary, they employed a 'crop and abandon' practice. Gardens were cleared and cultivated for two years and then left fallow, when they were colonised by weeds and woody plants. The land was then cleared again and turned into a permanent sweet potato garden, in which cultivation continued until yields fell to such a level that replanting was not worthwhile. The land was then abandoned; it was colonised by cane grass, which could be used for pigs, but it never regained its original vegetative cover. Cultivation moved further uphill, so that over time there was a belt of abandoned, degraded land separating the villages from their current hillside gardens. The Kakoli sustained an ecological balance with parts of their environment, but not all of it.

Feudal societies differ from primitive communist in many ways. For the present discussion, the most important is that they may have within them a growth process that puts increasing pressure on the environment. As in societies based on reciprocity, that process may be activated simply by population growth and the tendency to breed up to the limits which the environment can support. But in a rank redistribution society the problems set are greater because a proportion of the population, however small, comprises non-producers. If it is that proportion which is growing, then the entire burden of supporting it has to fall on the remainder of the population (the tenants). And if the landlords and their retinues have the highest material standards of living, then their offspring are more likely to survive and to have greater life expectancy than those of the tenants, with obvious consequences for the demands for food and other 'needs' won from the land.

Increased demand for agricultural production from this source leads to an alteration in the ratio between producers and non-producers in the agricultural economy, and can only be sustained in the long term by increasing the productivity of the former group. The same is true whatever the source of the increased demand; the monarch may call for a greater contribution to the country's military, for example, either to provide a more secure defence or to wage an aggressive campaign against others. Or the feudal establishment may wish to increase its material standards: greater investment in the built environment, for example, requiring more craftsmen who must be supported by others.

In feudal England all of these sources of demand were present, stimulating a range of agricultural innovations. For a substantial period, from the Norman conquest on, it seems that the environment was able to cope, for the population tripled between 1066 and 1348. Part of this increase was catered for by extensions to the settled area, and in part it was sustained by improvements in agricultural practice – such as the development of the three-field system and crop rotation. But according to one agricultural historian (Postan, 1973) by about 1300 the limits of this expansion had been reached and England, with about six million inhabitants, was overpopulated. Subdivision of land had proceeded to such an extent to cater for the increased population that holdings were in many cases too small to sustain the occupants and their families; at the same time, some of the more affluent landholders had been able to increase the size of their holdings and so increase their relative wealth, and in some areas industrialisation proceeded apace, based on local wool production. Further, much of the marginal land brought into use was unsuited to grain crops, and there was a shortage of animal manure as fertiliser. Others accept Postan's case that England's population was reaching its Malthusian limits at the time, but argue that the real cause of the problems was the unwillingness of the parasitic aristocracy to invest in improvements to agricultural technology. The pressure was ended by the arrival of bubonic plague in 1348, which presaged the major fall in population over the next three decades known as the Black Death; it was only from the sixteenth century on that growth recommenced, and the incipient capitalist system led to increased investment in improvements to agricultural productivity.

Whereas many people looking for evidence that land degradation occurs under most types of mode of production and not just capitalism focus their attention on contemporary peripheral areas of the world economy, Blaikie and Brookfield (1987b) have pointed to the important evidence provided by the histories of the Mediterranean region and of Western Europe in the last two millennia. But in such exercises it is often very difficult to evaluate the relative impact of land use practices and other variables, such as climatic change (as, for example, the so-called Little Ice Age of Europe in the late medieval period: Grove, 1988). With regard to the circum-Mediterranean area, however, Blaikie and Brookfield argue (with Shaw, 1981) that human intensive occupation of the area may have retarded rather than accelerated rates of erosion, and that it was only when and where management standards were poor – with terraces poorly maintained, for example, so that heavy storms could stimulate active degradation – that environmental deterioration occurred. Certainly such deterioration has occurred, because land that once supported forests (the cedars of Lebanon, for example: Mikesell, 1969) now clearly cannot, and what was the 'breadbasket' of the Roman Empire (the Carthage region) no longer sustains intensive agriculture. Thus it is not human 'interference' with the environment *per se* that promotes its degradation, but only badly managed 'interference'; the fertility of land with its 'natural' vegetation removed may be maintained if it is 'well' farmed, but not if it is opened up to erosive forces.

Similarly in northern Europe, Blaikie and Brookfield (1987b) suggest that the accelerated erosion that occurred in parts of France and Germany was the consequence of the interaction of human and climatic causes, rather than either one or the other. In the département of Haute-Marne, for example, there was substantial damage to the land in the 1780s. This, it seems, was the result of human response to a series of bad harvests, and a drought in 1784–5. Many cattle died because of the drought, farmers were unable to build up their stocks because of high prices, and the decline in livestock numbers led to a substantial decline in soil fertility (because of the lack of manure). Better management of the land was required to ensure that the pressures of increased demands could be met without land degradation, and it was the improved management practices of the agricultural revolution in the period from the sixteenth century (as, for example, with the enclosure movement in England) that allowed societies to increase the pressure on their environmental resources and to some extent escape the constraints that these resources posed to the existing level of environmental understand.

Another environment in which the case for bad management practices (themselves perhaps a response to environmental stress) rather than 'interference' with the environment *per se* probably led to degradation is where the so-called 'hydraulic civilisations' were established. According to Wittfogel (1956, 1957), such civilisations were characterised by large-scale water works built both to promote production (i.e. via irrigation) and to provide protection and flood control. There have been many such civilisations in arid and semi-arid areas; their social and political structures were distinguished from those of other feudal societies by the extent of state power required by the demands not just for large amounts of labour but also for it to be integrated in major public works – the irrigation and flood control systems:

> In hydraulic economy man extended his power over the arid, the semi-arid and certain humid parts of the globe through a government-directed division of labour and a mode of co-operation not practiced in agrarian civilizations of the non-hydraulic type . . . . The development of such a work pattern meant more than the agglomeration of large numbers of men. To have many persons co-operate periodically and effectively, there had to be planning, record-keeping, communication and supervision. There had to be organization in depth. And above the tribal level this involved permanent offices and officials to man them – bureaucrats. (Wittfogel 1956, p.156)

But this centralised control meant that 'the hydraulic farmer maintained a man–nature relation that involved unending drudgery on a socially and culturally depressing level' (1956, p.161) – a way of life Wittfogel later described as 'benevolent in form and oppressive in content' (1957, p.136). So where the control could not be sustained, and the management practices declined in efficacy, the hydraulic civilisations collapsed. (Wittfogel, 1957, implies that the failures often resulted from autocratic despots losing the support of the bureaucracy necessary to run the hydraulic culture.) It was not that an equilibrium with the environment could not be sustained but that the organisation of the society prevented it, in the long run – though some hydraulic civilisations lasted several millennia.

Blaikie and Brookfield (1987a) come to a similar conclusion with regard to the current situation in Nepal, where according to some observers the farming practices and destruction of forests to cope with population pressure are the causes of accelerated erosion and the increased flooding of the Brahmaputra and other rivers in India and Bangladesh. They point out that some commentators suggest that farmers, because of the pressures on them, choose management options which lead to accelerated land degradation. But some farmers, especially the richest, may be able to take other options which protect their land, so that 'poverty is the basic cause of poor management, and the consequence of poor management is deepening poverty' (Blaikie and Brookfield, 1987a, p.48).

According to this argument, the problem of land degradation under feudal and other rank redistribution societies is not simply that human 'interference' with the environment necessarily leads to such degradation; rather it is the nature of the social and economic system that encourages bad land management practices. This leads to a deterioration, rapidly and apparently continuously in a high-energy environment such as Nepal, but only rarely, and usually at times of environmental as well as economic stress, in temperate environments such as those of north-western Europe. Thus understanding of the origins of environmental problems requires an understanding of the nature of the social, economic and political organization which leads to the generation of those problems; the problems are not inherent to human 'interference' with the environment, but are the consequence of how that 'interference' is managed.

Games against nature

The environment provides all societies, not just those based on either reciprocity or rank redistribution, with limits to growth related to the available agricultural technology and land management practices. The stability of such societies depends on them learning the nature of those constraints and developing an appropriate set of agricultural practices. This is illustrated in a classic paper by Peter Gould (1963), which is relevant to the study of all decision-making in the context of an uncertain environment whatever the mode of production but is especially important in societies which have little ability to 'control' or modify the environment and so must learn to live with it.

Gould uses as his example a village in Ghana where, for illustrative purposes, years are either wet or dry. The farmers in that village know about five different crops, and experience tells them what yields they can expect in a wet and a dry year. Those yields (in arbitrary units) are:

Crop	Wet year	Dry year
Yams	82	11
Maize	61	69
Cassava	12	38
Millet	43	32
Hill rice	30	71

In a wet year yams offer the best return, but in a dry year the yield from them is very low. So should they plant yams, and gamble on it being a wet year; should they plant maize which has by far the highest average yield over the two types of year; should they plant yams in some years, maize in others, and so on; or should they divide their land among the crops, to minimise the risks of a food shortage in any given year?

To answer this question, Gould uses the concept of a 'saddle-point' from the mathematical theory of games; the saddle-point is a row minimum that is also a column maximum – it is simultaneously the lowest high point and highest low point (as illustrated in Abler, et al. 1971, p.480). Gould drew up a diagram comprising two scaled columns (Figure 4.1), with the wet and dry years forming the columns and the row scaling the yields for each crop. The saddle-point on the resulting diagram is the lowest point at the intersection of two crops, which is where maize and hill rice meet at a value on the yield scale of 54. This can be attained either by planting 77.4 per cent of the land with maize and 22.6 per cent with hill rice in every year (so that in a wet year the high maize yield compensates for the low hill rice yield, and vice versa in a dry year), or by planting all of the land with maize in 77.4 per cent of years, and all of the land with hill rice in the other 22.6 per cent. In the long run it doesn't matter, for the average annual production will be 54 units, but, as Gould puts it:

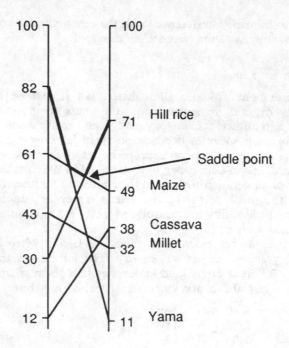

Figure 4.1 Graphical representation of the yields from the five crops in Gould's example, indicating the location of the saddle-point

when men have experienced famine and have looked into the glazed eyes of their swollen-bellied children, the long run view becomes somewhat meaningless. Thus, we may conclude that the farmers will hold strongly to the short-term view and will plant the proportions *each year* since the truly catastrophic case of hill rice and wet year could not then occur. (1963, p.293)

This planting pattern (the mathematics of which are laid out by Gould) is the 'rational' response to an uncertain environment which the farmers cannot alter and in which there is no ability to store food (the 'surplus' of a good year in which production exceeded 54 units) for the bad years that are bound to come. It was the development of the ability to store food, and also to transport it from areas of 'surplus' to those of 'deficit' that enabled societies to break out of the game against nature as portrayed by Gould, and to develop new games in which they could change the yields, and the probability of getting them whatever the climatic conditions, through environmental control.

Into Capitalism

The replacement of feudalism by capitalism as the dominant mode of production in Western Europe was intimately associated with increased productivity in agriculture, since the ability to produce food and industrial raw materials more efficiently was central to the growing concentration of people in non-agricultural occupations. The ability to transport and to store those materials was equally important, since capitalist expansion was built on both urbanisation and the growth of long-distance trade. Thus it was the willingness of those with power in society to invest in increasing agricultural productivity and the necessary restructuring of society which enabled the transition to capitalism, a process which markedly altered the relationships between societies and their environment: the agricultural and industrial revolutions of the sixteenth century onwards, that most associate with the transition to capitalism, saw the technocratic interpretation of the environment come into its own.

The nature of those changes in agriculture are clearly illustrated in England during that period, and in the expansion of English influence over much of the rest of the world (see, for example, Butlin and Dodgshon, 1989). From the sixteenth century on, and especially in the century after 1750, there were many institutional and technological changes in English agriculture, the results of much experiment and trial and error and the willingness of individuals to invest in such experiments in the expectation of substantial gain. Such experiments involved not only the relatively small, affluent elite but also a wide range of the farming population, as in the enclosure movement. In terms of agriculture practices, new crops were introduced and productive strains were developed. The new ones were mainly root crops, which were used as winter feed for livestock. This enabled much larger numbers to be retained through the winter rather than slaughtered in the autumn, and the greater volumes of manure thus produced could be used to fertilise the arable fields, increasing the productivity both of grain farming (the staple for human food) and of the root crops and hay that sustained the wintered-over animals. Other new crops, such as clover, were widely used because of their efficiency in fixing nitrogen from the atmosphere in the soil, thereby increasing its productivity during the fallow period. There were improvements in technology too, in the ability to work the land, for example the development of more efficient ploughs.

Alongside these technological changes were the institutional, introduced to improve the management of the land. The most important in much of England was undoubtedly the process of enclosures: the former open fields in which each tenant had a number of small strips of land were replaced by consolidated tenant holdings. Those holdings, with their enclosed fields (usually by hedgerows), allowed major developments in livestock farming in particular, with which came the creation of new ecosystems, such as those associated with the ubiquitous hedgerows of the English Midlands. Selective breeding was possible, and the productivity of the land was increased enormously by the development of high-yielding breeds.

The major difference between these agricultural developments and those preceding them was that they were not basically a response to the Malthusian spectre, to the society having reached what seemed to be the limits to growth. Rather they were the outcome of investments because people wanted to get the benefits that increased productivity brought in terms of what they could do with the yields from their land – from the additional money earned. This was especially the case with the large landowners, who wanted increased rents to spend on more conspicuous consumption (bigger homes surrounded by landscaped parks, for example) and to invest in the increasingly profitable trade and industrial ventures. Accumulation of wealth was their goal, and they promoted it by encouraging their tenants to want improved material standards, accessible to them through purchase if they invested in increased productivity. (Thus in many villages the tenants as well as the landowners favoured enclosure.) So the major land-owners, therefore, increased agricultural productivity on their own lands provided wealth that could be invested elsewhere (indeed, according to some analysts it was the existence of the land-owning pattern of several parts of north-western Europe and the possibility of accumulating large wealth from it that facilitated the emergence of capitalism and the industrial revolution there: Hechter and Brustein, 1980). Increased rents from tenants aided in that accumulation of wealth. The demands for greater rents stimulated the tenant farmers to increase their productivity, a stimulus much assisted by the fact that they were not just handing over tribute as in the feudal system but were able to earn additional income for themselves that could be spent on themselves, and invested in themselves too.

Productivity of land and labour

Progress under capitalism, as set out in the previous chapter, is achieved through increasing the productivity of labour, which creates greater surpluses per unit of input (usually measured as labour time). In part, that pressure to increase labour productivity can be assisted by increasing the productivity of the materials on which it works – the smaller the proportion that is wasted, the greater the returns from the investment. This is perhaps more clearly seen in agriculture than in other activities, because the productivity of the material – land – can be increased very substantially.

As already outlined with regard to the agricultural revolution in England from 1750 on, increases in the productivity of land have been very substantial in recent centuries, and are usually measured in terms of output per unit area. These have been achieved through the selective breeding of plants and livestock to obtain higher-yielding strains, and by changing the basic land use in many cases. The enclosure movement there was associated with a substantial switch away from grain farming largely for subsistence purposes, into livestock rearing (with the associated cultivation of root crops as winter fodder), because the returns from livestock (£s per hectare for the wool) were greater than those from grains and other products, reflecting the demand for industrial raw materials. Forest land was also eaten into, and its relatively low yields were replaced by either crops or livestock – a process that continues to the present day with the clearance of very large areas of tropical forest.

The changes which brought about increases in the productivity of land were largely associated with the plants and animals that it supported, and the developments known as the industrial revolution had few direct links with them. But increasingly industrial technology was applied to the task. A large chemical industry has developed in the twentieth century based on the production of fertilisers to be used to increase soil fertility more efficiently than animal manures, releasing farmers from the need to keep stock in order to produce their own fertilisers and, where it is economically sensible, turning the majority of their land over to arable farming: the fertilisers also allow this to be a permanent switch, removing the need for a fallow period (one year in three, or five, or seven). And technological solutions have been found in other areas; the introduction of relatively efficient movement of water up from the water table, for example, has allowed large-scale irrigation developments, as on the High Plains of the United States.

Alongside the investments aimed at increasing the productivity of the land (and thus indirectly of labour) have been those undertaken to increase labour productivity directly. Much of the machinery introduced to agriculture has been for this purpose, although some activities – such as sheep-shearing – remain labour-intensive. Hand-milking of cows has been replaced by machines, for example, allowing one person to milk very many more animals in an hour, and advances in the design not only of the machinery but also of the milking sheds (such as the herring-bone cowshed of New Zealand) have been promoted for the same reason. In arable farming, the development of machinery for planting, tending and harvesting crops has increased labour productivity greatly; no longer are very large gangs required to pick the hops in Kent or raise the potatoes each October in Scotland (the reason for a mid-term break in universities as well as schools) and combine harvesters do the work that formerly involved not only several tractor drivers with harvesters, but also those who threshed the grain and baled the straw. (According to Roberts et al., 1989, the pressures on American farmers to invest continually in new machinery to increase productivity means that they are on a 'technological treadmill'.) To accommodate the new machines, such as the combine harvesters (which also improve land productivity to some extent since they are more effective and less prone to waste than individuals), fields have had to be enlarged, destroying many miles of hedgerow field boundaries in parts of England, and bringing not insubstantial additional areas under production (see Goudie, 1986a, pp.84–6).

The extremes of these developments are what is known as factory farming, which involves an increasing divorce of animals from the land in livestock rearing. Instead of having free range in the fields, the animals are confined to buildings and are fed the products of those fields. Arable farming is generally much more efficient than pastoral farming in transforming the products of the land into food – the energy equivalent of the production of animal-based foods from a hectare of land is much less than that from arable use of the same area. This means that productivity can be increased very substantially indeed, since the land requirements of the animals (in terms of area occupied) are small and the same area of land supports a much higher stock density than if the animals freely roamed the fields. The pressure is then to increase the productivity of the arable land as much as possible, though mechanisation, the use of fertilisers, and field enlargement, to provide more food for the captive animals. And there are environmental consequences, such as the increased volumes of animal wastes (slurry) to be disposed of; in an increasing number of cases this is proving difficult, and the material is entering natural stream courses with consequences for water use.

More than in many other sectors of capitalism, therefore, it is possible in agricultural and pastoral activities to increase the productivity of both land and labour. As in all sectors, of course, the increased productivity of land results from the application of human labour, either directly – thereby increasing its productivity as well – or indirectly, through the use of 'dead labour' (machines). But the productivity of the land resource can probably be increased more in this sector than in any other, which is crucial in understanding the demands that are made on the land in the dynamic of capitalist society. If, as argued in the previous chapter (p.55), the continued health of capitalism depends on technological and organisational changes designed to ensure a continued flow of surplus value, then the ability to increase productivity via two routes in agriculture should be particularly attractive to investors; the result would presumably be that the crises of overproduction and underconsumption would be especially apparent in that sector.

Increasing Land Productivity

The capitalist dynamic requires increased productivity in order to survive. The move to greater productivity may occur at different rates at different times and places, and may be greater in some sectors than others. The next sections explore some of the ramifications of this statement.

Organisational change in English agriculture

English agriculture, as argued earlier, developed out of a feudal system in which the land held by the feudal lords was divided up into separate farms, the majority of which were allocated to tenants who paid an annual rental for the use of the land. Over time, some of those tenants purchased their land and became freehold occupiers, as the landlords decided to sell for a variety of reasons. Thus an increasing proportion of the farmed land became a marketable commodity, and the organisational structure of land ownership became more changeable, allowing changes in order to promote increased productivity. Nevertheless, for long periods relatively little altered.

Much has changed in recent years, however, as a major study by geographers in London has shown (Whatmore et al., 1987a). This begins by noting that although farms in Britain are predominantly owned and managed by individual families, the traditional concept of the 'family farm' (see, for example, Williams, 1963), only partly incorporated within the capitalist system, is no longer appropriate. Instead the situation now is of: 'a wide range of productive, labour and business relations representing neither an empirically nor a theoretically discrete category . . .'.

They suggest a typology based on the extent of what they call 'subsumption' in both the internal and the external relations of the farm unit. Subsumption involves the capitalist transformation of agriculture through one or both of: direct methods, involving the 'full commoditisation' (1987a, p.27) of labour relations and the influence over technical procedures by external capital; and indirect methods, involving the appropriation of some of the surplus produced on the farm by external capitals. The typology comprises four ideal types defined according to the degrees of direct subsumption of internal relations and of indirect subsumption of external relations:

(1) The *marginal closed units*, comprising farms low on both. Families own and manage the land and the business, provide most if not all of the labour, and have few debts. These farms are usually small-scale units, 'surviving on the margins of commercial agriculture' (p.32), and contain family members living partly on other sources of income (such as state benefits).

(2) The *transitional, dependent units*, which contain some hired labour and carry some debt; many are on the edge of viability and need more capital, and perhaps more land, in order to avoid being marginalised.

(3) The *integrated units*, in which capitalist relations dominate, with high levels of capital input and credit, and with contract marketing quite common. 'Such businesses are firmly set upon the technological treadmill and must continue to be dynamic and expansionist in order to remain viable' (p.33).

(4) *Subsumed enterprises*, which occupy the highest positions on both scales. The family farm has been taken over by corporate capital, is run by a manager and has strong links with external capital, for both technological inputs and marketing.

The authors then applied this typology, which in its ideal form implies farms moving from the first stage through the next two to the fourth, to three case study areas in southern Britain, showing that the movement had been greater in some areas (those close to London) than others (west Dorset: Whatmore et al., 1987b). As they move through the stages, so farmers increasingly become tied into the growth dynamic of capitalism, reflected not only by their mortgage and capital indebtedness but also by their links to chemical and pharmaceutical companies which are playing an increasing role in the food chain via the developments in biotechnology (Barlow, 1988a). As Barlow sees it:

The processes of technological change will be selective, hence the pattern of uneven development will be maintained and the trend towards regional monocultures based on the requirements of the food processing industry reinforced. (1988b, p.117)

Ecological imperialism

With land that has long been occupied and farmed within the capitalist mode of production, it is not always easy to achieve substantial increases in the productivity of either the land or the labour. Thus, in order to obtain the profits available from the sale of agricultural products to an expanding market, it may make more sense for those with capital to invest to put it into lands currently outside the capitalist mode, which offer great potential for both initial profits and rapidly increasing productivity. This is what happened in medieval England with the destruction of the forests and the draining of the wetlands. From the sixteenth century on, it happened on a much wider spatial scale, as an increasing proportion of the earth's surface was drawn into the capitalist system. As Richard Peet (1969; see also Chisholm, 1962) has shown, a global system of agricultural zones focused on the core of the capitalist system was developed during the nineteenth century, as advances in transportation technology (such as refrigeration) enabled long-distance movements to markets: in the early 1830s the average distance that butter imports travelled to London was only 262 miles, whereas by c.1910 it was 3120 miles; the comparable figures for wool and hides were 2330 and 10,900 miles.

The expansion took place in two basic ways. This section deals with the first, whereby people from the capitalist countries occupied the lands themselves and imposed their own organisation upon them. Most of those lands were occupied by either rank redistribution or reciprocity societies, which were in some way or another dispossessed of their ownership, and in some cases (such as the aborigines of Tasmania) virtually eliminated. Such processes characterise much of what is known in Britain as the 'New World', including most of the American continent, Australia and New Zealand, and parts of southern Africa.

In these lands of 'white settlement' the important feature for the present analysis is that the nature of the land use pattern imposed was geared almost entirely to production for markets elsewhere. This was particularly the case with Australia and New Zealand; the former was initially settled as a prison camp and the latter was reluctantly colonised by Britain when it was used as little more than a refreshment stop for whaling and other expeditions, but within a few decades each country had been transformed into a great food-producing appendix to the British Isles. This involved, as Powell persuasively argues, the development of images of those lands as 'attractive and bountiful rural landscapes' (1977); the purpose of settlement was to obtain that bounty for the British Empire. Not all lands had the same image, and there were conflicts in some places about the best way to organise the occupation of the land and reap its harvests. Powell (1970) illustrates this in his detailed study of the conflicts between the official vision of the settlement of western Victoria as a landscape of small farms in the image of rural England and the vision of the initial European colonists, who saw the land as organised in large sheep stations; the latter won. Similarly, in South Australia, as illustrated in Meinig's classic work, the pattern of settlement and land use resulted from a pragmatic learning process as people with a particular image of the rural scene came to terms with what to them was a new and fickle environment: he termed it 'a quick mass-testing of the land and the revelation of its qualitative patterns at an incalculable social and economic cost' (1962, p.207).

It was not just that the settlers organised land tenure and practised agriculture according to perceptions that they had learned in very different environments many thousands of miles away, and that what they produced was geared to the markets there, but also that they wrought major changes to the local ecosystems. One of the first detailed studies of this process was *The Invasion of New Zealand by People, Plants and Animals* (Clark, 1949). Its relatively neutral description was shunned by Crosby four decades later; his book is called *Ecological Imperialism: The Biological Expansion of Europe, 900–1900* (Crosby, 1986). When the pakeha occupied New Zealand they found no mammals and relatively few species of flora and fauna, as a consequence of the islands' long isolation. Those settlers brought with them not only the animals and plant species necessary to their agriculture, and destroyed much of the native population, but also introduced many other European flora and fauna, to create an environment as similar as possible to that left behind. All parts of New Zealand had (and still have) an Acclimatisation Society, whose purpose was to introduce and propagate 'innocuous' flora and fauna, both useful and ornamental: the first report of the Otago Acclimatisation Society summarised its work as to ensure that:

> the sportsman [sic] and lover of nature might then enjoy the same sports and studies that make the remembrance of their former homes so dear, the country rendered more enjoyable, our tables better supplied, and new industries fostered. (Swann, 1966, p. 3)

The outcome was the introduction of 130 species of birds, 40 of fish and 50 of mammals, of which 30, 10 and 30 respectively became established in the wild. One of the mammals introduced (to Australia as well) was the rabbit. It bred extremely rapidly and was the cause of much soil erosion, especially in the high country of the South Island (see Cumberland, 1947; McCaskill, 1969, 1973); so much so that both eating rabbit and owning rabbits as pets became legally proscribed.

The impact of the rabbit on New Zealand and Australian environments is just one example of the consequences of this ecological imperialism. As Crosby puts it, the Americas and Australasia have provided European-based societies with a major windfall during the last four centuries in the form of an environment that could be exploited for great gain. But the consequences of the pursuit of that exploitation have been great. The 'Dust Bowl' created in the Great Plains area of the United States during the droughts of the 1930s provides a clear testimony to this (Worster, 1979); there were fears in the summer of 1988 that it would be repeated, despite the many lessons on land use practices apparently learned from the first episode. The example of the Dust Bowl in the 1930s further illustrates the contention of Blaikie and Brookfield (see p.80) regarding the importance of management practices in the impact of human 'interference' on physical systems. According to Worster:

there was . . . a close link between the Dust Bowl and the Depression
– . . . the same society produced them both, and for similar reasons.
Both events revealed fundamental weaknesses in the traditional culture
of America, the one in ecological terms, the other in economic. (1979,
p.5)

He argues that no other word than 'capitalism' sums up the reasons for the
Dust Bowl; the inherent pressures of capitalism on the individual farmers to
increase their personal wealth through exploiting nature led them to ignore
all environmental limits, with the ultimate disastrous consequences, just as
'Wall Street ignored sharp practices and a top-heavy economy' (p.7) which
together contributed to create the Depression.

> In a more stable region, this sort of farming could have gone on
> exploiting the land much longer with impunity. But on the plains the
> elements of risk were higher than they were anywhere else in the
> country, and the destructive effects of capitalism far more sudden and
> dramatic. There was nothing in the plains society to check the progress
> of commercial farming, nothing to prevent it from taking the risks it was
> willing to take for profit. That is how and why the Dust Bowl came
> above. (1979, p.7)

Settler colonies such as Australia, New Zealand and the United States are not
the only milieux in which ecological imperialism has been practised. Indeed,
it has probably produced greater degradation of the environment in parts of
the world invaded by capitalists who either did not intend to settle there
permanently or later decided to leave. Some areas of plantation economies in
the humid tropics illustrate this; as Blaikie (1985, p.144) argues, the attitudes
that they developed led to rapid exhaustion of the natural resource base
before moving on, in a process somewhat akin to slash-and-burn agriculture,
except that the capitalists were probably less concerned that the soil's natural
fertility should be replenished by a period of fallow. Thus cheap land was
often available, and governments were prepared to subsidise the provision of
an infrastructure, thereby making the investment even cheaper. Alternative
investment opportunities elsewhere suggested that rather than seek to maintain the productivity of the soils, it was better to 'mine' them and move on,
an attitude encouraged by potential political instability which threatened the
security of long-term investments. So the commitment of the capitalist to the
environment being exploited may be very low, with the obvious consequences. And yet, as Blaikie (1989) argues with regard to removal of forests
from many parts of the Third World (the periphery in the pattern of uneven
development) today, local interests in the conservation of environmental
resources are difficult to defend against such ecological imperialism; the
short-term gains of the economic activity generated are accepted at the
sacrifice of the long-term health of the environment.

Capitalist penetration

In this second, and more widespread, method, lands formerly occupied by
non-capitalist modes of production are slowly penetrated by that mode –

not by their forcible removal, as with ecological imperialism, but by their incorporation within the capitalist world economy. This is, of course, how the peasant economies of many parts of Europe were replaced by capitalism, and contemporary developments are but a continuation, on a very large scale, of that process. But much of what is happening now is in tropical and sub-tropical, arid as well as humid, environments that are less able to withstand the increased pressures than the European temperate humid regimes.

This process of penetration comes about through contact between peasant and capitalist societies, in which each seeks to benefit from the other. The capitalist societies want to obtain the products of the peasants' land; the peasants want to obtain the material benefits of capitalist consumption. To achieve the latter goal the peasants must sell products, to obtain the income that they need to finance material purchases; if they do that, the capitalist societies get the increased volume of foodstuffs and other raw materials they require.

At face value, this appears to be a symbiosis that brings mutual benefits, but usually, in the long term if not in the short, the peasant societies are weaker and gain least. As stressed in the previous chapter, competition in the capitalist world calls for continued increases in productivity, in agriculture as much as in other sectors of the economy. Thus in order to increase their money incomes, and be able to sell in the capitalist markets, peasants must increase their productivity; they must put greater pressure on their land. This need is accentuated by the nature of the markets in which they are competing. The peasants can have little influence, if any, on the demand in those markets, but must respond to it; the crops and animal products that they offer for sale must be those that the outsiders want. And they are competing to sell to them in situations where they have no alternatives – if the outsiders don't buy, there is no sale. And so they are at the mercy of the market, and must respond to its signals. Their usual response, whatever the signal, is to try and produce more to sell, thus putting more pressure on their land.

Why is this so? Assume that a peasant family has decided that it needs a certain money income in order to live at the desired material standards. It thus produces enough to sell on the markets in order to yield at least that level of income. Neighbouring peasant families are doing the same, with the result that they sell and get the income they need. Others perceive their success, and decide to enter the market too. The result is that the supply:demand relationship is altered, in the buyers' favour, and the price falls. How does the individual peasant farmer react to this fall of income? The only sensible way appears to be to produce more, to increase productivity of land and labour. The result – even more products on the market, a further change in the supply:demand relationship, and a further deterioration in the price. There is continuing pressure to produce more, with clear consequences for the environment.

Sooner or later the market will become saturated, and not all that is produced will be sold. How then does the individual peasant family respond? A likely way is by seeking to increase market share, by undercutting competitors (in exactly the same way described in the previous chapter), which can only be achieved – if a constant income is to be sustained – by increasing productivity. Alternatives, such as collective action to keep prices high and production down (see Chapter 6) and the move into other products, are less likely to be undertaken, the first because of the difficulties of achieving it, the other because it involves substantial investment in some cases and a loss of income for a period in most – investment in buildings, equipment, livestock and even plants (such as orchards) may have to be written off before the 'natural' productive life was completed, and new investments may take time to yield returns (with forests this could be several decades).

But exactly the same will probably happen if the market is not saturated and prices are high. For some peasant households, the ability to earn sufficient income for their needs may be the only driving force and the potential for more will be irrelevant; they will not respond to the market by sending more products to it. Others will not respond because their contact with the capitalist system, its growth ideology, and the promotion of consumption via advertising will convince them that extra income is desirable, a conviction probably strengthened by the pressures outlined in the next paragraphs. Thus whatever the short-term situation, as peasants are incorporated into capitalism so they will continually seek to increase their production and income. After a good season, for example, yields will have been high but prices will have been depressed; to recover, more must be sold next year. After a bad season, with low yields, prices are relatively high and there is pressure to produce more next year and benefit from the greater income potential.

As peasants move into the capitalist system, therefore, so they become increasingly drawn into its dynamic, and in particular to the need to increase the productivity of both their land and their labour (see Bradley and Carter, 1989). This will probably lead them to further incorporation into the capitalist system, because they will realise (and probably be 'convinced' by outside agents) that the increased productivity they require can only be achieved by capital investment in agricultural practices. This means either that they must invest their income in the purchase of machinery and other capital goods rather than using it for immediate consumption, or, more importantly, that they must borrow money from within the capitalist system to facilitate the investments. Paying off the debts so incurred becomes a further pressure to increase productivity. And this will probably mean that they switch an increasing proportion of their land and labour resources into production for the capitalist markets and away from their own subsistence; more and more of their effort is involved in producing for exchange rather than for use values (Watts, 1983). Increasingly, then, they come to rely on the markets for their day-to-day requirements, which only increases the pressure further, especially when the markets for their own products become saturated and competition to sell becomes fiercer.

In general, the terms of trade move against peasant producers operating in the market system, especially over the long term. The terms of trade is the technical term for the ratio between the costs of imports and exports, which for an individual household is the difference between the cost of purchases and the income received from the sale of products. Within capitalism, this changed ratio often comes about because of the effects of inflation: goods cost more and so it is necessary to work harder to keep one's level of consumption up. Peasants on the edge of capitalism suffer from this; the goods they have been convinced that they need are increasing in price, and the only way they can cope is to increase their production. They are further disadvantaged because the trend in prices for foodstuffs and other raw materials is frequently downwards, as more and more production is encouraged to keep down the costs to the importers. The pattern of uneven development described in the previous chapter is based on inequality in the market-place, whereby the producers in the periphery are at the mercy of the purchasers in the core. As a consequence the terms of trade often move against the producers for two reasons: the costs of imports rise and the values of exports fall, and the peasant producers individually can have little impact on either.

The overall consequence of these pressures is greater demands on the physical environment, and its eventual degradation, as argued by Blaikie (1985) in his excellent analysis of the political economy of soil erosion. Thus, for example, the pressure to grow peanuts for the capitalist economy in parts of Niger led to accelerated soil erosion, both because this resulted in the displacement of pastoralists and the disruption of the ecological balance they had achieved with the environment and because the techniques used to produce the peanuts removed nutrients from the soil at much greater rates than they were restored by natural processes and by fertilisers. And in Botswana, a doubling of the cattle herd in the Ngwaketse district between 1963 and 1982 was the result of increased commercialisation of agriculture which, along with other extensions of the capitalist system and the incorporation of local labour into other activities, promoted major changes in the socioeconomic system (Figure 4.2). Grazing was no longer communally controlled, and pressures on the environment increased in order to earn incomes from beef cattle, but

> the increased cattle population reduces grass cover and encourages soil erosion, which in turn reduces the productivity of the grass. Fewer and cooler fires result which enables more seedlings of woody plants to survive. Reduced competition with grasses also aids the survival of seedlings. Once established, woody plants shade out grasses and intercept rainfall, so that grass cover is further reduced. The decline in grass cover reduces the productivity of cattle in the rainy season, so that more are needed for the same output. The increase in shrubs helps survival in the dry season, so that fewer cattle die. The vicious circle is completed. (Blaikie and Brookfield, 1987c, p.195)

This whole process of incorporation of the peasantry, its impoverishment and marginalisation in many cases, and the consequent degradation of the environment has been termed 'silent violence' by Michael Watts (1983) in his major study of northern Nigeria. It is silent violence because, as

Model of ecological change on a sandy loam soil initially carrying bushed and wooded grassland

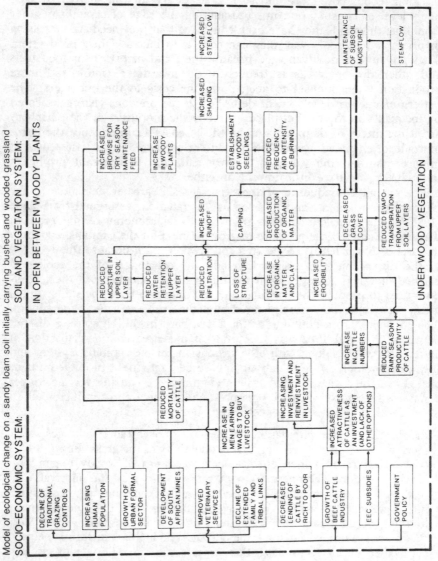

Figure 4.2 The origins of land degradation in Botswana

discussed more generally below, people suffer and die not because of intentional acts against them – what is called behavioural violence (see Johnston et al., 1987) – but because of the operation of the structure of the global economic system of which they are part. The argument regarding structural violence is closely linked to the concept of a core–periphery organisation of the capitalist world economy, in which the periphery is exploited for the benefit of the core. At a national scale this is shown in, for example, relative rates of GNP increase, state indebtedness and wealth accumulation. At the individual scale it is shown by differences in the quality of life, as exemplified by people's life chances. Thus, if the capitalist world economy can sustain an average life expectancy for French children of over 78 years, but of only 40 years for the residents of Sierra Leone, then structural violence is being enacted on the latter in order to improve the life chances of the former. Johnston (1989) has analysed these differences in life chances to show the amount of structural violence that is present in the contemporary world as a consequence of its core–periphery organisation. His data suggest that if the life expectancy of the French were enjoyed throughout the world, those born in 1985 could anticipate a total of 8,520,012 million more years of life than they will achieve because of the current differentials in life expectancy at birth; of those lost years, only 0.23 per cent will be in the nineteen countries designated as 'Industrial Market Economies' by the World Bank, which house some 8.7 per cent of the world's population.

Watts's (1983) work on the Hausa peasants shows how they had learned to survive in the fickle environments of northern Nigeria before British colonisation; they were able to cope with climatic uncertainty and food shortages. But then incorporation into capitalism eroded their coping mechanisms, so that they could not readily survive famines as they had in the past. Hence:

> The contradiction of colonial rule in Nigeria was that while the success of metropolitan capital depended upon expanded commodity production by households who subsidized the reproduction of their own labor power, the demands of capital and the effects of commodity production simultaneously undermined (and occasionally threatened) the survival of those upon whom it ultimately depended. There is, then, a structural relationship between famine and the political economy of colonialism that legitimately warrants the use of the term 'violence'. This structural causality and the absences and neglect that mark the history of famine in northern Nigeria . . . is the 'silent violence' . . . . (Watts, 1983, pp.xxiv-v)

As Watts points out elsewhere (Watts, 1989), this does not mean that Africa is in a chronic state of crisis, but it does stress once again the point that it is the nature of the relationship between society and nature, and specifically the way in which human 'interference' with nature is managed under capitalism, that is the cause of much land degradation and the appalling human consequences that stem from this.

Perhaps the clearest example of this degradation is the process of desertisation that has taken place in the Sahel region of Africa in recent decades, which led to the major famines that gained international media coverage in the early 1980s. (Desertisation is the preferred term of some for the process by which an area becomes a desert; they reserve 'desertification' for processes that clearly are catalysed by human 'interference'.) The nature of the causes of that degradation is a topic of much debate (see, for example, Hulme, 1989, on whether overgrazing has stimulated the onset of drought conditions). But many observers believe that increased pressure on the land in the semi-arid areas has contributed substantially to the creation of desert conditions: Hare, Kates and Warren refer to the process as

> the effects of interaction between mounting pressure on land and vegetation and the incidence of naturally occurring droughts, which are a normal part of desert margin climates. It is possible that desertification amplifies itself by means of the albedo feedback mechanism . . . [see p.38 above], but the large-scale climate is, in the end, able to reassert more humid conditions. Damage to ecosystems during desertification may, however, make the recovery of surface productivity lag well behind the climate. (1977, p.336)

Goudie has provided a model of how desertification has been stimulated in northern Kenya (Figure 4.3); the sedentarisation of nomads and their increased numbers are seen as the crucial human factor, and the increase in their cattle herds as the catalyst for land degradation.

Other Resources

The discussion so far in this chapter has focused on flow resources, and especially those of the land system involved in agricultural production, which Rees classifies as in the 'critical zone' (i.e. they are resources that can be exploited to exhaustion: see p.73 above). The arguments advanced apply equally well to other critical zone flow resources, such as fish and forests. But what of the other types of resources, the flow resources in the non-critical zone (that cannot be exhausted) and the stock resources?

Non-critical zone flow resources

Resources in this category cannot be exhausted, in that they are naturally self-regenerating – as with water through the hydrological cycle (though, of course, changes in the global environmental system can affect the amount of water available, in particular through the waxing and waning of the polar ice-caps). These resources can be degraded, in ways to be discussed in a later section, and they are limited in the extent of their use. Thus the problems with such resources reflect the extent of use and of degradation.

With regard to use relative to the limits available, there are pressures within the capitalist mode of production to increase use and therefore reduce the availability of the resource. The dynamo of capitalism, as previously described, depends for its continued operation on increased levels of consumption of goods and services. Thus it is necessary for people

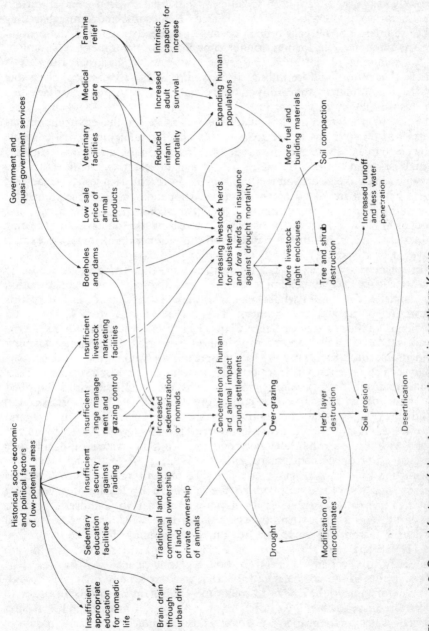

Figure 4.3 Causal factors of desert encroachment in northern Kenya

to be convinced of the need to consume more in general – hence the pro-growth ideology of capitalist societies – and for the producers of certain products to convince people of the need to consume more of what they have to offer. The latter is crucial because, as already argued, a static situation is rarely tenable for long under capitalism. In a competitive situation, if consumption of the good or service concerned is not increasing, it is likely that profits will be falling; if consumption isn't increased, the value of the investment in the production will fall, so everything must be done to ensure that more is consumed.

This growth syndrome has many consequences for the environment, as described on p.91 in the sections of this chapter referring to critical-zone flow resources. It usually involves the promotion of goods and services which draw on the environment to a greater or lesser extent in either the production or the operation of the product. In recent decades, for example, there has been increased use of electrical appliances, with consequences in the demand for the generation of power to be consumed in the home, and also of appliances driven by batteries, increasing the demand for the raw materials from which they are made and the production of toxic wastes that have to be disposed.

In some circumstances it is a non-critical zone flow resource that is being marketed. An excellent example is water, and its provision for consumption by capitalist companies whose goal is to make profits from the sale of this naturally occurring commodity. This is illustrated by Walker and Williams's (1982) study of Santa Clara County in California. There, as the land was settled and more intensively used, requiring irrigation for farming and promoting urban growth, so the demand for water grew, and increasingly had to be imported from outside the county boundaries. Much of the water is supplied by private companies, with the remainder either supplied by municipal agencies or self-supplied (e.g. from private wells). Walker and Williams suggest that the motives of these suppliers, both private and public sector, are geared towards promotion of increased water consumption, with little or no reflection on 'the economic value of water uses against costs of demand management' (1982, p.107). Agency zeal (the promotion of growth) and inter-agency competition are both cited as reasons for these attitudes, which are sustained by local water law; any right to use water granted to a company or agency in California must be taken up within three years, or the right is forfeit. Alongside these social and legal factors are those that are purely economic. 'The rule of profits' (p.111) means that short-term profits and long-term market growth are necessary to company success. Although public agencies do not exist to make profits in the normal sense, because they are largely financed through the sale of bonds, they have to make the equivalent of profits in order to ensure returns to their investors: 'A good record of growth makes raising capital easier and cheaper' (p.111). Thus continued expansion of water demand and delivery is typical of the county, leading Walker and Williams to conclude that *efficiency in water supply and water use is not a major policy concern* . . . . Inefficiency and overdevelopment will be tolerated or even encouraged if growth is anticipated or is proceeding apace. This is not to condone such inefficiency, only to see it in the harsh light of the real political–economic purposes . . . (p.117)

What we infer from this example is that many of the natural resources in the non-critical zone may be treated as commodities in the same way as the products of both stock and critical-zone flow resources. The implications for the environment can be profound, because the goal of the profit-makers is to accelerate the consumption of the resource. There are limits to that consumption, because of the finite amount of the resource available. Efficiencies can be gained, by ensuring as little waste as possible (perhaps through pricing policies) and by recycling the resource – which with water means using it as many times as possible during one sequence of the hydrological cycle (the example of the number of times water in the River Mersey is used between source and estuary is often quoted in this context; the number is probably apocryphal). Water is not only a scarce resource globally, and even more scarce locally in many parts of the globe; it is also a necessity for human reproduction. Thus the extent that water consumption – and by implication that of other non-critical zone flow resources – is promoted in order to enhance profit-making and wealth accumulation is critical, since it means that eventually choices will have to be made on how to use a limited amount of water available in an area, which could well be through the price mechanism of the capitalist market; the highest bidder would win, water would become more expensive, and the costs of survival to the individual would increase. Making those choices in any area could be delayed by importing water from others, as has increasingly been done during the last two centuries of rapid urbanisation, but paying for those investments and their upkeep means that the water becomes more expensive.

Stock resources

The critical issue with regard to stock resources is the rate at which they are consumed, and so denied to future users. The debates about those issues can be clarified in terms of two polar extreme positions. At the one extreme are those who argue for great caution in resource use and the need to avoid waste at all costs, because of the problems that will be faced if, or when, exhaustion occurs. In moral terms this is often expressed as protecting the resource base for future generations and only exploiting that part of it which can be justified; it is extremely difficult, of course, to develop normative standards of what is justifiable. (Sagoff presents the moral argument fully, claiming that environmental legislation is necessary in the United States to 'express Americans' perceptions of themselves as a nation, called upon, to an extent, to appreciate and preserve a fabulous natural heritage and to pass it on reasonably undisturbed to future generations': 1988, p.224.) At the other extreme there are those who argue that although the stock resources are finite in volume, that volume is so great, relative to past, present and anticipated future use, that there is no foreseeable problem of scarcity, especially since the lesson of the past is that we are likely, aided by increasing exploration and exploitation technologies, to discover more stocks than we are currently aware of. And in any case, the argument often continues, human ingenuity is such that even if a stock does become either exhausted or too expensive for continued exploitation, alternatives will readily be found.

Whatever the merits of these two arguments and the long-term availability of certain stock resources, there remain issues of their exploitation and the impacts that this can have on other aspects of the environment. To the extent that the stock resources are viewed as commodities to be sold in competitive markets – and most of them are in capitalist societies – there are pressures to exploit them as cheaply as possible in order to promote profitability. This can often have major environmental impacts, at least locally.

An extreme example can illustrate this. Banaba, or Ocean Island, is a small island in the Pacific, much of whose area has been covered over millennia with guano that has been transformed into phosphate of lime, as was the case on the nearby, better-known island of Nauru. That lime was an attractive stock resource, for there was great demand for phosphate as a fertiliser in Australia and New Zealand. Companies were launched to work the resource, employing local labour; as the resource was worked, so the other resource of the island – the land on which the Banabans grew their food – was slowly removed from them: as Binder expressed it, 'their little island diminished. In fact it was worse than diminished; it was packed into sacks and disappeared altogether . . . . Even where their precious food trees were spared, or replanting promised, the mining chasms made access impossible' (1977, p.55). The Banabans were persuaded by the local colonial administration first to give up their land and then, if they were not to remain as indentured labourers working in the phosphate mines, to accept resettlement in the Fijian islands. The latter happened with a shift to Rambi in 1946, whilst Banaba itself became a 'moon-scape nightmare of mined-out stark coral pinnacles' (Binder, 1977, p.183). When the initial agreement allowing mining of the phosphate was signed with the British Phosphate Commission, the earth and trees destroyed in that activity were to be replaced. BPC subsequently argued that this was impossible, and it has not been done. The result is that Banaba is now uninhabitable.

This example illustrates two major issues concerned with the winning of stock resources. The first is that removal of the resource has both direct and indirect impacts on the environment. The direct impact is just the removal, and the 'hole' that results. The indirect impacts are not just the consequences of that 'hole' itself, such as the subsidence in many areas of underground mining, including the removal of artesian water, but also the disturbance of other environmental systems. That disturbance may be temporary, and it is possible either to restore the systems to their original state or to create new, acceptable systems in their places (as with the rehabilitation of tip heaps alongside many coal mines to form grassy hills).

But such rehabilitation costs money, and that money can only come – in the absence of collective action (see Chapter 6) – from what would otherwise be profits. In a competitive situation, the organisation that threatens its profitability by returning some of the income into non-profit-making activities such as restoring the landscape threatens its own viability. This does not mean that it won't be done in some cases, that for a variety of altruistic reasons people will use part of their profit to enhance the landscape and so promote values other than those of the capitalist dynamo. But that can only done if the profits continue to be forthcoming. The need to make a profit from the exploitation of stock resources, in a competitive situation, means that there are strong pressures to minimise expenditure on clearing up the mess created by mining the resource.

Industrialisation and Urbanisation

A major feature of the expansion of the capitalist mode of production has been the immense growth in the range of commodities available for purchase and consumption. This involves the transformation, through increasingly sophisticated and complex industrial processes, of the raw materials obtained from the stock and flow resources in the environment. The processes themselves have considerable impact on the environment.

Wastes and pollution

Most transformation processes produce wastes, either parts of the raw materials that are not required or transformed aspects of the materials that are not integral to the new product being created. Some of those wastes may be of use in other production processes, and are consumed accordingly. Others are not, and so remain as by-products of the process. They can be classified into stock and flow wastes, in the same way that natural resources are classified. Each type provides a particular set of problems, in that they have to be assimilated by the environment, frequently to its detriment.

With stock wastes, the most straightforward problem is simply their disposal: they take up space. Thus ways of disposing of the ash from power stations have to be found, for example; in some cases this has been deposited in the 'holes' created by mining, but in others it has simply accumulated in piles. Such disposal is rarely insignificant in its local environmental effects. An ash-heap is clearly an alteration of the local geomorphological and ecological system; the ash put in a pit does not replace the soil that may have been removed. Some wastes which are naturally degradable through biological and mechanical processes are broken down into their constituent parts. This in turn may be problematic, since those constituent parts then taint the environment – as, for example, with the chemicals that enter water courses. Particular problems are created by wastes that are especially toxic and dangerous to other life forms – the wastes from nuclear power generation come into this category – and great problems of their disposal are being faced. Examples of the impact of allowing those wastes into the environment, as in the Chernobyl incident in the Ukraine in 1986, clearly illustrate the problems.

The problems with flow wastes are of a different order, since their entry to the environment is often more difficult to control than is that of stock wastes. It can usually be controlled, but at a cost, through the even greater sophistication of the transformation processes. The example of the emission of waste products from power generation through the burning of coal illustrates this. The by-products are released into the atmosphere, and the chemicals are then carried through the hydrological cycle to other locations where they are deposited through precipitation (the 'acid rain' phenomenon) and then enter local ecosystems, with consequent deleterious effects on plant and animal life. Controlling the emission of those wastes requires investment in 'cleaner' power stations, which have a reduced potential profitability because higher prices must be charged; it then makes the items produced with the power more expensive and threatens the profitability of industrial operations – which may have to invest in more expensive plant to increase productivity to counter the increasing costs. That new plant may be more energy-efficient which, as the example of water resource development showed (p.98), is not in the interests of the power industry. Furthermore, changes in the generation of power may involve the creation of new (probably stock) wastes that need to be disposed of, and will increase the demand for other resources to be used in the power station (such as lime as a bed for the burning).

Stock and flow waste generation is not confined to the production processes in capitalist (or any other type of) industrialisation. They are also consequences of consumption, either because not all of the product is consumed or because there are by-products of the consumption. An example of the latter is the production of CFC gases, through both the operation of electric refrigerators and the use of aerosol sprays; those gases, it is now believed, are destroying part of the ozone layer that protects the earth from certain types of radiation, with consequences for human health. With regard to wastes from consumption itself, most consumption is temporary only and the products are eventually discarded. This probably involves discarding them in their original manufactured state, as with a car or an item of clothing. The waste materials may be reusable, either to make the same product again (perhaps of an inferior quality, as with paper), or in the production of another product, or as a fertiliser for the soil (though again, the product may contain within it elements that will harm the environment, which have to be removed first).

Because the nature of capitalism requires the continued growth in the value of production, and thus in the volume of commodities consumed, the problem of wastes increases. The more that is produced, the more wastes that will be produced, both as a by-product of production and/or consumption and once the utility of the product has ended. Further, the growth dynamic of capitalism requires the production of wastes through consumption to be speeded up. In order to sustain profitability, people have to be convinced to discard items long before they are redundant; much clothing is discarded before it is so worn that it fails to fulfil its function, for example, and many motor cars are scrapped while they still could continue to be used for thousands of miles. (Vance Packard illustrates this graphically in *The Waste Makers*, 1961, with the forecast of factories on cliff-tops dumping their production directly in the sea below without it ever being 'consumed'.) The ever-increasing production of waste is part of the capitalist system, and calls for the application of human ingenuity to counter it if environmental degradation is not to proceed at at least the same pace.

Urbanisation

The by-products of industrial processes are one example of a larger category of products known to economists as externalities, which are the effects (usually unintended) of one person's actions on another, over which the latter has no control. Externalities may be positive, in which case the recipient gains something of benefit, free of charge. But many are negative, in that the recipient suffers the consequence of an action, which may involve a cost, and cannot prevent its occurrence. At the local scale, a negative environmental externality could be the ash from a fire falling on a neighbour's garden; at the international scale, the acid rain phenomenon is an example of the same relationship, with Britain presumed to be the producer of an externality and Norway the unfortunate recipient.

Most externalities are limited in their spatial extent; the further you are from the source of a pollutant, the less you are affected by it. Some may have a very wide impact, as suggested by the simulations of nuclear explosions (whether disasters or the consequences of bombs; Openshaw et al., 1983); a few may be global in their direct effect, but many more are indirectly, as the arguments summarised in Chapter 2 indicate. Because most are local, this means that there is a geography of externality production, and of receipt (which in the case of airborne pollutants means downwind of the source, which is why so many urban areas in Britain have their higher-status residential areas upwind of their industrial districts).

There are two important spatial scales in these geographies. The first is the global, and refers to the core–periphery division of the countries of the world into a pattern of uneven development. (Here the discussion refers only to the capitalist world, and avoids the issue of whether the whole of the earth's surface is now incorporated within the capitalist world economy. Advanced communist/socialist societies are the subject of a later section.) That pattern was initiated with the transition to capitalism in parts of north-western Europe. The core was established there, and the areas concerned have remained within the core to the present. The core has expanded, however, taking in most of Western Europe, most of North America, and Japan. The remainder is in the periphery, at varying levels of economic development, as defined on capitalist terms.

It is within that core that industrialisation emerged and the processes of transforming raw materials into commodities for consumption were launched. In many ways, therefore, it is in the core – widely recognised as the most 'advanced' areas of the world economic system – that most negative environmental externalities have been created through the production of pollutants as by-products of industrial processes, and where large areas of land have been made derelict. This is not to say that similar dereliction is not a characteristic of the periphery too, where the winning of resources has led to substantial modifications of the physical environment – as in the goldfields of Australia, for example, where it was not only the mining but also the separation of the gold by chemical processes that sterilised large areas of land. Thus the map of wealth in the world is well correlated with the map of environmental degradation caused by industrial, rather than agricultural, processes.

At more local spatial scales, the map of environmental degradation shows considerable geographical variability, within the periphery as well as the core. The major reason for this is the process of urbanisation, whereby the industries and the people who work in, and otherwise benefit from, them are concentrated in high-density concentrations to benefit from the internal and external economies of scale that characterised the growth of industrial complexes. The internal economies arise from the efficiencies associated with large size; the external economies arise from the efficiencies that result from proximity to suppliers, servicers and customers. Those urban areas are thus major concentrations of both the production of wastes and the generation of negative externalities. And the greater density often brings with it an even greater concentration of the pollutants, with major consequences for the local environment, as exemplified by the major smogs over cities like Los Angeles and Lima caused by the burning of fossil fuels, especially oil and its derivatives. Similarly, it is in the industrial cities that the rivers have received the greatest volumes of pollutants as the by-products of production and consumption processes, with the consequence that many have 'died' and been unable to support fish and other life.

Urbanisation has other major impacts on the environment because of the indirect consequences of replacing the 'natural' environment by a built one; the full range of these impacts is set out in detail by Douglas (1983). They are clearly seen, for example, in the difference between local climates in urban and rural areas, which is a consequence of differences between their two surfaces and the materials involved (see Chandler, 1965; Landsberg, 1981). Urban areas tend to be warmer than the surrounding countryside and even than the lower-density suburban areas, especially at night, because of the radiation of heat; this is exacerbated by the air pollution in towns, which helps to form a dome over them that traps the heat in. Cities also tend to be less humid because there is less evaporation, a consequence of the relative absence of vegetation, but because of the greater number of nuclei in the air above them, resulting from the emission of pollutants, they tend to have slightly more precipitation.

The building of urban areas interferes with other environmental systems, such as those involved in the movement of water. In rural areas some of the water received as precipitation goes straight into the streams, but much more is either stored temporarily in vegetation and soil or moves through those media only slowly towards the open channels. In urban areas the lack of vegetation removes that control (and also reduces the amount of moisture returned directly to the atmosphere via transpiration) whereas the covering of land surfaces by buildings and various paving surfaces denies water access to the soil. It thus moves rapidly across those surfaces into the water channels, so that in storms those channels have to cope with a much higher peak load than in the countryside; one result is greater erosion by urban streams and more expensive engineering works to compensate – with an increase in the 'natural hazards' of urban areas as the consequence (Perry, 1981, illustrates this for Britain, and both Jones, 1990, and Gardiner, 1990, outline human impacts on the environment of that small, densely occupied island).

Construction of residential and other areas means an extensive built-up area altering the environmental systems, and in many cases accelerating environmental processes and land degradation. Cooke (1984) has illustrated this in his detailed studies of residential development on the slopes around Los Angeles, which has substantially influenced the processes of soil erosion and slope movement.

Urbanisation has proceeded furthest in the core of the world economy, in that a greater proportion of the population there live in cities than in the countryside, but the periphery now contains some of the world's largest cities and some of the worst examples of environmental degradation as a consequence: Douglas notes the size of those cities, and records that

> The people of those cities will live in an environment created by human endeavour, often made unpleasant by the side-effects of human activity, frequently full of risks derived from crowding, inadequate housing and poor sanitation, yet by no means immune from the extremes of natural processes, such as floods, tidal waves, landslides and earthquakes. (1983, p.vii)

Until relatively recently, these major urban centres have been spatially contained as very high-density concentrations, clearly separated from the small settlements of the countryside. But with the growing mobility made possible by the car and the investment in road systems, urban development has sprawled over very large areas. The densities are relatively low, and the impacts on the climate and hydrology less than in the older cities, because of a greater area of vegetation and untarmacked soil, but the general spread has had many consequences for the natural environmental systems.

This outward expansion of urban areas has been associated in general with greater overall prosperity, which has a number of characteristics. One is that with the great increases in productivity most people are required to work fewer hours in the day, fewer days in the week, and fewer weeks in the year. This decline of demand for time at work has been compensated by the growth of leisure time and recreational activities. Much of this is reflected in the continued dynamic of the capitalist system, as the provision of leisure and recreation facilities becomes commoditised, at home and beyond. Part is reflected in increased pressure on the environment for recreational use.

Recreational use of the environment focuses on certain preferred landscape types, especially in areas of preferred climates (i.e. warm and sunny).

Mountainous areas and, especially, coasts with beaches are particularly favoured, and there has been increasing pressure to make these available to a growing number of people for short and long visits. Tourism is one of the most rapidly expanding service industries of recent decades, stimulating a great deal of built environment creation, again with clear direct and indirect consequences for natural environmental systems. The development of resorts throughout the Mediterranean countries illustrates this, with not only the provision of the accommodation and transport facilities that people are led to demand but also the transformation of large areas of the environment into 'pleasure parks' of some form or another. Even in the relatively remote landscapes, this increased pressure has substantial environmental impact, as in the erosion of the natural soil cover under footpaths in most of the favoured rambling areas of upland Britain.

The tourist industry is typical of recent trends in capitalism as it seeks to counter the problems of overproduction. People are increasingly being encouraged to take several rather than just one holiday a year, to travel further, and to demand a higher standard of facilities. Holiday resorts which previously operated for a few months only now cater for visitors year-round. As the demand for this continues to be stimulated, so the pressures it creates on the environment are increased too. To some, we are now in a post-industrial society and the evils of the polluted cities of the nineteenth and early twentieth centuries are behind us. Yet the growth industries of the present produce their own environmental externalities, as the capitalist dynamo speeds up the processes of consumption to which the environment is for ever committed.

Advanced Communism/Socialism

According to Marx's interpretation, one of the major features of the capitalist mode of production is its basis in the alienation of the individual, from other individuals and from nature. In pre-capitalist modes, survival depended upon community among individuals and community between individuals and nature; people were interdependent, and personal survival was conditional upon that interdependence. Similarly, people were dependent for their survival on the personal relationship with nature, since they drew sustenance directly from it. The essence of human being, according to this interpretation, was those two forms of interdependence. With the development of capitalism, however, people lost their essential human-ness because both labour and nature were commodified. People no longer relied on each other in any sense of reciprocity; instead they interacted through the buying and selling of their labour power. Similarly, their alienation from nature came about when nature and its products became commodities to be bought and sold. Thus, as Kolakowski expresses it:

> Marx's starting point . . . is . . . the fact that individuals are alienated
> from their own labour and its material, spiritual and social consequences
> in the form of goods, ideas, and political institutions, and not only from

these but from their fellow beings and, ultimately, from themselves. (1978, p.222)

Marx's goal was to end that alienation and to restore humanity to people by removal of the alienating mode of production – capitalism – and its base in the commodification of labour and nature. Thus communism, to be achieved through socialism, was to restore people to their pre-capitalist state, without denying them the opportunity to active high levels of material satisfaction. The implication is clearly that under that mode of production people will once again live in relative harmony with nature, in a condition of relative ecological equilibrium from which all of the environmental problems of the modern capitalist world will be absent. As Blaikie (1989) argues, there is little evidence that such harmony is being achieved in the present communist/ socialist countries, and plenty of evidence that environmental degradation there is as substantial as it is elsewhere. Komarov (1981) shows that although the Constitution of the USSR has in Article 18 the requirement that

> In the interests of the present and future generations, the necessary steps are taken in the USSR to protect and make scientific, rational use of the land and its mineral and water resources, and the plant and animal kingdom, to preserve the purity of air and water, and ensure production of natural wealth, and improve the human environment

and Article 67 states that

> Citizens of the USSR are obliged to protect nature and conserve its riches

nevertheless there has been a 'ravaging of nature', generating an 'ecological alarm . . . [that] cannot be too loud nor too premature' (Komarov, 1981, p.19). Similarly, Smil refers to land degradation in China as an 'ancient problem getting worse' (1987, p.214).

The reasons for this lie in the nature of those societies and their origins. As already stressed, in the ideal-typical sequences of societal development, socialism and advanced communism would come after capitalism and so benefit from its technological achievements. But that sequence has not been followed, and instead the 'overthrow' of capitalism in most of those areas preceded any true onset of capitalism itself. As a consequence, in those societies it has been necessary to replicate the technological achievements of capitalism (or at least a large number of them), a necessity accentuated by the political isolation of the advanced communist/socialist countries and a reluctance, if not outright refusal, on the part of the capitalist countries to share their accumulated expertise. Thus the industrial revolution has occurred not once, but twice, with the same consequences in terms of, for example, urbanisation and environmental degradation; further, because of large, and in several cases rapidly growing, populations the pressures to industrialise and to increase agricultural production have demanded a much faster response, and in much greater volume, than was the case a century or more ago in the core of the capitalist world economy.

Despite these pressures, it could be argued that the demands on the environment in socialist countries should be less because of the absence of the drive to create surplus value for the accumulation of wealth. Production in socialist societies is in order to meet socially defined needs, and although these go well beyond subsistence to high material standards of life, nevertheless there are no pressures to consume, no use of the mass media to convince people that they 'need' certain consumption goods and 'want' to replace those that they have – which are still serviceable and perform their function – by new models. So why are paths to 'development' being followed that are creating ecological disaster on the scale suggested? Komarov suggests that in part it is a consequence of the failings of centralised planning and the nature of the giant bureaucracies in Russia, where the most powerful individuals and agencies are those whose continued power depends on delivering high material standards to the population and whose ideology is very much based on growth, on investing what is available on economic development in order to 'obtain strategic advantage over the United States' (Komarov, 1981, p.135). Furthermore, he argues, there is major ignorance of the extent of the ecological disaster. The majority of the Soviet population is denied information, while the affluent 15 per cent enjoys high standards in clean environments, insulated from the ecological problems by 'the green fences around their suburban houses' (p.134). Meanwhile, the

> majority willingly suffers from the noise, the smog of those cities where they can find better paid jobs, where they can find some products to buy, let alone worrying about the carcinogens, allergens, or substances causing chromosomal mutations present there. (p.134)

Government experts know the extent of the ecological disaster, Komarov claims, but the power elite use their positions to ensure they are relatively untouched by it.

> Five to six per cent of our society has access to natural products . . ., special drinking water, and special swimming pools with filtered sea water (without oil and phenol) . . . . Hence for us everything will always be ecologically all right. In fenced wild forests there will be enough 'wild boars' to hunt; in lakes screened by underwater nets there will be fish for anglers. And no matter how Baikal is degraded, they will try to keep a few bays in virgin splendour, with pines on the high banks and the purest water . . . . (p.134)

It could be argued that the anti-alienation component of communist ideology should have ensured a different approach to the relationship with the environment, what Blaikie and Brookfield call a 'distinctive socialist environmental management' (1987d, p.208). This has certainly not happened, and all of the evidence suggests that environmental despoliation has been as extensive in the East as in the West. Part of the reason for this has been the pressure on the authorities in the East to achieve the aimed-for high material standards rapidly, in order to maintain the loyalty of the population and to prove to the West that it could be done. Further, there was little accumulated capital available and the industrialisation programme (including the industrialisation of agriculture) had to be achieved as efficiently (i.e. as cheaply) as possible; the extra costs of industrialisation without negative environmental externalities could not be afforded (even if they were appreciated). Finally, industrialisation and urbanisation undoubtedly have substantial negative impacts on the natural environment, so that any programme of increased commodity production, whether capitalist or socialist, is bound to affect not only the store of stock resources but also the nature of flow resources.

In Conclusion

A first conclusion to be drawn from this chapter must be that any form of social organisation is going to have substantial impacts on the natural environment and the equilibrium of the systems that comprise it. With some modes of social organisation, their primitive technology means that their impact is likely to be relatively limited, and very much subject to the perceived environmental constraints within which they live. But as technological advances occur, so the potential for significantly altering those environmental systems increases, perhaps at an even greater rate than the technological advances themselves.

Marx was aware of this a century ago, as is clear from his brief remarks on the changing relationships between people and nature indicated at the outset of this chapter. He saw the penetration of agriculture by capitalism as replacing 'old-fashioned' methods by scientific ones, and as a consequence:

> it disturbs the circulation of matter between man and the soil, i.e. prevents the return to the soil of its elements consumed by man in the form of food and clothing; it therefore violates the conditions necessary to lasting fertility of the soil . . . all progress in capitalistic agriculture is a progress in the art, not only of robbing the labourer but of robbing the soil; all progress in increasing the fertility of the soil for a given time, is a progress towards ruining the lasting sources of that fertility. (1977, pp.474–5)

That robbery can be limited to some extent, through the application of human ingenuity and technological expertise. But, as has been argued here, the pressures to allow those alterations to proceed in order to facilitate the advance of the mode of production are very strong, and the limitations have been relatively ineffective. To bring them about needs a collective determination to succeed, and it is to the discussion of the nature of collective action that we now turn.

Chapter 5
Collective Action and the State

Free and open markets may be the key to financial success. But if they are to operate fairly and honestly, someone has to write the rules and to see they are rigidly enforced. (Queen Elizabeth II, speaking at the Guildhall, London, reported in *The Independent*, 11 February 1989)

Two major arguments have been advanced in the preceding chapters. The first is that because the environment operates as a vast complex of interlocking systems and sub-systems, environmental problems must be countered collectively, rather than individually. The externality effects of environmental use, over both space and time, are such that their generation can only be effectively tackled by society at large. Thus, although individual initiative in the attack on environmental problems is desirable there are major limits to it, especially within competitive modes of production (see Johnston, 1986a, Chapter 2), and viable approaches to both solving existing environmental problems and preventing the creation of others must involve collective agreements. The second argument is that the creation of environmental problems is not only a consequence of the human struggle for survival, but is also increasingly a product of the predominant mode of social organisation (capitalism) through which that struggle is co-ordinated collectively.

These two arguments lead to a paradoxical situation, to some extent at least. Collective control of the environment is necessary, if it is to be conserved and kept in a condition capable of sustaining human life at high material standards; such collective control would seem to require mitigating the demands made on the environment by the unceasing quest for greater profitability in the production and circulation of commodities. But if that quest is constrained, the mode of production may well fall into decay. Profitability must be promoted, which means promoting environmental stress, unless ways can be found of simultaneously reducing environmental stress and expanding the production of surplus value. The promotion of profitability is also a collective concern, as will be argued here. Thus, it would seem, at one and the same time we need collective action to promote profit-making and collective action to promote environmental protection.

Whether the two are compatible we leave to a final chapter; the concern here is to appreciate the basis of collective action, with particular reference to the role of the state.

Collective action can be brought about in three ways.

(1) *Voluntary, ad hoc agreement.* In this category are all agreements where a group of interested parties come together, develop an appreciation that collective action is necessary, and then undertake such action. This occurs very frequently in almost all aspects of human life, and at all spatial scales; examples range from sporting bodies agreeing on the criteria of eligibility for selection to a national team to members of a family deciding to share the costs of residential accommodation for an elderly parent. Central to all of these agreements are three characteristics: (a) they are entered into voluntarily; (b) they are *ad hoc* agreements only, developed for a specific purpose and having no influence on any other activity; and (c) they need not be entered into by all interested parties.

(2) *Voluntary acceptance of a central power.* In this category come all those agreements that are made by a single body; agreements that cover a wide range of topics, and are binding on all constituent members of the body. People accept the standing of that body to legislate in certain areas, and agree – perhaps grudgingly, and perhaps without formally registering their acceptance – to abide by its proposals. By far the major example of such a body is the state, an institution with sovereign power within a defined territory, which may be accountable to the residents of that territory in a variety of ways, as for example through the process of election for the right to run the state and through a constitution which limits the state's powers and reserves all other power to the people. The state makes decisions in a wide area of activities, and separate decision-making fora do not have to be established for each issue, as is the case with the first category.

(3) *Imposed from without.* With this form of collective action, the majority of those involved have no say on whether action should be taken on an issue, and in what direction. There is an individual or body of individuals with the power to impose rules of behaviour on others, and power to ensure that they obey those rules. Such bodies range widely in size and scope. Our concern here is with bodies that have power over large populations. Most are known as states, but they differ from states as described in the previous category in that the affected individuals have no guaranteed influence over those who have power within the state.

Our particular concern here is with the state, and especially the state as defined in the second of these three categories. Appreciation of the nature of the state, and of its necessary role in the capitalist mode of production in particular, is central to the present chapter. This requires first an understanding why in many circumstances the first of the above categories is not workable, and a state is necessary to ensure that the required collective action takes place.

The Logic of Collective Action

The basis of the case for a state, or at least some independent body that insists on people taking certain actions, is the work of a number of theorists on the logic of collective action. In effect, they argue that people acting individually will not necessarily do that which is in their individual best interests; they need others to impose rules to ensure that they do act in their own best interests, which is also the collective best interest. Some theorists suggest that this is not a general conclusion, but it is sufficiently important as an underpinning of the theory of the state to merit substantial coverage here.

Thomas Hobbes and Leviathan

The classic statement of this position was provided by the seventeenth-century philosopher, Thomas Hobbes, in his book *Leviathan* (first published in 1651). He argued that we are all concerned with our own survival but, to some extent at least, some people's success will be to the detriment of others, because their search for the means of survival could involve them seeking to impose their power on others. Because all want to survive, all will want to be powerful over others, in order to ensure their survival; the result is that everybody is wary of everybody else and everybody feels insecure. To quell their insecurity, everybody then seeks to increase their individual power over others, which in turn only heightens the insecurity. In a market society this power is sought through market operations, with the result that:

> everyone can and does continually compete for power against others. Every man's [sic] power resists and hinders other men's search for power, so pervasively that any man's power is simply the excess of his above others' . . . . Everyone seeks to transfer some of the powers of other men to himself, or to resist the transfer of some of his to others. And he does not do it by open force but by a market-like operation which sets every man's value at 'so much as would be given for the use of his Power'. (Macpherson, 1968, p.38)

Hobbes's analysis of this continuous search for power over others concluded that it would be destructive or, as he put it, there would be

> no place for Industry; because the fruit thereof is uncertain: and consequently no Culture of the earth; . . . no Knowledge of the face of the earth; no account of Time; no Arts; no Letters; no Society; and which is worst of all, continuall feare, and danger of violent death: And for the life of man, solitary, poore, nasty, brutish, and short. (Macpherson, 1968, p.41)

To avoid lives that were 'solitary, poore, nasty, brutish, and short', he argued, individuals would be prepared to give up some of their natural freedoms: 'the right to do or take anything and invade anybody – provided everyone else would do so at the same time' (1968, p.43). In other words, people would be prepared to enter an implicit contract with a sovereign power, which would act to restrain the competition for power that was in the end going to destroy that which people were seeking to achieve from it – high material living standards. They would accept the power that the state exercised, and the punishment it delivered to those defying its power, because they realised that such obedience was both in their own individual long-term good and in the general good. The nature of that obedience was laid down in nineteen 'laws of nature', and it was the role of the state to enforce those laws.

Rational action and game theory

Hobbes's work has been carried forward in recent years by a range of theorists. Seminal among them was Mancur Olson, in *The Logic of Collective Action*. He began his argument by observing that

It is often taken for granted, at least where economic objectives are involved, that groups of individuals with common interests usually attempt to further those common interests . . . . But it is *not* in fact true that the idea that groups will act in their self-interest follows logically from the premise of rational and self-interested behaviour. It does *not* follow, because all of the individuals in a group would gain if they achieved their group objective, that they would act to achieve that objective, even if they were all rational and self-interested. Indeed, unless the number of individuals in a group is quite small, or unless there is coercion or some other special device to make individuals act in their common interest, *rational, self-interested individuals will not act to achieve their common or group interests.* (1965, pp.1–2)

One can deduce as Hobbes's did, from this proposition that, as Olson hinted, a coercive power is needed to ensure that interests are promoted, and that rational individuals will accept this. Rational people should accept the argument and be prepared to enter into a social contract with the state as the coercive power erected to further that end.

The validity of Hobbes and Olson's proposition is frequently illustrated with reference to a simple 'game' in the mathematics of game theory known as the *Prisoner's Dilemma*. Michael Laver (1981, pp.47–50) gives a clear introduction to this. Two men suspected of committing a serious crime are apprehended while committing a less serious crime. The police have no conclusive proof of their guilt in the more serious crime, and so want each of them to provide that proof by implicating the other. They are interviewed separately, and the police do not allow them to meet and confer. The deal that the police offer to each is as follows:

If you implicate your accomplice in the serious crime, and he is convicted, you will go free; if you do not, you will be convicted of the lesser crime in any case, and will go to jail. (Laver, 1981)

The arrested men know that if both stay silent, both will be convicted of the lesser crime, for which the punishment is one year in jail. They also know that if one implicates the other, the squealer will go free and the convicted man will get ten years for the serious crime. Finally, they estimate that if both squeal, each will get eight years. This produces what is known as a payoff matrix, which indicates the likely consequences of each of the two alternative actions for each individual – stay silent or squeal; these combine to produce four possible outcomes.

		Prisoner B	
		Stay silent	*Squeal*
	Stay silent	1,1	10,0
Prisoner A			
	Squeal	0,10	8,8

The numbers in the four cells of this matrix indicate the outcome for each of the suspects, according to their decision whether to stay silent or squeal; the first number indicates the sentence that Prison A will get, and the second indicates the sentence that Prisoner B will get. Thus, according to the top left-hand cell, if both stay silent each will get a sentence of one year's imprisonment for the lesser crime. If Prisoner A stays silent and Prisoner B squeals, then, as the top right-hand cell shows, Prisoner A will get 10 years and Prisoner B will go free: similarly, if A squeals and B keeps silent, A goes free and B gets 10 years (bottom left-hand cell). Finally (bottom right), if both squeal both get eight years.

What should they do? They face a dilemma, hence the name of the game. They would be best off collectively if both stay silent, because each then will get one year in prison. But each has to gamble that the other will stay silent too; if he doesn't, then the one who does keep quiet gets 10 years. For each, the best thing to do is to squeal, whatever the other does. Thus if Prisoner A squeals, he will get off free if B stays silent, which is better than getting one year if he (A) stays silent too; if Prisoner B squeals, A will get eight years, which is better than the ten if B squeals and A stays silent. Exactly the same calculations hold for B: whatever A does, B will be better off if he squeals. So both squeal, and both do eight years. If both had stayed silent, both would have done one year, but because neither could trust the other not to squeal each had to take the course that assumed that the other would. And so, as Laver puts it:

> both do time for . . . [the more serious crime], despite the fact that both would be better off staying silent and simply doing their time for the . . . [lesser crime]. The pursuit of individual rationality inevitably leads to an outcome which is deplored by both criminals. (1981, p.49)

What if the police had allowed them to confer? Wouldn't they then have come to a pact to remain silent? Perhaps, but each still might have been uncertain whether the other would break their agreement and go for the deal. Mutual co-operation would be to their individual benefit, but unless that co-operation was enforced in some way, neither could trust the other to stick to the agreement.

The general conclusion to be drawn from this simple example is that mutual co-operation, which will benefit all of the parties involved, will not be the strategy chosen by people acting individually. It is in their self-interest to co-operate, but the rational pursuit of that self-interest as individuals leads to the decision not to co-operate. Only enforced collective action will lead to the optimal outcome.

That general conclusion has been applied to a wide range of situations, and used both to make the case for the state, thus developing Hobbes's ideas, and to show the limitations of the state. With regard to the former, the Prisoner's Dilemma has been used to develop the argument for the provision of what are known as public goods – state-supplied goods and services which are made available to all and for which all pay (according to the rules adopted within the state regarding 'from each according to his ability to pay') out of their taxes. For example it may be in the interests of all employers within the territory of a state that every employee be literate; illiterate people cannot do any of the available jobs. Thus the first thing that any employer would have to do is train an employee in the skills of literacy. But why should an employer take on this cost?; why not leave it to other employers to do the training, and then, given the freedom of individuals to sell their labour to whom they wish, offer jobs to people once they are trained? (Employers could even offer a small premium in wages, which would still cost less than the cost of training.) As a consequence, no employers would offer literacy training: all want literate employees, but none is prepared to pay for the training because the others may not. Those who do not pay would gain a competitive advantage (their production costs would be cheaper) – such individuals, who benefit from the expenditure of others while making no contribution themselves, are known as *free-riders*. All would, however, accept the situation where compulsory literacy training was provided for all by the state, and all employers would pay a 'fair' contribution for that training through their taxes. Their individual needs would only be met if all were required to pay for them. They could, of course, be required by the state to provide training themselves, rather than pay for the public good. However, they would know, because of the obedience owed to the state, that all would be doing the same: there would be no free-riders, no employers obtaining benefits while they let others bear the costs.

An illustration of the Prisoner's Dilemma showing the limits of the state is given by Brams's (1975) example of two nation–states involved in an arms race. In this context, the payoff matrix used earlier can be applied: for 'Prisoner' read 'State' and for 'Keep Silent' and 'Squeal' read 'End the Arms Race' and 'Continue the Arms Race' respectively. For each state, the best solution is for both to select the 'End the Arms Race' option, because the ultimate consequence of that path (war) might then be avoided and each would have more resources available to devote to other state activities (or to return to its citizens, through lower taxes). But neither can afford to select that option unless it trusts the other to. Trust is the crucial word; the countries may enter into a treaty on arms limitation, in the same way that the prisoners might have conferred, but how can they be sure that the other party will keep the treaty, since there is no 'super-state' which exists to insist that this is done? Thus, as Brams argues, states will be very reluctant to opt out of the arms race; if there is no certainty that the adversary will do the same, then 'the nation that disarms will relinquish control over its fate and thereby suffer its worst outcome' (1975, p.34).

Of course some states do opt out; Switzerland has done so, by taking a neutral stance during both of the world wars of the present century. But to do that means trusting that the neutrality will be observed, which was not the case with every state that adopted such a position in those conflicts; Swiss neutrality was of value to the adversarial powers. And many that opt out do so knowing that their security is protected, or at least guaranteed, by other countries that remain in the arms race. But what about those latter countries; don't they sometimes seek detente and indicate a willingness to trust the others to opt out with them? Geopolitical analysis (e.g. Kennedy, 1988; Taylor, 1989a) suggests that such a willingness to negotiate will occur only at times when the adversaries are all under stress. In a two-nation arms race, for example, if both are suffering budgetary problems as a consequence of the costs of the arms race, then one may be prepared to respond to the other's overtures with regard to reducing the pace of, if not ending, the arms race. But the problem of trust remains; if, as a consequence, one becomes stronger than the other economically, it can reinvest in the arms race and gain an advantage.

The Prisoner's Dilemma has been presented here as a 'two-person game', and is thus an oversimplification of the situation in most circumstances. But it can be extended to involve many players, so becoming much more complex. The basic message remains the same, however. Indeed if anything it is enhanced; where large numbers of individuals are seeking rational personal outcomes, their inability to be sure that their competitors will not take decisions that are in neither the collective nor their own individual good, and will not involve free-riding, will mean that rational decisions lead to sub-optimal solutions. This is well illustrated by an argument of direct relevance to the study of environmental issues.

The Tragedy of the Commons

'The tragedy of the commons' is the title of a classic, though some believe flawed, paper by Garret Hardin (1968), which has been developed by several authors as a paradigm example of the Prisoner's Dilemma (e.g. Laver, 1981; Taylor, 1976). Taylor introduces it with the simple example of two users of a water supply who also pollute that supply. They could cease pollution, at a cost, but is this in their individual interests? The payoff matrix (expressed in monetary values, here termed £s) is as follows:

User B

	Not pollute	*Pollute*
Not pollute	2,3	1,4

User A

	Pollute	4,1	3,2

According to this, it is in the interests of each user to pollute, because the returns from doing so exceed those from not doing so, whatever the other does: if A pollutes, the return is £4 if B does not, compared to £2 if A does not either; if B pollutes, then the return to A from polluting too is £3, compared to £1 if A doesn't pollute. Thus each user prefers to pollute, whatever the other does. In addition, each prefers the other not to pollute, because there are externalities involved. B's pollution spills over on to A, for example. Thus whereas A's return is always greater when polluting, it is greater when B is not polluting, presumably because B's production costs are higher and B is thus less competitive. Thus although pollution may not be desirable, especially in the long term, it is in neither's interest not to pollute, even if it is guaranteed that the other will not: voluntary co-operation does not seem sensible, so if pollution is to be ended it must be an imposed solution.

Hardin's paper generalises the point that Taylor draws from it, and also develops a moral message: the paper's subtitle is 'The population problem has no technical solution; it requires a fundamental extension in morality'. (His source is an earlier portrayal of the same problem; Lloyd, 1833.) Hardin argues as follows. There is an area of common land, on which herders can graze cattle. Each herder will seek to graze as many cattle as possible. Eventually, the carrying capacity of the common land is reached. This should result in stability, but instead 'the inherent logic of the commons remorselessly generates tragedy' (Hardin, 1968, p.1244). Why? Because all herders are seeking to maximise the returns from their cattle. Since the positive consequences of adding an additional animal to the commons go to the herder owning the animal, whereas the negative consequences are felt by all herders, the result is a net gain to the individual who increases herd size. Assume that when the common land is at its carrying capacity each animal produces a return of £1. An additional animal gives a return of only £0.9999, because the amount of grazing to be shared by all the animals is slightly less. Because the value of all animals declines very slightly, the negative costs of going above the carrying capacity are incurred by all. If herder A adds an animal above the carrying capacity, therefore, increasing her herd size from 20 to 21, the additional income is £0.9999. The loss of income from the reduced value of the other 20 is £0.002 [£20 – (20 × £0.9999)], so the net outcome is that A's returns increase from £20 to £20.9979. It is thus clearly in A's interest to add that twenty-first animal. All the others, who do not increase their herd size, will suffer a loss of income – to £0.0001 for every animal owned, as a consequence of the depletion of the grazing resource.

It is thus in every herder's interest to increase herd size, even though this takes the common land above its carrying capacity, means that every animal is worth less, and eventually may mean the degradation of the commons. As Hardin expresses it:

the rational herdsman [sic] concludes that the only sensible course for him to pursue is to add another animal to his herd. And another; and another . . . . But this is the conclusion reached by each and every rational herdsman sharing the commons. Therein is the tragedy. Each man is locked into a system that compels him to increase his herd without limit – in a world that is limited. Ruin is the destination toward which all men rush, each pursuing his own best interest in a society that believes in the freedom of the commons. Freedom in the commons brings ruin to all: (1968, p.1244)

And, Hardin claims, the evidence that this is the case is there for all to see, as in the continued depletion of fish stocks so that 'species after species of fish and whales [are brought] closer to extinction' (p.1245).

The tragedy of the commons, to Hardin, is an example of the general argument, illustrated by Taylor's smaller case of pollution, that in a finite world individual rational action fails to recognise that finiteness, with tragic consequences for all. (The tragedy of the commons can be expressed as a Prisoner's Dilemma game also, with herder A against the rest, and each herder playing herder A in turn.) Hardin used the 'tragedy' to develop a wider argument regarding the carrying capacity of the earth itself, that the breeding habits of the human population are exceeding the earth's capacity to sustain the additional numbers, and that if this growth is not controlled the ultimate tragedy will be upon us – genocide. Human history shows, he argues, that successively what was treated as a common resource is no more. Initially the land from which food was gathered was treated as a commons, but now in most parts of the world it is enclosed and its use restricted. The commons was also used as a place for waste disposal, but increasingly we are realising the perils of polluting those commons and seeking to restrict the previous unconstrained dumping of wastes into the environment. As he puts it:

Every new enclosure of the commons involves the infringement of somebody's personal liberty . . . . But what does 'freedom' mean? When men mutually agreed to pass laws against robbing, mankind became more free, not less so. Individuals locked into the logic of the commons are free only to bring on universal ruin: once they see the necessity of mutual coercion, they become free to pursue other goals. (1968, p.1248)

This leads him to conclude that just as societies agreed to reduce access to the commons in terms of both food-gathering and pollution, so they will agree to:

The necessity of abandoning the commons in breeding. No technical solution can rescue us from the misery of overpopulation. Freedom to breed will bring ruin to all . . . . The only way that we can preserve and nurture other and more precious freedoms is by relinquishing the freedom to breed, and that very soon.

This, of course, is a solution recognised by the governments of India and China in recent years, but the evidence that it is a solution widely accepted by the people there is equivocal; there are many claims that China's 'one-child family' policy is failing.

How, then, do we avoid the tragedy of the commons, in specific instances and in the generality of Hardin's final argument on population control, given that 'If *everyone* would only restrain himself, all would be well; but it takes *only one less than everyone* to ruin a system of voluntary restraint' (Hardin, 1974, p.562). Hardin's answer (1968) to the question 'How to legislate temperance?' is a policy of 'Mutual coercion mutually agreed upon'. In this, he defines coercion not in its popular usage as 'arbitrary compulsion imposed by distant, non-accountable decision-makers' but rather as mutual consent to do what may be considered undesirable in itself, because the alternative is much worse:

we are not required to enjoy it, or even to pretend we enjoy it. Who enjoys taxes? But we accept compulsory taxes because we recognise that voluntary taxes would favor the conscienceless. We institute and (grumblingly) support taxes and other coercive devices to escape the horror of the commons. (Hardin, 1968, p.1247)

In other words we accept the necessity of a state, which will require us to obey policies framed to avoid the tragedy of the commons, but we accept that necessity because we have been convinced of it through rational argument. This means the use of education to promote an ideology that will sustain the commons, the environment: 'One of the major tasks of education today is to create such an awareness of the dangers of the commons that people will be able to recognize its many varieties, however disguised' (Hardin, 1974, p.562).

In his second paper (1974) Hardin takes the lifeboat metaphor as a key to develop his theme; the lifeboat is unable to support all on board, and so unfortunate decisions have to be taken on who should survive. To him, 'Spaceship Earth' is equivalent to the lifeboat, requiring decisions to be made on that scale. Thus, he concludes,

so long as there is no true world government to control reproduction everywhere it is impossible to survive in dignity . . . . Without a world government that is sovereign in reproduction matters mankind lives, in fact, on a number of sovereign lifeboats. (1974, p.568)

This raises a major problem with regard to environmental policies, to which we return later in this chapter.

Is a State Needed?

The conclusion to be drawn from the argument so far in this chapter is that a coercive sovereign institution (a state) is necessary to ensure the future of the natural environment; without it, people, acting rationally and in what seems to be in their own best interests, will put such pressures on the environment that its quality will be degraded. But is this necessarily so?

In this book on rational ecology, Dryzek (1987) identifies nine different ways of co-ordinating human societies, each of which can be applied to environmental use. He evaluates each according to five criteria: (a) negative feedback, defined as returning to a desired status quo in the case of changes, as with the action of a thermostat; (b) co-ordination across all parts of the ecosystem, so that solution of a problem in one place does not merely transfer it to another; (c) and (d) robustness and flexibility, to cope with the (perhaps unexpected) spatial and temporal variability in ecological circumstances (robustness and flexibility are substitutable according to Dryzek); and (e) resilience, so that if there is a major shift in environmental circumstances the system can be steered back to its initial operating range. His evaluations of the nine are as follows.

(1) Through the operation of *markets*, and use of prices, which are characterised by consumer sovereignty and the unconstrained pursuit of self-interest, producing the results so starkly laid out by Hardin. As Dryzek concludes: 'Private enterprise, consumer sovereignty markets may have their good points, but . . . ecological rationality is not one of them' (p.86). People will not pay for environmental protection voluntarily, as a rule, and as a consequence eat into their potential profits.

(2) Through *commands* issued from an administration. He argues that these may be satisfactory for dealing with 'familiar, routine and static problems' (p.108) and that they are well suited for the rapid mobilisation of resources to meet an immediate problem within those categories, but that 'Highly structured organizations are at a loss, though, when it comes to dealing with high degrees of uncertainty, variability, and complexity'.

(3) Through a set of formal rules, laid out as *laws*, to which all adhere. Laws can be robust, and can co-ordinate, thereby meeting two of the criteria. But robustness may be at the expense of flexibility, so that laws cannot perform well under the other criteria.

(4) By the promulgation of desirable *values*, through moral persuasion, a procedure which Dryzek finds wanting in practice and unlikely to succeed in theory, again because success on some of the criteria is likely to lead to failure on others (substantial flexibility makes co-ordination difficult, for example).

(5) Through what he calls 'partisan mutual adjustment' via a mechanism of '*Polyarchy*'; the latter term is used as a synonym for what most term 'democracy', in which collective choices are made by the majority view of a large number of actors with competing interests to promote. Dryzek has more faith in such a system than in either markets or administrations, because its negative feedback and co-ordination devices are superior, but the polyarchies that exist are, he claims, 'far better at responding to signals from General Motors or the Daily Mirror than to messages from ecosystems' (p.131), because of their association with market economies.

(6) Through formal *negotiation*, with co-ordination achieved via

bargaining. But this mode fails on the other criteria, for reasons stressed by the game theory arguments; what sanctions are there to require people to stick to bargains?

(7) Through *force*. War might be an efficient way of achieving negative feedback, as Malthus suggested, but could it produce global co-ordination, and wouldn't it call forth a large administration, with all the attendant problems? (Furthermore, the idea of war as a way of solving environmental problems appears to be contradictory, given the ecological impact of some recent wars, such as that in Vietnam in the 1960s.)

(8) Through *radical decentralisation*, or the promotion of anarchy, with societies lacking formal administrative structures. This is the argument developed by Schumacher in his influential book *Small is Beautiful* (1973); if societies are locally self-reliant they will need to develop closer harmony with their environments than is the case with modern global society, and thus promote ways of living that meet the criteria of negative feedback, flexibility, resilience and co-ordination (the last through co-operation, to the mutual benefit of all). But Dryzek finds that such anarchic solutions fail on the robustness criterion; in the face of states with strong repressive apparatus, anarchic societies are doomed to failure, so unless there can be a global revolution the solution will not work.

(9) Through *discussion and practical reason*, which would take place in an open society where interest groups are unable to structure the decision-making agenda and deny people full, unbiased access to relevant knowledge. An open society is an emancipated one, in which people have control of their own destinies, but alone, Dryzek feels, it will not lead to the solution of environmental problems, in part because it will be pragmatic in its approach to problems and will therefore lack co-ordination. However, an open society with its problem-solving mechanisms is attractive if practical reason is introduced, because this will lead to agreement on common interests, purposes and values. Once that has been achieved then the solution of problems can be set within a firm framework; if that framework promotes ecological values, then small scale, open societies may be able to ensure equilibrium between human societies and their environments.

Dryzek provides an agenda for tackling the problems of surviving within and sustaining the earth's physical environment in which the 'most prominent items are decentralization in the form of substantial local autonomy and self-sufficiency, open and discursive "communicatively rationalized" social choice, and (perhaps) limited bargaining'.

Clearly, achievement of the items on this agenda will involve major shifts both in the organisation of production, distribution and exchange and in the nature of political institutions. Such may be attainable long-term goals. In the meantime, however, we face the problems of living in societies characterised by markets, administrations, laws, polyarchies, bargaining, and some use of force. The argument so far in this book has been that markets lead to environmental degradation, but that states might prevent that. In the absence of any alternatives, we must then turn again to a consideration of the state.

Alternative games

Before doing that, however, it is necessary to ask whether people may not adopt the practices that Hardin says are necessary, of their own free will; might they not act altruistically, because in the end that is in their self-interest too? This issue is faced by Taylor (1976) and he argues that in certain circumstances such behaviour might be forthcoming. Laver describes those circumstances in the following way. Assume not one game of the Prisoner's Dilemma but a sequence of several involving the same participants, as in the arms race. Each player may take the following position:

> I'll start off by cooperating. Thereafter, I'll do whatever you did in the previous game. If you cooperated, I'll cooperate; if you damaged me, I'll damage you. (Laver, 1981, p.50)

In this situation, if you choose a damaging strategy you become worse off. If your adversary declines to increase arms in a given period, but you do invest, then in the next period the adversary will too, and you will need to respond; you are both damaged in the long term, even though individually you may have gained a short-term advantage. But if you don't invest either, a status quo is maintained: as Laver says: 'If none are armed, or if all are armed, there is a stand-off. Clearly an unarmed stand-off is preferable to an armed stand-off, since it is cheaper' (1981, p.51).

The lesson to be drawn from this would seem to be that people might be prepared to enter into agreements not to increase stock on the commons beyond the proven carrying capacity, not to breed beyond a certain level, and not to pollute a water supply. But, Laver goes on to argue, Taylor's analyses suggest that such co-operative strategies are only likely to develop when the number of individuals involved is small; the smaller the group, the lower the probability of a 'wildcat' defection and the greater the problems of monitoring adherence. Further, the individuals involved must perceive that the immediate benefits to be gained from defection are small relative to the long-term gains of continuing to adhere to the agreement. The more 'future-oriented' people are, the greater their likely commitment to the bargain. But how 'future-oriented' are people with regard to environmental issues, especially when their decisions to limit profits may affect not only immediate returns but also long-term survival (in a competitive market, not in an ecological sense)?

In an arms race, of course, one defector out of a small number of countries involved in an agreement to limit investment on weapons would almost certainly be sufficient to lead all to abrogate the treaty. But in the sorts of situation illustrated by the tragedy of the commons, the defection of a few out of a very large number might not be fatal – assuming that the few were not extremely strong relative to all others. Thus if 1000 herders had access to the commons, and all had approximately the same number of animals, if one or two increased their herds above the carrying capacity (we assume that this is known) the degradation would probably not be very severe. A few free-riders can be accommodated, just as the London

Underground does not become non-viable if a few fare-dodgers succeed; the problem is how to ensure that there are only a few!

Before turning to a fuller discussion of the nature of the state, we need to look at two other games that Taylor has introduced. Both, he points out, involve the existence of a privileged sub-group within the group under study, such that there is: 'at least one sub-group whose members collectively find it worthwhile to provide some amount of the public good by themselves' (1988, p.10).

If the public good is action either to solve or to avoid environmental problems, then these games suggest that individuals will act with the sort of coercion that a state would impose, through self-interest and not altruism.

Taylor's presentation of these games involves the classification of the individuals involved into two groups, those who *co-operate* (C in the payoff matrices) and contribute to the costs of environmental programmes, and those who *defect* (D) and fail to contribute. The first game is the game of *Chicken* (whose name is taken from the 'real' games, played by both children and adults) in which the payoff matrix is:

Individual 2

	C	D
C	3,3	2,4
D	4,2	1,1

Individual 1

Here each individual gets a greater return from co-operating than not, irrespective of what the other person does; individual 2, for example, gets a return of 3 units from contributing towards the costs of the environmental programme if individual 1 contributes also, which is better than a return of 2 units if individual 1 defects.

To illustrate the relevance of Chicken, Taylor gives two examples. In the first, there are two neighbouring cultivators, whose crops depend on the maintenance of drainage ditches which divide their two properties. Either can do all of the work, but would prefer to share it with the other; but the consequences of neither doing it are so dire – involving the almost complete loss of the crops (the D,D option in the payoff matrix) – that one would do it even if the other did not. Thus both will contribute, without being forced to – although it could be argued that one might gamble on the other doing it and decide to free-ride. The latter involves what Ward identifies as a reputation for toughness,

> a reputation for sticking to commitments not to cooperate . . . . Tough players are often able to force the other player to bear the costs of providing some public good all by himself and are therefore themselves able to enjoy the benefits of free-riding upon his actions. (1987, p.23)

If toughness worked, then clearly some coercion would be needed to ensure that the free-rider met a fair share of the costs; but Ward's conclusion is that a toughness strategy will work in certain circumstances only. (For another example, see Dufournaud and Harrington, 1989.)

Taylor's other example involves the case of two factories which emit polluting wastes into a lake. If only one pollutes the lake, the lake survives, but if both do, a critical threshold is crossed, and the lake 'dies'. Each factory owner can either co-operate by not polluting, or defect by polluting. Each would prefer to defect, and free-ride on the other, but the potential catastrophe if both defected is such that each will unilaterally decide to co-operate. This is an example of what Taylor calls a 'lumpy good', in which there is a discontinuous relationship between the amount of pollution and the consequence (as suggested by bifurcation theory – p.30). Again, however, it is possible for one individual in the game to 'act tough', and gamble on the other not doing so, which is the situation that led to the virtual extinction of certain species of whale (Taylor and Ward, 1982 – though note that these authors suggest that the experience with the commercial extinction of the blue whale because of 'toughness' by both Japan and the USSR was a learning experience which ensured that a similar fate did not befall other species). Where the Chicken situation occurs, Taylor and Ward are more optimistic that at least some of the individuals involved (in a game of n players) will co-operate than is so where the Prisoner's Dilemma is operative: 'the only convincing possibility under which *none* of the public good will be provided in Chicken games is that of risk-loving players pre-committing themselves simultaneously to no-cooperation . . .' (1982, p.370).

But, of course, this is not to say that all of the costs of the needed environmental programmes will be met. Further, it is often in people's short-term interests to adopt non-cooperative strategies, not just to free-ride on others but also in the ideology of the technocratic fix that underpins much of capitalism in particular, which is that if one resource is exhausted another will be found ('invented') to replace it.

The other game introduced by Taylor (1988) is that of *Assurance*, which has two payoff matrices, depending on the situation. In the first situation (Case I), neither of the players can provide the public good alone – perhaps because it is too expensive; in the second (Case II), either can provide some of the public good, giving benefits to each, but the one who does co-operate and make a contribution receives less in return that the costs. In both cases, if neither contributes, there is no benefit at all. The two payoff matrices are:

		Case I					Case II	
		2					2	
		C	D				C	D
	C	2,2	–2,0			C	2,2	–1.1
1					1			
	D	0,–2	0,0			D	1,–1	0,0

In both cases the cost of contributing to the public good is 2 units and the benefits are 4 units, so that the total net gain available is 2 units. In Case I, if both contribute, both make the maximum net gain; if only one contributes, that person loses 2 units of investment, and neither has any gain. Thus for any gain at all, co-operation is essential. But people will only co-operate if they perceive the benefits, implying that all perceive the public good as desirable. If some do not, then they have no stimulus to contribute, and will only do so if coerced, presumably by a state which has accepted the arguments of those who favour the public good. Taylor's example of Case II is of two individuals sharing a vegetable patch; one person's weeding alone cannot control the weeds entirely, but it enables some crops to be grown by both, so the return from only one person weeding is just one unit. Thus if one person weeds but the other doesn't, the former suffers a net loss and the other a net gain. The implication would seem to be toughness again, and a free-riding benefit. But for both players there is a better return from co-operating, whatever the other does, than from not doing so, which suggests that each should undertake weeding, to their mutual benefit.

Although in some situations it seems that individual and collective goals coincide, so that people will co-operate in the provision of public goods, which include those that sustain the environment, nevertheless in many cases this may not occur, at least not initially. It could be that after a period of learning people come to appreciate the benefits to be gained from voluntary co-operation, but during that period the environment may be irrevocably degraded (as with the extinction of the blue whale). The conclusion must therefore be that, in environmental issues involving a complex, interacting set of global systems, individual action will not prevent the problems of resource deterioration from emerging, and that whatever the attractions of Dryzek's agenda its achievement in the foreseeable future is unlikely. Thus, following Hardin, a state appears to be a necessity.

Understanding the State

The state is a universal phenomenon in the capitalist and the advanced communist/socialist contemporary worlds, which suggests that neither of those modes of production could operate without a state. Why is this so? And why is it that the modern state is so large and apparently all-powerful, implicating itself throughout the daily lives of people, in the spheres of both production and consumption (civil society)? Such questions have increasingly concerned social scientists, leading to the production of a substantial number of enquiries into the nature and function of the state (e.g. Alford and Friedland, 1985; Dunleavy and O'Leary, 1987). The following section draws on those sources to develop an appreciation of the role of the state, particularly of the state in capitalist society, which is essential in order to understand how it might operate in the context of the solution of environmental problems.

At the outset, it is necessary to be clear what is meant by the state. Dunleavy and O'Leary (1987, p.2) give the following comprehensive definition, identifying the state by five characteristics.

(1) The state is a recognisably separate institution or set of institutions, so differentiated from the rest of its society as to create identifiable public (i.e. state) and private spheres.

(2) The state is sovereign, or the supreme power, within its territory, and by definition the ultimate authority for all law, i.e. binding rules supported by coercive sanctions. Public law is made by state officials and backed by a formal monopoly of force.

(3) The state's sovereignty extends to all the individuals within a given territory, and applies equally, even to those in formal positions of government or rule-making. Thus sovereignty is distinct from the personnel who at any given time occupy a particular role within the state.

(4) The modern state's personnel are mostly recruited and trained for management in a bureaucratic manner.

(5) The state has the capacity to extract monetary revenues (taxation) to finance its activities from its subject population.

These five characteristics make it clear that the state's sovereignty is territorially defined. What they fail to stress is that the state is necessarily a territorial body, that it could not operate if it were not and that its territoriality is part of its power base (Mann, 1984); these points are important to later discussion.

Dunleavy and O'Leary's definition of the state makes clear what it is, but not why it is. States perform many functions, not all of them in the same way – just as there are different ways of seeking to make profits in the sphere of production and of organising civil society (p.68), so there are different ways of doing what the state has to do, and the state may do other things that it does not have to do. Clark and Dear (1984, p.43) collapse the many activities of the capitalist state into three basic operational objectives:

(1) *to secure social consensus* by guaranteeing acceptance of the prevailing contract by all groups in society;
(2) *to secure the conditions of production* by regulating (a) social investment to increase production in the public and private sectors, and (b) social consumption to ensure the reproduction of the labour force; and
(3) *to secure social integration* by ensuring the welfare of all groups, but especially the subordinate classes.

These objectives are very similar to those developed earlier by O'Connor (1972), but they are placed in a clear priority order. Initial attention here will focus on the second and third, however.

The state and the sphere of production

Capitalist society is founded, as already stressed, on the creation of saleable commodities, from which a profit can be realised. Both the creation of the commodities and their sale for profit involve market-place transactions. Why does the state need to be implicated?

Part of the answer to this question can be provided by reference back to the Prisoner's Dilemma. Buying and selling in all but the more primitive of market systems involves taking things on trust. Individuals agree to sell their labour against a contract that they will receive a wage at the end of a given period of work – usually a week or a month. Manufacturers buy a machine from another manufacturer against a contract of sale which guarantees that the machine will be able to do certain tasks, if properly used, and should last a certain (usually only vaguely specified) time. But what if these undertakings are not met, if the labourers' wages are not paid, or the machines fail to perform satisfactorily? What recourse do the injured parties have if contracts are not honoured? The honouring of contracts is one of the nineteen 'Laws of Nature' identified by Hobbes in *Leviathan* – 'That men performe their Covenants made' (Macpherson, 1968, p.201). But, in Hobbes's terms, it needs a Leviathan to ensure that they do so perform. If there is no recourse to redress from broken contracts, it may not be in the interests of people who make them to keep them. In the long term, they may suffer; a manufacturer whose machines fail to satisfy may get no further custom from the dissatisfied customer, who in turn may encourage others not to purchase from the same source, but the short-term benefits of not providing what was agreed may outweigh these other considerations. With the contract for labour, the sanctions within the market-place may be less severe, especially if the supply of labour exceeds the demand so that it is a buyers' market; failing to meet the terms of one contract is then unlikely to prevent others coming forward to sign new agreements.

One way to try and counter the failure to honour contracts is for those affected to act collectively. In the case of the machinery sales, for example, if all manufacturers of a certain product joined together in an organisation and agreed to co-operate on issues of mutual interest, the experience of one of their members might lead them to initiate a collective boycott of a machine manufacturer who failed to meet the specifications set out in a contract sale. But individual manufacturers could decide not to join, and even having joined might decide not to participate in the boycott, because it is not in their interest so to do (they might get preferential treatment from the machine seller). With regard to the labour example, the individuals concerned could combine in a trade union and bargain for collective rights; employers might then be more bound to honour contracts entered with a stronger bargaining body, but there might be some prepared to work outside those bargains. In both cases the groupings are voluntary, and there is still no requirement for the contract to be honoured.

The honouring of contracts can only be achieved if the alternative to not doing so is punishment, punishment substantial enough to make it un-attractive to break them. (Thus, for example, newspaper editors may implicitly enter a contract not to libel individuals, because the law requires them not to. But they may be prepared to break that law, and commit a libel, because the cost of so doing – the redress they are required to make to the injured party – is less than the additional income obtained from sell-ing the libel through their papers' circulation.) There must then be an institution that can create rules with regard to contract compliance that hold for all contracts entered into within the territory where that law holds; that institution must also have the power to hear cases against accused malefactors and impose punishments if the accusations are found to be valid. That institution, with sovereign power over the population of a defined territory, is the state.

This example of contract compliance is but one of a very large number of issues which relate to the successful operation of a market economy. More generally, that market economy needs an infrastructure within which it can operate. In part that will be a physical infrastructure – markets cannot function unless there is a transport system, though the transport network need not be state-provided. In part, it will be an abstract, facilitating infrastructure. Transactions in a market economy are almost all negotiated in a common currency and in a common set of weights and measures, for example. People signing contracts which involve payment at a date in the future want an assurance not only that they will be paid on the due date but that the value of what they are paid will not be less than they expect in real terms (i.e. in the purchasing power of the currency). Thus stability of the currency is highly desirable, and ensuring this is a major task for the state; as in many capitalist countries in recent years, the British state has been concerned to control the rate of inflation (the rate by which money loses its value) in order to promote profit-making. People, it is argued, are much less prepared to invest in a capitalist venture which will be profitable at some date in the future if the nature of that profit is uncertain. An as far as possible inflation-free future is thus a requirement for successful attempts at wealth accumulation, and if those attempts are not initiated, the health of the population involved, and eventually their potential for survival, is in jeopardy.

The provision of this facilitating infrastructure is an example of what is widely known as the provision of *public goods* by the state. The need for this is often brought about, it is argued, by 'market failure', whereby the private producers fail to provide for themselves that which they need. In some cases they could not provide it: it would be very difficult, if not impossible, for example, for individuals to provide themselves with the security that a national defence system gives, yet without that security they may not be prepared to make a long-term speculative investment; similarly, it would almost certainly be unworkable for many different currencies to be circulating in a country. In other cases it might be possible for the private sector to provide the needed good or service, but for some reason it fails to do so, even though it needs it. The earlier example of the provision of literacy training, using the game theory framework (p.115), illustrates this; all employers want literate workers but none are prepared to pay for the training voluntarily in the fear that their competitors may steal a march on them by free-riding. But if they are forced to meet the costs of the training, because all others are, then they are content. And so the state is an acceptable body to ensure that market failures are rectified, by requiring all to meet the necessary costs.

The longer-term problems of the capitalist mode of production, as stressed earlier, are linked to its inbuilt crisis tendencies. Such crises affect not only those who suffer from them directly, such as the manufacturers of goods for which the market is no longer expanding, but also all others in society indirectly, through the multiplier process: fewer people have money to spend, less goods are consumed, smaller profits are obtained, and so on. It is in no one's interest for this to happen, and yet it is within no one's grasp to prevent it. Prevention might be achieved collectively, however, via the sovereign power of the state. For example the profitability of certain groups of manufacturers might be enhanced if they could get access to cheaper sources of raw materials. The state might assist this by subsidising their search for such sources; type examples of this include the monopoly that the British government gave organisations such as the East India Company and the Hudson's Bay Company over trade in certain parts of the world, monopolies that were backed by the state's domination of the use of armed force and, even more so, by the colonisation of areas to ensure uninterrupted access. This involved the state in the creation of the core–periphery structure of the world. Alternatively, the state might assist in a restructuring of the economy, by helping investors to write off redundant stock and fixed capital, and by investing in research which might lead to the invention of marketable, new products. Or the state might become a large-scale purchaser – as happened at the end of the 1930s when many states invested heavily in rearmament programmes and stimulated demand in their economies.

The health of a capitalist society depends on successful accumulation strategies by those searching for profits from investments. But the market system of capitalism, if not regulated and sustained by the state, will in the longer term fail to deliver the needed profits. For the capitalist system to work, an independent body must keep it healthy.

This imperative stretches beyond the regulation of what Clark and Dear term 'social investment' in the sphere of production to the sphere of civil society, involving what they call 'social consumption' to ensure the reproduction of the labour force. Labour is a necessity, and so it must be reproduced. This requires shelter almost everywhere. The provision of housing can be undertaken through the market, with people investing in homes either to sell or to rent. If they are to be sold, then there must be buyers with either substantial sums of money available for the purchase of an expensive product with a long life expectancy (including the land on which it is built, which has an infinite life expectancy, and is in fixed supply) or the ability to borrow the money needed to finance such a purchase. If neither is available, the homes for purchase may not be built. With regard to homes for rent, the returns on the investment come slowly, over the long life of the building; alternative investments may generate quicker profits, and mean that houses are not built. This is yet a further example of market failure to provide a necessity – homes for the needed workers. The state may then be called upon to remedy the failure, either by creating the conditions that will encourage the provision of housing – subsidising its construction, perhaps, or subsidising the purchase and/or rental in some way – or by providing the housing itself.

Employers want healthy workers, because they are more productive. They may be able to obtain a continuous supply, because of an excess of labour available over that demanded, in which case they may be prepared to do little about their employees' health and discard them when their productivity declines. But if that strategy is not available, they may have to spend on keeping their workers healthy. As with the training example quoted earlier, they may not be willing to do this unless required to, which involves the state in either enforcing health expenditure by employers or ensuring a health service for all, so that potential as well as actual workers are healthy. Similarly, state activity may be the only way of ensuring that the products on offer are safe for the population to consume, hence the legislation of minimum standards for the preparation of foodstuffs, for example. The state must ensure investment in civil society as well as in the sphere of production.

The state and social integration

As well as the tendencies to crisis inherent in capitalism because of the problems of overproduction and underconsumption there are further problems caused by the inbuilt antagonism between the buyers and sellers of labour – what Marx terms the class conflict. Each category is dependent on the other: if it cannot buy labour, the employing category cannot produce commodities and so realise profits that can be translated into wealth; if they cannot find employers to purchase their labour, members of the employee category cannot obtain the income with which to purchase the means of reproduction and survival. This interdependence means that in the long term the two parties must reach agreements, otherwise all will lose. But in the antagonisms that precede such accommodations, it is the employer category that has the greatest power. Those selling their labour power have little to fall back on if they are out of work, and savings are rapidly depleted; the stock of wealth held by most in the employing category means that they are better able to weather periods without income, and so can hold out longer (in a strike, for example). Or they can reinvest that wealth elsewhere, and obtain surplus from putting other people's labour to work; capital is more readily switched than labour in many circumstances.

The nature of this unequal relationship between the two categories means that the employed group are potentially hostile towards the capitalist mode of production, and hence could be mobilised to support political and other programmes designed to bring about its downfall. Capitalism can be presented to them as an exploitative system in which, although their absolute living standards may rise in certain circumstances of high productivity and buoyant markets, their position is always relatively insecure. To counter that potential mobilisation, and its threat to the social order of capitalism, the state is called upon to legitimate the mode of production, and win the grudging support of those who ostensibly stand to gain least from it. This can be done in a variety of ways, many of which are associated with what is popularly known as the welfare state.

This legitimation function involves the state acting to protect the interests of members of the employee category, basically by guaranteeing them a minimum level of welfare below which no individual and family will be allowed to fall. In particular, welfare programmes are designed to give assistance to those who have fallen on hard times through no fault of their own. For example, in Britain programmes of unemployment and supplementary benefits are used to provide subsistence level incomes for those unable to obtain work, and a range of other benefits are provided for those whose earned incomes are lower than a prescribed level deemed necessary for basic subsistence; particular attention is paid to those who either cannot earn themselves but are dependent on others, such as children, or may have nobody on which to depend, such as old people.

Alongside aspects of the welfare state provided to protect the weak in periods of hardship, which may be so structured to ensure that people do not become dependent on them and lose the incentive to work, are other aspects designed to assist all people in the search for better life chances. The public education service is a good example of this. In a capitalist society there is a strong meritocratic ideology, which argues that success comes to those who earn it and is equally available to all with the right qualities and attitudes. In a meritocracy, potential ability to succeed in a wide range of occupations is associated with educational attainments; the better educated are those fitted for the more demanding, and thus better paid, jobs. Thus if access to the relevant education is equally available to all, then all are being given equal chances to compete and succeed in the meritocratic rat race. A public education system is thus promoted among the population as being provided by the state for all irrespective of background, class or place; it is part of the legitimation function, since it allows the state to present itself as the champion of the relatively underprivileged. Similarly, a public health service can be presented as in the interests of all.

Payment for these public services comes from the state's exchequer, which obtains its income from taxation. To the extent that the taxation system is progressive – the more money people earn, and the greater their wealth, the greater their tax contribution – then it can be argued that the rich pay more. To the extent that the benefits of the public systems are provided either equally to all or biased towards those in greatest need, it can be argued that the poor receive more. Thus the welfare state can be justified as redistributive from the rich to the poor, which again presents the state as the champion of the relatively underprivileged in capitalist society.

Acceptance of this role for the state involves the poor seeing the state as their protector; while it fills this role, and they are relatively satisfied with the outcome, they are prepared to accept the mode of production, or at least not to question and challenge a system that produces wealth by exploiting them and continually demanding greater productivity from those of them who are in work. The more affluent, who are in most cases either employers or managers whose incomes come from ensuring that capitalist enterprises operate successfully, accept that they pay a higher proportion of the costs of the welfare state, in order to achieve the needed quiescence; they may question the level and range of welfare spending, but not the principle on which it is based.

There is something paradoxical between the two roles of the state discussed so far – the promotion of accumulation and the legitimation of the mode of production. Expenditure on the latter comes to a considerable degree from what would otherwise be profits. But those who would receive those profits are convinced that it is sensible to have the welfare state, for two reasons. First, it is in their interests to have a quiescent labour force which accepts the nature of capitalism and is prepared to work within it, particularly when the costs of that are being met by everybody. Secondly, many aspects of the welfare state are public goods which the state has to provide because of market failure. The public education system is a good example; as well as being a part of the state's legitimating role it also subsidises the training of skilled employees for the capitalist enterprises. Thus the latter may question the level of expenditure, and perhaps the detail of how it is used (they don't like the teaching of social sciences that call the legitimacy of capitalism into question, perhaps), but they will not challenge the provision in principle, because they benefit from it too.

Securing social consensus

The education system plays a part in the third state function, too. In order to operate successfully a society must be orderly, stable and secure. To achieve those ends, all members must accept a set of laws and rules within which they will act. They must submit to a rule of law, a system for arbitrating between opposing claims and making decisions, including determining punishments that will be accepted; and they must be prepared to serve, if called upon, to defend that system and its members from outside aggressors.

Part of this function thus involves establishing a legal system and set of laws, a policing system, and a defence force, which can provide the needed order, stability and security. The laws, for example, will define the nature of property ownership: what individuals can own, what they can and cannot do with their property, and under what circumstances they can be required to yield part or all of their property to others, including the state. Legal, police, defence and security systems must enjoy the support of the population (or at least not be challenged by them) in order to operate, and it is a function of the state to ensure such support. This is best achieved by gaining acceptance of the systems by people during their most formative years of socialisation – their childhood and early adult years. This can be done in two, linked, ways. First, the state-provided or state-sponsored education system can be used to promote an ideology entirely supportive of the systems, presenting them in a positive light as operating in everybody's individual and collective good and ensuring that people accept the disciplines of obeying the legally given orders of the various components of the state apparatus. Secondly, this socialisation can be bolstered by ensuring that it is backed up in the home, where many of the disciplines have to be put into operation, and in the various media (popular and otherwise) which circulate within the state.

Why the state?

Why is it the state that undertakes these tasks, rather than some other body that is not independent of both the sphere of production and civil society? The reason is that many of the things that the state does would not be accepted by at least some of the individuals affected if they thought the state were acting for particular interest groups only. Thus, for example, if the state were part of civil society and dominated by members of the employee class, while the latter might accept its legitimating activities the members of the employer fraction, whose wealth is derived from success in the sphere of production, might not; employers might feel that the state was biased towards one group only and might either direct their investment elsewhere or seek to take the state over themselves. On the other hand, if the state were dominated by members of the employer class, then its attempts to legitimate the mode of production to the members of the other fraction could be seen as presenting one group's interests only; the employee class, in turn, might be less prepared to accept the rule of law that the state represents.

So the state must be presented as objectively neutral from the interests of any one group within the population, and instead seen as working in the interests of all. If it is explicitly 'owned' by one section of the population, its legitimacy is open to challenge. Further, the state must be seen as independent of those in positions of power within it. In democratic states (to be discussed in more detail in the next chapter) these comprise two groups of people. The first are those employed to run the state, to operate its laws but not to enact them. They, as Dunleavy and O'Leary's definition of the state makes clear (see p.126), are engaged for their managerial capabilities and are accountable to the other group of powerful members of the state, and through them to the population at large. They should not be seen as promoting the interests of certain groups over others, but merely as administering the state efficiently. The second group are the politicians, those elected in some way by the population at large to define the parameters within which the state will be run, and to be answerable to the electorate for that definition and its perceived success, or lack of it. Thus the state in such circumstances does not 'belong' to either group; it 'belongs' to the whole population, who determine collectively how it will conduct itself and fulfil the tasks that are set (usually only implicitly) for it.

This independence of the state is seen by some as a 'charade', for a variety of reasons. Some argue, for example, that the employer and managerial classes clearly do dominate the state, and even if they don't 'own' it their power is so disproportionate that they in effect do have complete control, with the electoral process no more than a window-dressing and meritocracy so manipulated that the ideology of equality of opportunity is really a myth (see Dunleavy and O'Leary, 1987, Chapter 4). More fundamentally, others argue that since capitalism is an unequal, exploitative mode of production, structured to advance the interests of the wealthy few to the detriment of the majority, then if the state is promoting capitalism it is necessarily promoting the interests of the few over the rest. To them, the only way to alter that situation is to capture the state and, through a programme of socialism, change the mode of production so that there is no class division and all are indeed treated equally.

The limits to the state

As has been stressed earlier in the discussions of the sphere of production and civil society, capitalism is not a determinate mode of production in which a certain behaviour pattern is required in order to promote the underlying dynamo, the accumulation of wealth. The driving forces are there, but there are many ways in which they can be taken forward. In the sphere of production, for example, there are many options open to those who make investment decisions – what type of commodity production to invest in, how to organise the production, and where to make and to market the product; in civil society, similarly, there are many options available for the conduct of life away from the workplace. And the same is true of the state. As has been argued, a state is necessary to capitalism, and it must play the three roles just discussed. But how those roles should be played, how the script should be interpreted, is up to the personnel who run the state and, to the extent that they are accountable to an electorate, to the population at large.

The degrees of freedom of the state personnel extend beyond the necessary roles of the state as defined here. It is necessary that those roles be played, and that the state ensure the health of the mode of production within its territory. But the state is not confined to those roles alone, and if the personnel involved wish to take on additional roles then they are able to do so, as long as playing those roles is acceptable to those to whom they are accountable and does not significantly impede the necessary activity. Thus those in charge of the state may bring to that task certain imperatives that they want to carry through other than their economic–political functions, or they may be convinced by others that certain additional roles are desirable and would be widely supported.

What other roles might the state personnel adopt? In a major essay on the nature of power in society, Michael Mann has suggested that organizational power, 'the capacity to organize and control people, materials, and territories' (1986, p.2–3), can be categorised in two ways, according to its use. He distinguishes first between *extensive* power, which is 'the ability to organize large numbers of people over far-flung territories in order to engage in minimally stable cooperation', and *intensive* power, which is the 'ability to organize tightly and command a high level of mobilization or commitment from the participants' (p.7). Secondly, he distinguishes between *authoritative* power, which involves obedience to commands emanating from the state elite, and *diffused* power, which is spread through a population without necessarily any commands but rather 'an understanding that these practices are natural or moral or result from self-evident common interest' (p.8). This leads to the following typology of what he terms 'forms of organisational reach':

	Authoritative	Diffused
Intensive	Army command	General strike
Extensive	Military empire	Market exchange

Thus in an army command, power is intensively used, and is authoritative; it is limited to the troops being commanded, however, whereas in a military empire there is wide general control but the command structure does not penetrate far into everyday life. In the two examples of diffused power, the general strike is intensive, concentrated on a particular group only and diffused since it is accepted by those involved as the thing to do, not enforced upon them. And the system of market exchange is extensive, since it penetrates most aspects of life (as described in Chapter 2), and diffused, because again it is accepted as the way of doing things, not imposed by a command structure.

Extensive, diffused power is typical of modern capitalist states, especially of those in Western Europe and North America. The state influences very many aspects of daily life in both of the other spheres, but it does so not through the issuing of commands that must be obeyed but rather by developing understanding about what should and should not be done. Understanding about what? According to Mann, there are four sources of power involved – economic, ideological, military and political. *Economic power* is that involved with the organisation of production, distribution, exchange and consumption and, as discussed here in detail, is the base of the capitalist mode. The state exercises economic power in order to facilitate the operation of the capitalist system. *Ideological power* involves the transmission of a set of ideas that allow people to give meaning to their existence; it provides the concepts and categories with which to appreciate that which is perceived. These social forms are in part related to the economic power, since capitalism requires a state-backed ideology to sustain it. But they can extend well beyond the economic sphere, to cover all other aspects of life; they usually have a moral base in a religion, and many states promote a particular set of religious norms, either explicitly or implicitly. In so doing, the state influences life far beyond the basic structure of market exchange. *Military power* involves the application of organised physical force; it too can be used to promote the market system (as in colonialism) but it may be used by the state personnel in other ways, to promote ideas and goals independent of the economic sphere – as in Britain's defence of the Falkland Islands in 1982 and the Argentinian invasion of the Malvinas to promote a national identity. Finally, *political power* involves centralised organisation of social relations, which again may not be a necessary adjunct to the economic sphere, as with state involvement in the organisation of sport.

The personnel in control of the state have available to them an organisation that can be used to structure life within the state's territory in a whole variety of ways. In deciding how to exercise that power, those involved draw on the four sources itemised above, and in so doing benefit from the experience of those who preceded them and acted similarly. They are part of the process whereby a culture is reproduced, where culture is defined as the entire corpus of ideas that underpins life in a society. That culture must incorporate and facilitate the mode of production, but it will almost invariably extend well beyond that task. And it can be changed, if the state personnel are determined enough and what they propose is acceptable to the population. Such culture change may well involve changing attitudes towards the environment. A society's culture, as described in Chapter 1, certainly embraces such attitudes, and so the state can be used to change them.

States and Territories

The arguments developed in this chapter clearly indicate the necessity of a state for the capitalist mode of production. But they say nothing about either the number of states or the size of individual states. It is necessary to have more than one? Is the present system of states a desirable configuration?

From the outset, it is important to realise that the state is necessarily a territorial body, that in order to function as it does it needs to have a clearly defined territory over which its sovereignty holds. The reasons for this are relatively straightforward. The state is involved in the exercise of power, which is influence (if not control) over people. It does this largely by setting norms and enacting laws to which all of the people it has power over must conform, with the sanction that they will be punished if they do not. How then is that power efficiently exercised; what strategies can be used to ensure that the laws are obeyed, that the norms of behaviour are accepted, that the ideology is absorbed, and so on?

Territoriality, according to Sack, is a widely used strategy involving: 'the attempt by an individual or group (x) to influence, affect, or control objects, people, and relationships (y) by delimiting and asserting control over a geographic area' (1983, p.56).

He suggests ten 'tendencies' that explain why territoriality comes to the fore as a strategy for obtaining control. Among them are: the ready classification that territory provides – a person or object is either within or outside the territory; the ready identification of the territory, through a boundary marker; territory provides a means of reifying power, by linking it with an inanimate object which displaces attention from the real objects in the power relationship; the apparent neutrality of territory, and the impersonality of relationships which use of the territoriality strategy thus involves; and the ability to engender identification with a territory, which thereby legitimises the control.

While territoriality is not the only strategy available to the state in its exercise of power, it is one that has been almost universally adopted, which suggests that it is probably the most efficient. Thus associating a state with a defined territory enables it to exercise its power; in particular, it allows it to exercise its military power, and it could well be argued that only a territorial identity allows that exercise. Similarly, the state's exercise of economic power is clearly facilitated by its association with a territory; its regulatory and other policies then apply to all economic activities within that defined area. Because those two types of power are so readily exercised through a territoriality strategy, this gives additional strength to the state elite in their exercise of ideological and political power; they have a firm base within which to influence the culture of a people, and since their work is especially judged on their economic performance (as detailed in the next chapter), this gives substantial freedom for the other activities, which may include promoting ideas about and policies on the environment.

Territoriality has a further advantage: it enables people to identify in a particular way and promote their collective interests, which might not be impossible but certainly would be difficult if other strategies were used. Thus Harvey (1985b), for example, discussed the value of what he calls 'regional alliances', of members of particular interest groups in a defined area collaborating, through the state, in what he terms a 'spatial fix', to promote the interests of those within the area against interests of those elsewhere. This leads to the development of geopolitical strategies which associate the state with promoting the interests of its residents beyond its borders (see p.129).

The association of the state with a territory is probably a necessity; it is unlikely that its roles could be conducted otherwise. But what territory? Clearly the present set of states is just one of an almost infinite number of possible configurations, and there is nothing either 'natural' or 'desirable' about it. It has evolved out of pre-capitalist and other formations and from the geopolitical rivalries of those exercising the four types of power. And it continues to evolve, as new states are created (Bangladesh, for example) and others consider whether to submerge their separate identities (as in the European Community). It exists, and is a firm framework within which economic, political, military and ideological power are exercised.

Regulating the System of States

Division of the world into a set of territorial states is efficient in many ways, therefore. But it is also inefficient in some, because the state boundaries are artificial and interrupt the operation of systems that have a wider spread. This is increasingly becoming apparent today as the organisation of capitalism becomes more and more global in scale, and the economic roles of individual states are restructured as a consequence (Johnston, 1986b). It is also becoming more apparent in the field of environmental policy, and recent work has illustrated the problems caused.

Environmental systems, as stressed from the outset of this book, are global in their interaction; no part of the earth is independent of all others, and no system or sub-system is constrained by 'artificial' political boundaries. Thus tackling environmental problems requires inter-state collaboration in many situations (on the difficulties, see Dufournaud and Harrington, 1989). But in a large number of cases global solutions appear to be required; as Hardin argued (p.119), global government is needed to attack global issues. How can this be done?

We can use the tragedy of the commons and Prisoner's Dilemma metaphors once again to illustrate the problems. In this application, the individual actors are the states in the world. Each state is making a demand on the world's environment, treating it as a commons, and in making those demands may be degrading the environment not just within its borders but globally. So it is in the interests of every state to agree to environmental controls, but it may well be that in certain circumstances some states at least are not prepared to impose such controls – either because they do not see it as in their interests to do so, whatever the others may do, or because they do not believe that an agreement can be effectively monitored, that some might break it.

Laver has illustrated these problems with two examples. In the first he analyses international co-operation in outer space, what he terms the 'tragedy of the celestial commons' (Laver, 1986). Outer space can in some ways be treated in the same way as land resources on earth, but unlike terrestrial land it is not under the jurisdiction of a state. Like terrestrial land, it is a scarce resource that can be destroyed by exploitation:

> Whether we are talking about the use of the Moon as an ultra-clean research laboratory or as a source of raw materials, whether we are talking about orbital space stations as providing vital communications nodes or surveys of scarce terrestrial resources, we are talking about a set of problems with essentially the same underlying structure. (1986, p.361)

– which is that of the tragedy of the commons. But there is one crucial difference: the actors in outer space are states, and there is no 'effective international government' that can regulate (through the use of effective sanctions) what those states do in outer space.

In the absence of such an international body, the only way of obtaining protection for extra-terrestrial environments is by international co-operation through treaties and other agreements. Two of these have been formulated by the United Nations Committee on the Peaceful Uses of Outer Space (COPUOS) – one is termed the Outer Space Treaty here, and the other the Moon Agreement; the first defines outer space as a commons and the second seeks to make the moon a collective territory, using phrases such as

> equitable sharing by all States Party in the benefits derived from [lunar] resources, whereby the interests and needs of the developing countries, as well as the efforts of those countries which have contributed either directly or indirectly to the exploration of the Moon, shall be given special consideration.

But the Moon Treaty has not been ratified by either the USA or the USSR, and so is an agreement between countries which lack the ability to exploit the moon's resources. Why haven't the two countries which have the proven technological capability of exploiting those resources signed the treaty? Laver suggests that it is because:

'Public' appropriation of common resources by all, the potential solution under treaty law, can be resisted by the strong, who anticipate that they can dominate the anarchy that results if neither public nor private appropriation is possible. (1986, p. 368)

Since none of the states that are signatories of the treaty is able to exercise its theoretical right of equal access to the resources, the two that are exercising that right feel no obligation to conform and share their gains.

In his other example, Laver (1984) focuses on two cases of the use of what we may term 'lower space'. The first concerns radio broadcasts, which use particular frequencies within the spectrum that cannot be polluted but which are of easy access and are fixed in amount. As the demand for broadcasting increases, the possibility of the exhaustion of the available frequencies increases too, which leads to calls for co-ordinated collective action to achieve optimal use. Such international collective action has been in operation since 1906 through the International Frequency Regulation Board (IFRB), whose decisions governments respect and operate, because it is in their interests so to do. ('Free-riding' is not feasible, because 'pirates' can have their use of the frequencies 'jammed'.) The benefits of belonging to the IFRB are perceived by all governments, which are prepared to implement its rules; there is no need for an international state or similar regulatory body in such cases, because all are members and all members respect the rules. Such a solution of a potential tragedy of the commons requires the absence of gains from free-riding, however, and the necessity of the resource.

The second case refers to the placing of satellites into geostationary orbits around the earth, to which access is currently limited to those states able to afford the expensive technology and which are therefore obtaining a monopoly over a limited resource – such satellites must be located 36,000 km above the equator. As yet, no international action has been proposed to regulate that limited commons, but many states see that they are being effectively, and potentially permanently, excluded from a resource by those which already have access to it and who see no benefits from agreeing to share it with others. The relative affluence of the latter states allows them to be potential free-riders, and to reserve for themselves the major gains of access.

Two further examples illustrate the relevance of Laver's arguments to the use of terrestrial environments. The first concerns the resources of the *Antarctic continent*. To date there has been no exploitation of those resources, beyond the fishing, whaling and sealing activities around the shores, so that although several states have claimed sovereignty over parts of the continent they have not been concerned to enforce those claims strictly, since there are no perceived benefits from doing so. Thus in 1959 they all signed the Antarctic Treaty, along with other countries which have no territorial claims on Antarctica but are prepared to support the general principles. Under that treaty, the continent is not to be used for military purposes and is to be freely accessible to all for scientific work. The signatories have agreed to share the commons. But the treaty contains no reference to economic exploitation, particularly of the extensive mineral resources known to be there, because at present it is either not technologically feasible or not economically desirable to exploit them (the winning of oil in the Arctic suggest it is probably the latter). Thus in 1988 an attempt was made to extend the treaty by adding an Antarctic Minerals Convention, which is intended to ensure that when such exploitation is proposed it will be judged against strict environmental standards, to prevent a scramble for resources and the likely degradation of the environment that would ensue. Nine countries signed the convention in Wellington, New Zealand in November 1988, but four more only indicated that they would sign soon (including the United States and the United Kingdom) and Australia later decided not to sign. Will all sign? And will signatories necessarily honour the Convention? The experience of the United Nations Universal Declaration of Human Rights suggests not (Johnston, 1989); it may be, however, that states will enforce policies to prevent the use of CFCs in the production of aerosol sprays and refrigerators, because of the potential dire consequences of not doing so. (This may be a good example of an Assurance game; p.124.)

Laver's examples and the evidence of the Antarctic Treaty therefore lead to doubts about the probability of international collaboration on certain types of environmental problems. These are backed up by the second example – recent experience of the attempts to get international agreements on oceanic resources. Several conferences on 'The Law of the Sea' have been convened under the auspices of the United Nations since the Second World War, as a response to the growing technical ability to exploit maritime resources and for states to defend coastal waters against outside users. Until that time, the *de facto* operating law was that of 'the freedom of the seas', and only a small coastal zone, a few miles wide, was claimed by states as their 'territorial waters' over which their sovereignty held (see Schachter, 1986). But in 1947 Chile claimed a 200-mile zone to protect its fishing industry (especially the whaling industry) from competition with other fleets, two years after President Truman of the United States had expressed concern over the exploitation of both fish stocks and hydrocarbons from the zone of the continental shelf, the relatively shallow area of sea around most coasts. These events stimulated the search for global agreement over the exploitation of resources within and beneath the oceans.

The search for agreement was done in a series of conferences on 'The Law of the Sea' convened by the United Nations (UNCLOS): the first was held in 1958, the second in 1960, and the third, which continues, began its deliberations in 1973. The major problem was to decide whether the seabed was just unclaimed territory which could, like the land surface, be claimed by states which wished to establish sovereignty there, whether it was a 'commons' open to all and which no state could appropriate, or whether there was no relevant custom and practice and international law had to be written *de novo* to cover the sea-bed. Agreement was eventually reached on the definition of sovereign limits: states could claim Exclusive Economic Zones, within which they have rights to the resources of the seabed, up to 200 miles wide. (This led to many definitional problems and legal cases, as fully illustrated by Prescott, 1985.)

Much more difficult to handle was the ownership and access to resources beyond those Exclusive Economic Zones, in the area known as the 'high seas'. This became particularly relevant as technological advances made it possible to exploit the mineral resources on and beneath the sea-bed, although as yet it has not proved economic to do so: according to Dubs 'the seabed resource is there in munificent abundance – but there are no miners who will exploit that resource in the next two or three decades' (1986, p.95). To date, the proposed treaty to govern that exploitation has not been supported by all states although, according to Schachter (1986, p.54), the non-signatories remain committed to the concept of treating the sea-bed resources as a common heritage whose exploitation should be organised through international agreement. The proposals in the treaty are that the resources should be treated as common and their exploitation governed by an international authority which would receive a large share of the net proceeds of the operations. That share of the proceeds would be distributed among all countries by an elected council of 36 states (for fuller details see Prescott, 1985, p.124ff).

The United States was among the countries which declined to sign this 'Law of the Sea' treaty. Its reasons were given by President Reagan in 1982, and covered five problems (Dubs, 1986, pp.113–14): the provisions would deter exploitation of the resources, because of the appropriation of a large part of the net proceeds by the authority; the constitution of the council would not give to the United States and other countries 'a role that fairly reflects and protects their interests'; amendments could be passed even if the United States disapproved – no veto was allowed; there was the possibility of national liberation movements and other 'undesirables' benefiting from the distribution of the net proceeds; and the absence of assured access in the future discouraged states from investment in the necessary technology for exploiting the resources (see also Clingan, 1986). As with the Moon Treaty, therefore, the powerful states in the world have been unprepared to sign a treaty which recognises certain resources as a 'common heritage' because to do so would mean renouncing some of their power. They refuse to adopt what others see as the optimal way of using and protecting those resources and achieving the optimal outcome of a Prisoner's Dilemma game; through the process of uneven development that characterises the capitalist mode of production they have obtained a position whereby they can protect their interests and potentially hasten the tragedy of the commons.

These examples refer to environmental issues affecting a large number, if not every one, of the current mosaic of states on the earth's surface. As argued in Chapter 2, the nature of environmental systems is such that a problem generated in one place is likely to have indirect, if not direct, effects on most others. Nevertheless, in many cases the impacts of environmental problems are small for the great majority of states and only a few are directly involved. In such situations, while it may be desirable to have an international court which can adjudicate between rival claims, and whose decisions would be accepted as final by all parties and in all states, negotiation between the states concerned could allow resolution (if not solution: see p.171) of many problems if they recognise the benefits of co-operation, as illustrated by the Assurance game (p.124).

Two countries that have set up a mechanism within which to resolve environmental issues are Canada and the United States. In 1909 they signed a Boundary Waters Treaty which established an International Joint Commission, comprising three members from each country. It can only consider issued referred to it by the two federal governments together and it makes recommendations only (see le Marquand, 1986); its major function is as a fact-finding body, with the perceived quality of its work giving its pronouncements high status, but it can also act as a facilitator, helping conflicting parties in the two countries (which may include state/provincial as well as federal governments and also private-sector concerns) to reach accommodations. The utility of the commission is entirely dependent on its standing and the willingness of the parties to disputes to accept its advice, and some observers (e.g. Carroll, 1986; Sewell and Utton, 1986) believe it to be an inadequate mechanism now, because of mutual distrust in the two countries. Wherever this is the case, the absence of a supranational state will mean that local as well as global environmental conflicts involving two or more separate sovereign jurisdictions will be characteristic of Prisoner's Dilemma rather than Assurance games.

The State in Advanced Communist/Socialist Societies

Throughout this chapter the discussion has been either explicitly or implicitly to do with the state in capitalist societies. But much of what has been said applies to advanced communist/socialist countries too. States, clearly, are necessary to the economic activity of the latter, as already suggested (p.135); they are involved in the exercise of political, ideological and military power; they are actors in international negotiations over the environment; and they need a territorial identity in order to achieve their goals.

Where the advanced communist/socialist states differ is in the absence of large numbers of separate economic actors to be regulated within their societies. Their regulation is done by central planning, which determines what shall be done where, and in what quantities, and provides the resources to enable their plans to be achieved. Thus the tragedy of the commons and Prisoner's Dilemma metaphors do not apply to activities within those states (except that most have some residual private land, much of which is farmed in the same way that tenants farmed under feudalism), and issues of environmental use do not require state involvement in the regulation of individual activities. Instead, it is the nature of state plans themselves which are the sources of such environmental degradation as may occur, and it is the attitudes of the state personnel towards the environment that are crucial. They must weigh up the environmental consequences of their plans against the economic and social objectives that they set, and determine to what extent they are prepared to commit resources to ensure relative harmony with the environment. They too are seeking to ensure the production of an increasing range of commodities, with all the implications for environmental use, although the decisions on what to produce are made on utilitarian rather than profit-making criteria. That difference apart, the pressures on the state with regard to environmental use are similar to those in the capitalist world; they must balance the imperatives of their mode of production against the damage that they do to environmental systems.

In Summary

The purpose of the present chapter has been to explore the nature of the state, and its necessity to the health of the capitalist and advanced communist/socialist modes of production. Although the state is a necessary institution for these, and it must perform certain roles, there is no necessity for it (which means the people who control it) to act in particular, predetermined ways: just as a Shakespeare play requires certain roles to be filled, but leaves it to those directing and acting in the play to interpret those roles, so an advanced economic system requires a state, but leaves it to the people involved to interpret the role of the state. It is to that interpretative role, and the ways in which others can influence it, that we turn next.

Chapter 6
State Operations and Environmental Problems

> No generation has a freehold on this earth. All we have is a life tenancy with a full repairing lease. (Margaret Thatcher, speaking to the Conservative Party Annual Conference, September 1988)

A conclusion that could be drawn from the previous chapter is that the degrees of freedom allowed to the state within the mode of production mean that if certain environmental attitudes occupy a central place in a national culture, then relevant policies to promote those attitudes can be implemented by the state. Thus the goal of those seeking to promote certain attitude sets is to ensure their place within the national culture. To appreciate the extent to which this is feasible, we need to understand how the state works. This is the purpose of the present chapter, again using environmental issues as the focus of the examples.

Democracy or Not

To most people in the English-speaking world, the states within which they live are democracies, briefly defined as rule by all. Thus if a particular goal is desired by a majority of the population, this should be reflected in the state's policies; if it is not, this suggests that some groups have veto power within the state, which then negates the concept of democracy. However, no state has democracy in the true sense. Many have little or no democracy at all, as defined in the following section; the remainder have what is termed representative democracy, in which rule is by a small group on behalf of all, for the simple reason that involving everybody in the running of a complex operation such as the state would not be feasible. It is necessary to explore these two caveats in a little more detail.

The geography of liberal democracy

Representative democracy, according to Berg is

an ideal type of national decision-making system whose members (above some minimum age level) enjoy equality of self-determination. (1978, p.156)

and self-determination is defined as follows:

An individual has self-determination to the extent that he [sic] is not excluded from making decisions that are relevant to him and to the extent that he makes or effectively participates in the making of such decisions. (p.167)

This is translated into the concept of liberal representative democracy, defined in Article 21 of the (unanimously adopted) 1948 United Nations Universal Declaration of Human Rights:

Everyone has the right to take part in the government of his [sic] country, directly or through freely chosen representatives

and

The will of the people shall be the basis of the authority of government; this will shall be expressed in periodic and genuine elections which shall be by universal and equal suffrage.

These statements of principle lead to statements of the institutional guarantees necessary for the existence of liberal representative democracy, set out by Dahl (1978) as follows:

Necessary Condition I: The Formulation of Preferences:

Institutional Guarantees Required:
Freedom to form and join organizations:
Freedom of expression;
The availability of alternative information sources;
The right to vote and to compete for votes.

Necessary Condition II: Signifying Preferences:

Institutional Guarantees Required – the above plus:
Free and fair elections;
Freedom to stand for public office.

Necessary Condition III: Equal Weighting of Preferences:

Institutional Guarantees Required – the above plus:
Institutions which ensure that government policies depend on voting and other popularly expressed preferences.

How many countries meet these criteria?

Several studies have been conducted in recent years seeking to portray in some way the geography of liberal democracy (for reviews, see Johnston, 1989; Taylor, 1989a). One of the single variables most frequently used to indicate the existence of a democratic regime is the use of free and fair elections to produce a government, whereby no political parties are proscribed, transfers of power are orderly and occur only as a consequence of electoral defeat/success, all of the seats in the parliament can be contested by all parties, there is a universal, adult franchise, there is a fixed timetable for holding elections, campaigns are open and free from intimidation, and voting is secret. Under strict observance of these criteria very few states would qualify. (Does the House of Lords disqualify the United Kingdom? Does gerrymandering and other manipulation of the electoral system in the United States disqualify that country?) Allowing some small deviations from the ideal, however, there are still, according to Butler, Penniman and Ranney (1981) only twenty-eight countries with more than three million inhabitants which qualify as liberal representative democracies.

If we look at a map showing the location of those countries (Figure 6.1), we see that, with very few exceptions (India is the most obvious), they are concentrated in what are known as the 'advanced, industrial western countries'. This suggests to some that liberal democracy is a 'natural' consequence of the process known as 'modernisation', as specified in Rostow's classic study of *The Stages of Economic Growth* (1971): studies show that level of modernisation and level of democracy are closely correlated (e.g. Coulter, 1975), and that the core–periphery structure of the world economy which is characteristic of global capitalism has liberal democracy concentrated in its core (Bollen, 1983). From this it is possible to infer that as modernisation spreads into the periphery, liberal democracy will follow.

Several critiques of this argument (what Taylor, 1989b, calls the 'error of developmentalism') have been presented. Here we concentrate not on the arguments on whether there can ever be economic equality in a capitalist world (on this, see Hirsch, 1977) but rather on the 'achievement' of liberal democracy. Implicit in the arguments of Coulter and others is that liberal democracy is a 'natural' consequence of modernisation; once a certain level of modernisation has been achieved, democratic guarantees will be fulfilled. But the evidence is that in all of the countries in which liberal democracy now exists it has been yielded, slowly and grudgingly, by an elite, as the price to pay for social consensus within the state and to sustain the legitimacy of the mode of production. A few of the British settler colonies, such as Australia, Canada, New Zealand and the United States, are partial exceptions to this. Their establishment came after the granting of substantial democratic freedoms in Britain, which were immediately implemented in the new countries; but the struggle for some democratic rights – notably universal suffrage for both sexes – continued.

This process of struggle for democratic rights is well illustrated by the slow transfer of power in the United Kingdom: first, from the absolute monarch to the major landowners; then the incorporation of the urban bourgeoisie; and, following this, by the struggle towards universal suffrage and the removal of all qualifications other than adulthood and citizenship. Even with the achievement of universal franchise, there were claims that the electoral system was 'rigged' in some places to devalue the votes of certain groups relative to those of others, as in Northern Ireland up to the 1970s, and even today Scotland and Wales are over-represented in the House of Commons relative to England. In the United States, too, there has been a struggle to enfranchise groups implicitly disenfranchised,

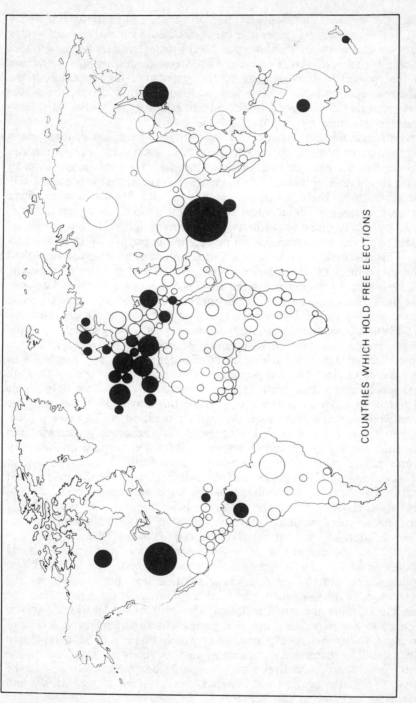

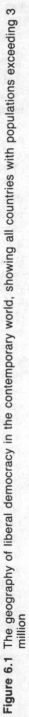

Figure 6.1 The geography of liberal democracy in the contemporary world, showing all countries with populations exceeding 3 million

despite the explicit statements of the country's constitution. For many years, for example, the governments of the southern states employed a literacy qualification to exclude the blacks from registering as electors (before the civil war, slaves counted as possessions and as only a fraction of a free person in the counting of the population for determining the number of representatives a state was entitled to). In addition, the actual process of registration was made difficult, to dissuade the blacks from seeking to exercise their civil rights.

This struggle for civil and democratic rights is seen today in many parts of the world. In some it appears to have been successful; many countries in South America have elected governments, for example, though in most this is a recent development, and the evidence suggests that it is quite likely to be temporary. There, as in several African and Asian countries, there have been periods of democracy followed by periods of autocratic rule, usually by the military or with its clear support following an 'irregular' transfer of power (i.e. a transfer not agreed by the population in a free election). This alternation of democratic and non-democratic rule can be linked to the situation of those countries in the periphery of the world economy.

An ideal-type representation of the sequence suggests something like this. There is a non-democratic government in power, which denies people some, if not all, of the civil rights agreed in the United Nations Declaration. There is popular agitation that those rights be granted, and the strength of the mobilisation of opinion is such that the stability of the regime is under threat and maintenance of order is difficult. Thus those in power decide to yield it to the population (who may seek to seize it through armed force), and a democratic regime is established. This not only grants civil rights, in order to generate consensus, but also seeks to advance the general welfare of the population through legitimation policies (see p.130). As a result, the costs of capitalist operations in the country increase, and outside investors may question whether to leave their capital in the country, especially if there is any possibility of some form of state take-over of their assets (as in Chile under the Allende regime). To the extent that withdrawal occurs, so the policies of the state are undermined, general prosperity is threatened and the welfare policies begin to fail, because they cannot be afforded without punitive levels of taxation, which in turn further discourage investment. This can lead to popular protest, and demands for government action which cannot be met; the economy stagnates, inflation may become rampant, and law and order is difficult to maintain. Eventually a non-democratic solution may be imposed, by the military and its allies (usually the local capitalists, whose profits are also under threat, plus the middle classes who prosper under them); this is presented to the population not as a permanent situation but as a way of restoring stability and prosperity, after which there will be a return to democracy. The latter may eventuate; just as likely is a failure of the military government to deliver either prosperity or general welfare, and the growth of popular protest and demands for a return to democracy and freedom (as in Chile in the late 1980s).

The small number of countries in the core of the world economy have escaped this sequence through their achievement of high levels of prosperity (though, of course, relatively few have not seen some deviation from the ideal model of democracy in the last four decades, as in France in the 1950s). That high prosperity has at least in part been achieved through the creation of a global capitalist economy with its core–periphery structure, and it is doubtful whether the core could be substantially enlarged – though its membership may change over long periods. Thus, according to this argument, it is likely that under the capitalist mode of production only a small number of countries, in the core of the world economy, will qualify as liberal democracies according to the criteria laid out earlier. In the remainder of the world, democracy is a luxury that cannot be afforded for long, and civil rights, welfare state policies and self-determination (the hallmarks of what Taylor, 1989c calls liberal–social democracies) must take second place to the maintenance of a fragile stability based on an exploited situation.

Types of non-democratic state

The great majority of states in the world are classified as non-democratic. But within that category there is considerable variation. All are run by a bureaucracy, an administrative class with its own culture; democracies are run by bureaucracies too, but with the major difference that those bureaucracies are subject to political, and hence popular, control. Among the non-democratic states, it is the nature of the group to which the bureaucracy is responsible that is the criterion used to differentiate them here. Five main types are identified.

(1) The *military dictatorships*. In these power resides in the military forces, who provide the ruling elite from negotiations within the military, without consultation with the population at large. There may be conflicts within the military, and occasional transfers of power, bloodless or otherwise, from one faction to another, and there may be consultation with outside bodies and powers, some of which may influence strongly, if not 'control', those in charge of the state apparatus. In most cases, military control is the result of a take-over at some stage from a civilian, frequently a popularly elected, government, as described earlier. The military sees its main task as maintaining law and order, if necessary by repressing opposition to its policies, and by the denial of civil and human rights. Strongly linked to those law and order policies will be economic policies designed to facilitate capitalist accumulation, and thus to benefit a small civilian elite and sustain its support; that elite, and the associated middle class, will provide senior members of both the military and the bureaucracy. (In a few cases, as described later, the military may promote other modes of production.)

(2) The *semi-feudal dictatorships*. Power in these countries resides in the major landowners, and there is no tradition of popular participation in the running of the state. Civil rights are largely disregarded, at least in the context of liberal democracy, and authoritarian rule is common. The senior ranks of the bureaucracy are drawn heavily from the families of the ruling elite.

(3) The *self-sustaining bureaucracies*. In these, groups from within the population win control of the bureaucracy, and rule as a consequence, with military support and little accountability as it is understood under liberal democracy. Access to the bureaucracy, and in particular to its senior levels, is carefully controlled by those in power, to ensure no challenges to their rule.

The best examples of this type of rule come from the advanced communist/socialist states, where the bureaucracy is controlled by the Communist Party (or some close equivalent). Only members of the Party can qualify for powerful positions, and membership is closely vetted to ensure that those who join accept the attitudes of the ruling elite. Most of those states originated through either popular revolt, led by an elite who were to become the bureaucratic class, or military imposition of such rule by another state where it already existed; the particular form of rule is then legitimated by the ideology of the *people's democracy*. In a classless society there is no split of the population into mutually antagonistic groups, and so no need for alternative parties competing to run the state; there is just one party, which reflects the popular view as expressed through its deliberations, and the legitimacy of that approach is secured through elections in which only the one party fields candidates. Clearly, then, the degree to which it represents the popular wishes and enacts them through the bureaucracy is a function of the party's openness. To the extent that it, through the bureaucracy, can control the flow of information and the agenda of what political debate there is, so the party is in many ways a self-perpetuating autocratic body.

Such party-run bureaucratic states need a strong and loyal police-cum-military in order to sustain their legitimacy and to avoid challenges to the imposed social consensus. Where the state has recently been created – probably replacing a liberal democratic state, a military dictatorship, or a retiring colonial power – the military presence may need to be large and the military may play a major role in the operation of many parts of the state apparatus. This was seen in several African and Asian countries in recent decades, and in those Eastern European countries which threatened to step out of line from the externally imposed ideology. The military dominance should, ideally, be a temporary stage prior to the development of a state ideology which will achieve popular legitimation of a people's democracy.

(4) *Nation-based part-democracies*. In these, control of the state is reserved to one group within the population, and other groups either play a subsidiary role only or have no say at all in the operation of the state apparatus. Most of the examples of this type of government occur in countries that have more than one national group within their borders, of which at least one is denied equality of civil and political rights. The clearest example is South Africa, where one racial group has seized control, gives limited rights to two other small groups, and denies any power within the state to the largest of all (which forms a majority of the population). The powerful group operates a liberal democracy, though one that is carefully manipulated to ensure continued support for the ideology and dominance of the bureaucracy.

Avoidance of possible conflict between racial and other groups in new, post-colonial states has been the cause of much effort to create constitutions in liberal democratic situations whereby all national groups participate in the state and none feel the need to impose themselves on the others. Thus the Fijian Constitution was written to achieve harmony, mainly between the (larger) Indian and native Fijian populations, but when that produced a government in which the Indians were in a majority (in 1986–7) the Fijians, who controlled the military, overthrew the government and insisted on a new constitution that would ensure their dominance of the state apparatus (Lawson, 1988).

(5) *Colonial states*. In these, power resides in another country, which has occupied the territory and, almost certainly, imposed itself on the native population. It controls the military and the bureaucracy, in association with a local elite which allies itself to the colonial power in order to promote its own interests: to the extent that the senior positions in the military and the bureaucracy are not occupied by citizens of the colonial power, whose loyalty is to the home state, they are filled from that comprador elite.

Influencing the State

Two basic types of state have been identified: the liberal–democratic and the bureaucratic. If policies to solve existing environmental problems and to avoid the creation of others are to be promoted, therefore, there is a need to understand how those states operate and how they can be influenced. Most attention is focused here on the liberal–democratic states.

The politics of liberal–democratic states

Within liberal–democratic states, the freedom to organise and campaign in elections means that people with different views are able to create political parties which present their programmes to the electorate. In complex societies, where frequent recourse to the population is not possible and methods of representative democracy have been evolved, such parties are necessary to the running of the state, for two reasons. Firstly, they allow the election of blocks of representatives to the legislature, who can be relied upon to vote together on most, if not all, issues, and so give some stability to the allocation of power within that body. Secondly, they allow the electorate to be presented with coherent programmes for the conduct of the whole of the state's business, and not *ad hoc* policies for particular, perhaps transitory, issues. Together these form the keystone for the adopted method of running most of what are known as parliamentary democracies. After an election, power to run the government, and hence control the bureaucracy, is allocated either to the party which has a majority of the members of the legislature or to a coalition of parties which is prepared to work together and which has majority support in the legislature, as expressed through votes of confidence. (In states with two houses of the legislature, as in Australia, constitutional arrangements determine which has primacy if the majority party is not the same in both. Other states have power distributed among several parts of the state apparatus – as in France and the United States where both the President and the legislature are separately elected and may be in conflict over the direction of policy; constitutional arrangements there determine which has the ultimate power, and under what circumstances.) Thus the representative system of liberal democracy involves the population allocating power to political parties according to their relative importance in the legislature.

A major task of the political parties is therefore to mobilise the electorate around their political programmes. Such mobilisation could start anew at the time of each election, when the parties have to go to the electorate for their approval. This would not be in the interests of the parties, however, for it would mean they had no stability of support. What they want is as many voters as possible committed to their political programme, and for those voters to express that commitment in the ballot box. This they achieve through processes of political socialisation, whereby people are raised in milieux within which the political parties, either directly or through associated agencies (such as trades unions in certain circumstances), seek to educate them and win their strong support, if not even greater commitment as expressed through membership of the party and willingness to act for it in a variety of ways.

How are the political programmes around which parties seek to mobilise support formulated? Each country has its own unique features that have influenced the development of those programmes, but in an important essay two political scientists suggested a general model of the development of what they term *electoral çleavages* (Lipset and Rokkan, 1967). An electoral cleavage is a division of a society on electoral grounds; the people on one side of the cleavage are mobilised to support one party, whereas those on the other side are mobilised by a further party which both presents an alternative political programme and opposes that of its rival. Lipset and Rokkan's major contribution was their classification of those cleavages into four major types.

In their comparative analysis of Western European political systems, Lipset and Rokkan suggest that electoral cleavages have developed as a consequence of two major periods of revolution. The first was the national revolution, with the development of the nation–state and a centralised state apparatus as necessary to the promotion of capitalism. This promoted two major cleavages, of which only one might be present in some states. The first was between the dominant and the subservient national groups, with the former taking control of the increasingly centralised state apparatus and the latter being relegated to a subsidiary position, creating what is widely termed a core–periphery cleavage. The relative importance of this cleavage depended on the degree to which different national groups existed within the state's territory, or were later incorporated within it as part of the process of nation-building, and the degree to which the dominant nation was able to impose itself on the others and erode their identity. The second cleavage was between the supporters of the new basis of ideological power, the centralised state, and those of the old, the church. If the first cleavage were present then parties would develop to represent the interests of the different national groups and to promote political programmes which favoured them; similarly with the second, parties emerged to promote either the secular or the religious control of the state and its ideology. If both were present, there could be at least four parties (one representing the secular dominant nation, for example, and another representing the religious subsidiary nation).

Following the national revolution came the industrial revolution, which substantially changed the contours of most societies. Again, Lipset and Rokkan suggest that two major cleavages may have emerged from this period. The first was between the two major economic interest groups – the landowners whose wealth was obtained from agriculture and the sale of its output; and the industrialists, whose wealth was based on manufacture. To the extent that these two groups wanted different political programmes (protection for one, free trade for the other, for example) so they could be mobilised to support different parties, producing an electoral cleavage that was basically a division between town and country.

The final cleavage in Lipset and Rokkan's schema followed the industrial revolution but particularly the enlargement of the franchise. As an increasing proportion of the population joined the electorate so there was the potential to mobilise voters across what has become known as the class cleavage, with those who sold their labour power on the one side (often known as the working class) and those who bought or managed it on the other (the middle class).

Lipset and Rokkan argued that the relative importance of the first three cleavages depended on the nature of the different societies, and that they provided the matrix into which the fourth was set following the franchise enlargement. In some countries the class cleavage virtually eradicated all others, and Great Britain is usually presented as a paradigm example of this, whereas many others have remnants of at least one of the preceding three (as in the Netherlands and Switzerland). In a few other countries particular local circumstances saw the development of cleavages outside the orbit of the model. In the Republic of Ireland, for example, the main cleavage has been between two parties which had opposing views on the validity of the 1922 settlement with Britain, but increasingly class issues have intruded (O'Loughlin and Parker, 1989). And in the United States, federal politics was long dominated by regional differences, which in part reflected a core-periphery division (Archer and Taylor, 1981) but also resulted from the wish of southern whites to sustain their racial superiority. Nevertheless, class differences are also present, and have been observed in voting at the state and local scales (Hodge and Staeheli, 1989).

More recently, further 'revolutions' have taken place, which have either introduced new cleavages or led to the replacement of the preceding ones (Harrop and Miller, 1987). The first of these can be called the 'welfare state revolution'. As political programmes designed to ensure the legitimacy of the capitalist mode of production among the 'working class' were advanced, so a growing proportion of the electorate became dependent on that welfare state provision and were mobilised to support its continuance (on this in Britain, see Dunleavy and Husbands, 1985), against those who promoted free market operations. Secondly, there was the growth of what some see as a 'post-industrial' stage of capitalism, in which affluence is widespread, material concerns less important, and class politics is replaced by 'value politics' (Harrop and Miller, 1987, p.175). This 'value politics' may include support for environmental causes, and will be the focus of more detailed examination later.

The contest for power

Each liberal democratic state has one or more electoral cleavages, therefore, the nature of which reflects the history of its political system, the major social divisions within both its sphere of production and its civil society, and the activities of the political parties (including major individuals within them in some cases) in mobilising voters around particular causes and political programmes. The goal of each party is to establish a core of support on which it can rely in most, if not all, electoral circumstances; from that core it can extend its campaign to others either less committed to any particular party or apparently prepared to switch parties. The larger the core the better, of course, but the larger the core the greater the probability that it will be heterogeneous in composition and thus difficult to hold together.

While political parties would ideally like voters to be committed to them without question, they realise that such undying loyalty is unlikely (and increasingly so given the greater social and spatial mobility within society). Voters must be socialised to support a broad-based programme that leads them to identify with the party and its attitudes towards the particular issues of the day; mobilising voters around specific issues may generate substantial support while the issue is salient but may make it difficult to sustain that support when the issue is of less importance to most people. Thus parties develop a general ideology, based for example on an appeal to people in a particular social class (with the party perhaps making a substantial contribution to the development of that class identity, so that class and party go together). From the core of support that this provides, they can then develop programmes relevant to issues that may be localised in both time and space.

Having created an identity on one side of an electoral cleavage, a party then has to compete with others for votes at elections. The goal clearly is to win as many votes as possible, so that it wins a majority of the seats in the legislature and can form the next government. This competition for votes means, as a seminal analysis of Anthony Downs (1957) showed, that to some extent the parties must conceal their separate identities in order to capture sufficient votes. Downs's analysis proceeds like this. Assume that the members of the electorate are arranged on an attitudinal scale from left to right; the closer they are to the ends of the scale, the more 'extreme' they are in their views. The cleavage in the society is between right and left, so that each of the two parties has its core of identifiers to one side of the median point of the scale. In order to win power each party must

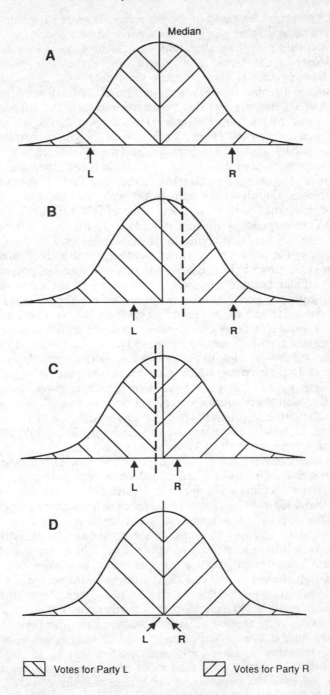

Figure 6.2 An illustration of Downs's argument regarding the nature of party competition

win the votes of at least half of the electorate. If more than half 'live' closer to it than to any other party, then a party has no problem; the problem is for the other party, which would seem to have no chance at all of winning. Whatever the distribution of attitudes on the scale, the parties will come close together as they compete for votes.

Assume a distribution of voters on the attitudinal scale as shown in Figure 6.2(A). Assume also that voters are rational, and support the party that is closest to them on the scale. Thus a party aiming to win majority support must place itself closer to over half of the voters than its opponent. The two parties start somewhere to the left and the right of the centre respectively; both have the support of about half the electorate, but neither can be sure of winning. And so what do they do? Party L starts the strategy (B) by shifting slightly to the right on the scale, and therefore putting itself closer to more than half; it 'invades' some of R's 'territory'. Party R feels that it has to respond by moving towards L (C), thereby not only 'regaining' its territory but also trying to 'invade' some of L's. As this strategy continues, so the parties come closer together, until both occupy a position in the middle ground (D), fighting for votes on election programmes that are very similar because they want the support of the same voters.

This argument of course makes a number of possibly unrealistic assumptions about voter and party rational behaviour, but as a general picture of party competition it bears considerable similarity to the situation in many liberal representative democracies (as suggested in Butler, 1960; see also Johnston, 1979a). Moving to the centre carries the possibility of alienating support at the extremes, which may mean that the voters there either abstain or support a party established to win those votes; to avoid either possibility, each party must keep contact with its 'wing'. But not to move towards the 'middle ground' opens up the possibility of a 'centre party' occupying it, and (if a majority of the electorate is 'middle of the road') garnering a large number of votes as a consequence.

Many societies have more than one cleavage, but Downs's analysis still works in a multi-dimensional attitudinal space rather than the simple one-dimensional attitudinal scale shown in Figure 6.2. But in such situations it is often hard for any one party to come close enough to sufficient voters to win the support of a majority, in which case they have to content themselves with a substantial legislative presence, in the realisation that no other party will have a majority of seats either. The formation of a government then involves the creation of a coalition of parties based on their power within the legislature and their willingness to co-operate with other parties (and thereby perhaps bargain away some elements of their programme in order to get support for others in the joint government programme). In general, the larger parties have most power in such bargaining but, as a great deal of mathematical analysis has shown (see, for example, Johnston, 1982c), some small parties may 'hold the balance of power' and thus have a great deal more bargaining resources available to them in the coalition formation process than they have seats.

Downs's analysis treats the electorate of a country as a whole, so that the task of a party is to win as many votes as possible. This implies that the number of seats a party obtains in the legislature is a function of the number of votes that it gets, a situation generally termed proportional representation. The relationship between votes and seats won is frequently far from perfect, however, as a consequence of the particular form of the electoral system used. Each country practising liberal representative democracy has its own electoral system which differs in some details from all others. Yet the basic features of those systems can be related to three main characteristics.

(1) *Constituency size.* The main difference is between systems based on single-member constituencies, such as those for the British House of Commons and the US House of Representatives, and those which use multi-member constituencies, such as the Irish Dail. In both Israel and the Netherlands there is but a single constituency – the entire country.

(2) *Method of voting.* The main difference here is between those systems in which electors merely indicate their most preferred candidate or party and those in which they are required to give a rank order of their preferences for some if not all of the candidates/parties.

(3) *Method of distributing seats.* On this characteristic, electoral systems differ in the way that they translate votes won into seats won. With some, such as the list systems of several Western European countries, the differences are relatively minor and relate to the formula used to allocate the seats. In others they depend on the other characteristics. Both Australia and the UK have single-member constituencies, for example: in the UK a plurality system is used, where each constituency is allocated to the candidate getting the largest number of votes, which may well not be a majority; in Australia a preferential voting system – the Alternative Vote – is used to ensure that more people prefer the elected candidate than any of the others.

These three characteristics make for an interesting diversity of electoral systems, especially when they are combined into hybrids (as in West Germany). Our concern here is not with their details (on this, see Taylor and Johnston, 1979), but with their political consequences.

It is often claimed that a country's political system is very much determined by its electoral system, a claim refuted by detailed analysis (as in Bogdanor and Butler, 1983). Nevertheless, as Rae's (1971) comparative analysis showed, whereas plurality, single-member systems such as the British are likely to produce legislatures in which a single party has a majority of the seats despite not having a majority of the votes (what Rae calls a 'manufactured majority'), in systems where the seats are distributed proportionally to votes majorities in the legislature are rarer and coalition government is common. Further, systems such as the British favour a political system dominated by two parties only (Gudgin and Taylor, 1980), especially where a single electoral cleavage dominates too; 'third parties' find it difficult to win seats in such situations.

The contest for votes

This discussion of electoral systems is important to an appreciation of the use of the state in the attack on environmental problems. Before turning to that topic explicitly, it is necessary to look at the bases of political competition.

In the contest for votes at national elections in the liberal representative democracies, almost all of which are in the core of the capitalist world economy, parties are offering themselves to the electorate as willing and able to operate the large and complex state apparatus and sustain it in its basic functions of securing social consensus, promoting capitalist accumulation, and legitimating the mode of production. They don't campaign on those terms, yet those clearly are the basis of their appeal, which is more popularly expressed in slogans such as 'Life's Good Under the Conservatives: Don't Let Labour Ruin It' and 'Britain is Great Again: Don't Let Labour Wreck It'. Thus the salient issues at most elections relate to the three basic functions. At different elections, different aspects of the functions may take precedence. At the 1979 general election in the UK law and order was high in many voters' minds and in the party campaigns, following the 'winter of discontent' and the many strikes in the preceding months, whereas at other elections the rates of inflation and unemployment have been crucial issues. Thus, for example, in analysing a great volume of survey and polling data, Sarlvik and Crewe (1983, p.272) identified four major 'issues that counted' during the 1970s in the UK: strikes, unemployment, rising prices, and law and order; at the 1983 election, attitudes and policies towards the welfare state and defence were also salient (Dunleavy and Husbands, 1985).

The importance of a small number of general issues related to accumulation, legitimation and consensus has been demonstrated by a substantial volume of work undertaken by political scientists and others into the relationships between these and voting/party support. (A general review is given by Weatherford, 1986.) In the United Kingdom, for example, work on the three elections won by the Conservative party in 1979, 1983 and 1987 provides clear evidence that those satisfied with their current and forthcoming financial situations were much more likely to vote for the incumbent government's return than were those who were dissatisfied and pessimistic (Johnston and Pattie, 1989), thereby accounting to a substantial extent for the growing spatial polarisation of the British electorate (Johnston, Pattie and Allsopp, 1988).

What these analyses suggest is that certain sets of issues are likely to dominate the electoral agenda because of the functions of the state in capitalist societies. One issue may dominate at a particular election. It may not be directly linked to the three main functions – either because it is of immediate importance to the electorate or because the parties do not differ on the salient issues. This is rare, however, and it is difficult for parties to manipulate the electoral agenda away from issues of general concern. An example of this is provided by the Australian general election of 1978, which followed the dismissal of the Whitlam government by the Governor-General. Whitlam sought to focus the electorate's attention on the constitutional issue raised by the dismissal, but the opposition won because of its attack on the economic policies of Whitlam's government.

Bringing environmental issues in

So how can environmental policies be brought to the forefront of the political agenda? How can parties and governments be forced to give priority to solving environmental problems and to preventing others being created? For the moment we assume that the existence of the problems is not controversial, and focus on the political process of promoting policies.

The following general strategies would appear to be open to those seeking to promote environmental policies.

(1) Convince one of the existing parties – and preferably a major one that is likely to win electoral power either on its own or as a major partner in a coalition – to adopt, and be committed to implementing, a range of environmental policies. In this way the environmentalists would be allying themselves with a party that already has a core of support among the electorate and has a programme in place that covers the generally salient issues in the electoral contest. The problems that they would face are: will this adoption of environmental policies make it more difficult for the party to win further support, and even lose it support from among its core, so that it is not prepared to promote these policies vigorously?; and what will happen when the party loses power, and the policies may then be dropped by the new government?

(2) Convince all of the major parties that they should adopt environmental policies because of their importance to the future prosperity of people, and thus to the long-term promotion of accumulation. Success with this strategy would appear to ensure a prominent place for environmental policies whichever government is in power, and the threat of withdrawal of support from the pro-environmentalists should those policies not be promoted vigorously might be an effective sanction. The viability of that sanction, however, will depend very much on whether environmental issues are so salient to the electorate that they are prepared to withdraw support from a party on those issues even if they are satisfied with its performance on others, notably the economic.

Parties can outflank this strategy to some extent by all adopting a pro-environmental stance, thereby effectively removing it from the political agenda; if all parties agree on an issue, then it cannot be used to discriminate between them, unless evaluation of their performance on that issue will be salient when they next appear before the electorate for support. This has been the situation in the United Kingdom in recent years, as both Brotherton (1986) and Owens (1986) have shown. With regard to conservation, for example, Brotherton provides quotes from each of six parties published in 1983 which he says are 'interchangeable: any of the six parties could have made any of the six statements' (p.151). But his analyses lead him to conclude that:

> although all six parties view conservation as a desirable goal, it is, for all but one [the Ecology Party, now the Green Party], subordinate to more important aims and ideals. As a result, conservation policies are not always framed in terms of what is best for conservation. At the very least they must be compatible to the party's ideology; and, if possible, they

will positively promote this. Conservationists may not like it. But conservation policies reflect party ideals, not conservation commitments. (1986, p.159)

Thus, for example, he suggests that the main concern for Labour and the Scottish National Party is with the inequalities of wealth that are the consequence of land ownership, while Conservatives are really interested in championing the freedom of farmers, along with other individuals, to use their property as they wish. Thus the commitment to conservation would seem to be of 'fringe importance' to the parties only, and is included to ensure that they can't be accused in electoral debates of 'not caring'.

Owens also identifies a 'greening' of the positions of all parties, producing 'a striking similarity in the rhetoric across the political spectrum' (1986, p.200). This is because, she argues, the parties are accommodating their positions to changing social values, without making any major commitment to action:

all parties have tried to accommodate the new concern without confronting any fundamental contradictions between their own values and ideology and those of 'green' politics. The result is a certain blandness of environmental policies across the board.

But she suggests that to accuse the politicians of blatant opportunism may be an oversimplification, in part because there are not that many votes in 'green' issues (although the material cited in Chapter 1 suggests a substantial change in a short period). Rather:

An alternative explanation is that environmentalists have been presented with a 'window of opportunity' by a particular combination of circumstances: a new party [the SDP] seeking 'untrodden' policy grounds; a handful of prominent 'single issues' (lead in petrol, green belts, acid rain, nuclear waste); and the significance of some of these issues in marginal seats. Recognising the opportunity, committed individuals within the Alliance have actively colonised environmental ground and other parties, fearful of losing votes, have followed suit. (1986, pp.200–1)

Thus when the Prime Minister made a major speech promoting pro-environment attitudes in autumn 1988, and followed this in the next spring with a conference aimed at ending the use of CFCs, the other parties could not condemn the policies and rhetoric but only suggest that her conversion was 'too little, too late', that her policies were not going to work because they clashed with her government's ideology, and that they (the other parties) were much 'greener than she'.

(3) Create a new party that will have environmental issues as its major concern. This has been done in several countries in recent decades, led by the West Germans and the French: as Porritt and Winner (1988, 212) express it, the Green Party in West Germany (Die Grünen) has 'seized hold of the imagination of all those even remotely interested in green matters. They have been a beacon of hope' (though they continue by observing that 'they have in many important respects made an appalling mess of things in their own country').

The success of a 'green' party depends on two factors. First, it must convince electors that, of the many issues on the political agenda, environmental problems are the most salient, but that other parties do not give them the highest priority in their manifesto commitments and likely policy directions. Voters should therefore opt for a party whose manifesto makes it clear that environmental issues are the most important facing society. Secondly, on the assumption that it will not win a legislative majority, the green party must be able to influence government policies and thereby ensure action against environmental problems.

The West German electoral system was particularly suited to the emergence of such a party with regard to both of these issues, which is not to imply that it is necessarily either the only place for a relatively successful 'green' party to emerge, nor that it had to be successful there. (The first 'green party', according to Hay and Haward, 1988, p.431, was founded in Tasmania in April 1972, one month before the foundation of the Values party in New Zealand.) In the West German electoral system each person has two votes, one for a constituency member (elected as under the British system) and one for a regional party list; the final composition of the Bundestag is proportional to the distribution of the second set of votes. Thus it is possible for the electorate both to vote for one of the major parties and to indicate that they are 'pro-green', a possibility that isn't available in most other countries, where to vote 'green' is not to vote for any other party. It is easier to convince people to vote 'green' in West Germany, since by doing so they are not effectively disenfranchising themselves from influencing the process of government formation, which they would be doing by voting for the 'greens' (or any other minority party) in other electoral systems. In Britain, on the other hand, a vote for the Green Party can be interpreted, and is by members of other parties, as a 'wasted vote': some are prepared to 'waste' their vote because of their commitment to the party and its principles; others may vote for the Green Party in constituencies where their vote was likely to be 'wasted' anyway, because it was a safe seat for one of the major parties.

The importance of the electoral system in the development of 'green party politics' is stressed by a number of authors. Rudig and Lowe, for example, argue that:

> The British system makes it relatively easy to form a political party and to field a small number of candidates. The financial threshold of the deposit makes it difficult for small parties with limited resources to mount a larger electoral challenge, and the first-past-the-post system makes it very difficult for new parties to achieve any representation. (1986, p.277)

Their analysis of the British Ecology Party (as the Green Party was then called) is largely pessimistic, leading them to give their article the title 'The 'withered' greening of British politics'. Apart from the problems presented by the electoral system, they concluded that the stimulus for radical 'green' politics had been weak in Britain in the 1970s and 1980s because

> low economic growth and industrial inefficiency have constrained the

development and the expansion of environmentally controversial projects . . . [which in any case] were sited in a way which reduced the potential for local opposition. Where strong resistance to particular projects did arise, the authorities were relatively quick to withdraw the plans. (pp.281–2)

So the focus of 'green' politics in Britain has been particular, and probably localised, projects rather than a general mobilisation around environmental themes; governments are adept at limiting political change when such a local project is strongly countered; and the British economy was in such a condition that few such projects were being launched in any case. (Rudig and Lowe might also have noted that the British electorate appears to be convinced that economic issues, and especially personal economic issues, are those on which they should judge the performance and promises of political parties.) Green politics there will flourish only in periods of prosperity, it seems; only the affluent will vote for policies to limit the creation of environmental problems. Similarly, in their analysis of a Tasmanian campaign, Hay and Haward conclude that:

Little can be claimed beyond the obvious: that the green vote flourishes in areas where both blue collar workers and the very affluent are comparatively *under*-represented . . . green values have little attraction to either the conspicuously affluent or the traditional working class. (1988, p.445)

This limits those who can be mobilised around environmental issues to the 'humanistic intelligentsia' (the term is Gouldner's, 1979) who are 'tertiary educated, urban, relatively affluent, professional and employed in those parts of the public sector not engaged in provision of the production infrastructures' (p.445; they thereby exclude what they and Gouldner term the 'technical intelligentsia', who are directly involved in production). Hay and Haward do note optimistically that the humanistic intelligentsia is rapidly growing in its relative size, and has interests very different from those of the 'traditional middle class'.

Rudig and Lowe suggest that environmental parties, in order to succeed, will need to broaden their appeal:

environmental parties will thrive to the degree that they can absorb other issues and cleavages. Where the New Left, regionalism, or agrarian interests have failed to form their own strong organizations or promote their demands successfully by other means, they might become attracted to the idea of a green party. (1986, p.283)

They note in particular for the British case the failure of the Ecology Party to embrace the anti-nuclear movement, many of whose members remained active in the established parties (especially Labour and Liberal). To advance this argument, they quote the case of the West German Die Grünen, which occupied political ground vacant because of the failures of the New Left and which, when in the Bundestag, represented the peace movement and campaigned for the welfare state, as well as promoting 'green' issues.

Whether 'green' parties elsewhere can act in the way Rudig and Lowe describe for the West Germans depends on the legislative context. In some situations their votes may be crucial because no party has an overall majority and therefore the 'greens' may be wooed to join a coalition. In this, they will undoubtedly be required to bargain away some of their proposed policies (if not their principles) in order to get others accepted and enacted. To what extent should they be prepared to bargain? Should they be prepared to bargain at all? These are the sort of questions that have been raised for Die Grünen, and have led to substantial public differences within the party. The main split is between those who recognise the need to accommodate with the other parties in order to achieve any of their goals (hence they are termed the realists, or *realos*, whose goal is to achieve radical reform through bargaining within the system – their programme, according to Papadakis, 1988, is one of 'self-limiting radicalism') and those who prefer to stand by their principles and not compromise (they are thus the fundamentalists, or *fundis*). Each faction faces a major problem. The fundamentalist strategy may fail because the group becomes isolated within the legislature and has no impact at all on policy; it may get publicity for its members and their cause by their legislative presence, but if they deliver nothing they may then be punished at the next election by all but the staunchest supporters. The realist strategy may fail because the stronger parties are able to accommodate most of the 'green' policies, probably in a watered-down form. Further, unless the party holds some 'balance of power' in the legislature, so that its votes are crucial to the government parties, then its long-term, substantial influence is likely to be slight. In the late 1980s the situation was favourable, however, especially in some of the Länder rather than the national Bundestag (see *The Independent*, 13 March 1989) and in this context the *realos* appear to have won the debates within the party (*The Independent*, 6 March 1989).

(4) Influence individual members of the legislature, irrespective of party. In most legislatures party organisations are strong and dominate the conduct of business; the degrees of freedom for the individual members are few. They may, however, be able to achieve substantial gains acting individually, by promoting legislation that wins sufficient support to be enacted; the abortion legislation piloted through the British House of Commons by David Steel in 1968 using a Private Member's Bill is an excellent example of this. So lobbying of individual members may lead to particular successes, but major policy changes (such as outlawing nuclear power generation) are unlikely to be achieved in this way.

One electoral system where the party organisation is not as strong as elsewhere is the American, in part because of the division of powers between Congress and the President. Individual members of Congress thus are able to promote measures that particularly concern them, and can mobilise the support of other members by promising to support their pet measures in return. In this process, known as log-rolling, support is most likely to be forthcoming for measures that are local in their impact – i.e. that affect the individual member's constituency only. Thus there has developed the practice known as the pork barrel, whereby individual members promote the interests of their home districts and states, thereby seeking to advance their own re-election chances by winning favour 'back home': pro-environmental groups could promote local interests through this channel, and win environmental improvements (as illustrated in Ferejohn, 1974; Johnston, 1980a). Further, they could extend the American system of pressure groups 'rating' the performance of members of Congress (in particular their voting records on salient issues) and indicating whether they they endorsed candidates' re-election campaigns, especially in the primary election within their own party. The endorsed candidates are those whose records are consistent with the pressure group's own programme, and the goal is to have as many candidates as possible from each of the two main parties who are acceptable to the group's position.

(5) Influence the population at large. This can have two components. One is the general process of influencing attitudes, whereby the local cultures changes; this topic will be discussed later, here the focus is on the second only – influencing the population at large in ways that can be expressed through the electoral system.

This strategy is especially important where the political system requires the government to consult the electorate on specific issues; in some places the electorate can insist on its opinions being considered. Such routine consultation usually involves the use of the referendum or similar device. Referendums are virtually unknown in some political systems, such as the British, but are widely used in others. In Switzerland, for example, referendums on certain issues are compulsory (the government cannot act without first getting popular approval) whereas on others they are optional, and are usually only held if a fixed number (currently 100,000) of citizens demand that the electorate be consulted. Whatever the origin of the referendum, its result is binding on the government, though in some cases this means that support for the referendum must be given not only by a majority of the electorate but also by a majority in a majority of the 22 cantons (Aubert, 1978). Thus in recent years environmental groups have had referendums held on a range of issues, including control of pollution from cars and twelve car-free Sundays a year: most of these have failed because, as Aubert describes it, such 'initiatives are usually over progressive issues . . . and the majority of the people, are even more conservative than the parliament' (1978, p.46).

Referendums are not used by the federal government in the United States, but they are in several of the states, with again the facility for citizens to require ballots on certain issues, the results of which will then bind the state or local government. As in Switzerland, they have been used by environmental groups, but with limited success (Ranney, 1978). California is one of the states where the facility is available and frequently used, and the procedure became widely known through the success of 'Proposition 13' in 1978, which limited the tax-raising powers of local governments. Again, environmental proposals were placed on the ballot papers in the 1970s and 1980s, with limited success (the main success was the measure that achieved protection of the coast from further development). Failure to carry such initiatives in part reflects the same conservatism among the electorate that Aubert noted in Switzerland, but it is also a consequence of the nature of the campaigning over the issues. Many of the proposals could, if enacted, severely impact on the profitability of individual enterprises, and in many cases these spend very large sums of money campaigning against the proposals (Lee, 1978). Such campaigns are frequently successful, especially since the proponents of the policies have much less resources available to them. In many cases the issue is polarised as between protecting the environment and protecting jobs and prosperity, and when presented in that light, large numbers of people vote for the latter. They are, after all, socialised into societies in which the dominant ideology is pro-accumulation.

Environmental issues and the electoral system: a summary

The conclusion to this section is very largely a pessimistic one with regard to the promotion of policies designed to protect the environment through the electoral system. Elections are conducted in liberal representative democracies in the context of a dominant ideology created and upheld by the state into which people are socialised, and around salient aspects of which (accumulation, legitimation) they are mobilised by the major political parties. As suggested here, some successes have been achieved in getting 'green' policies adopted and 'green' influence in the legislatures, but these have been relatively limited and the prospects for more are not great. So what are the alternatives?

Alternative Modes of Influence in Liberal Democracies

The 'classic' model of liberal representative democracy has the state as an elected body, accountable to the electorate, and only to the electorate. Governments are elected to achieve certain goals, and they are evaluated on their performance at the next election, relative to the potential of other parties who wish to form the next government. Thus the voter is sovereign, in the same way that in a market-place the consumer is supposed to be sovereign.

This theory of voter sovereignty is but a partial representation of the situation in reality, just as the theory of consumer sovereignty is only a partial representation of the situation in capitalist markets. In the latter, the producers and sellers of goods not only respond to the consumers' preferences, they also seek to mould those preferences, to get the buyers to want certain goods, and to prefer certain brands to others. Similarly in an electoral system, the 'sellers' (the political parties) seek to mould the opinions of the 'consumers' (the electorate). What is the nature of the mould that they use, and how is its construction influenced? As already discussed, political parties seek to mobilise support around particular versions of the dominant ideology (we thus exclude parties which challenge the dominant ideology). This is not done in a vacuum; the parties are promoting sets of attitudes that are relevant to various interest groups within societies; as the theory of electoral cleavages illustrates, most political parties emerged to represent major interest groups within society – church vs. state; town vs. country; farmers vs. manufacturers; workers vs. employers; state tenants vs. home owners; and so on. Some of those parties remain tied to particular, relatively narrow, single-issue interest groups only, but the great majority have developed broad programmes presented as representing the interests of major groups within the society.

Two questions follow from that basic presentation of the nature of political parties. How do they respond to changing economic and social circumstances? And how do they respond to conflicting claims from within the major interest group(s) that they serve? On the first, the normal mode of response is to listen to cases presented to them by the interest groups affected by the changes and to respond with policy changes where these are deemed necessary; such changes, if they are to be credible to the electorate over the long term, should be consistent with the party's general ideology. (Though developments in the New Zealand Labour Party after it won power in the 1984 general election indicate that this is not an inviolate rule: Johnston and Honey, 1988.) With regard to the second, the parties may either listen to the conflicting claims (from different groups within manufacturing industry, for example, or from both industrialists and trades unionists) and decide on balance which to support, or they may prefer to listen to certain groups only, because they are more sympathetic to their views.

There is a very great range of interest groups, large and small, within a complex capitalist society, and any party has to be selective in deciding which it pays attention to; it may well employ its own advisers to evaluate the claims and to hear the detailed arguments, and of course the civil service bureaucracy also exists to give advice. Thus achieving goals within such a society through political action means having access to those with political power and being able to influence them accordingly. Such success and influence can be obtained in a variety of ways. One is to treat it as a commodity, to be bought (and sold) like any other. Those wanting influence may obtain it by contributing to a party's funds (either directly or indirectly, by providing free or cheap services) and promoting it or its candidates at election time. Many countries seek to regulate this, to ensure that political parties, and thus governments, are not entirely in thrall to those with money in society, but most parties depend to a greater or lesser extent on donations from those who expect to get benefits (in a general sense if not specifically directed at them) from the party's actions when in power. Thus members of Congress in the United States may find that success in the 'pork barrel politics' brings with it substantial local donations to their re-election campaign funds.

Such direct 'buying' of influence is supplemented, very substantially in many cases, by other modes of achieving particular policy directions. For example, political parties strongly committed to the free operation of markets will be prepared to consult those interest groups which share that commitment. The consultation may be formal and organised, but in many situations it need not be. The members of such parties are likely to have many interests in common with those who will benefit from such policies, and they are likely to come from the same backgrounds and residential areas. Informal contacts between acquaintances and friends thus supplement, if not replace, the formal processes of consultation, and are often crucial in obtaining a particular goal.

Given the important function of the state in promoting accumulation, interest groups representing capitalists and their close allies are likely to want to ensure that government policies do not threaten profitability. So it is sometimes a surprise to observers that whereas the British Labour Party draws a substantial number of its MPs from trades union backgrounds, relatively few Conservative MPs are drawn from the world of business (most are from the professions, especially law and accountancy). The paradox is in part explained by the links between many members of the professions and the operations of capitalism, and also by the common backgrounds of many of the Conservative MPs and the business people whose interests they serve. The latter do not need to bother with politics, it is argued, because members of the Conservative Party are well aware of the general interests of business, and are readily accessible informally to make sure that particular points are brought home. Furthermore, it is contended, although the civil service is ostensibly neutral it too draws heavily, especially in its upper echelons, from the social and economic backgrounds that give strongest support to the Conservative Party, so that it too can ensure that the agenda before the government is treated sympathetically from a pro-business point of view.

The nub of this argument is that while elections produce governments, it is interest groups that influence them. This mode of operation is known as *corporatism*, whereby 'corporations' (the representatives of particular fractions of workers, professions and business) seek, and frequently achieve, major influence on the actions of governments. It involves, as Dunleavy and O'Leary (1987, p.193) describe it, non-elected elites seeking power over elected elites. The result is government via elite collaboration, in which the process of elections plays only a small part.

Corporatism involves more than elected governments being strongly influenced by interest groups, for those groups may also undertake some of the tasks of government. Thus, according to Cawson it involves not only situations in which:

> organizations representing socio-economic interests are permitted a privileged position by public authorities in a bargaining process over public policies which takes place in usually informal institutions outside the reach of formal democratic controls such as parliamentary scrutiny or ministerial responsibility (1987a, p.154)

but also an 'abdication' of power by the state, so that (Cawson, 1987b, 105): 'In exchange for favourable policies, the leaders of the interest organizations agree to undertake the implementation of policy through determining the co-operation of their members' (1987b, p.105).

The result is what O'Sullivan terms a neo-corporatist state, involving both the decentralisation of state sovereignty and the replacement of the 'command–obedience' method of government by one of 'consultation–commitment' (1988, p.9: the terms are Ionescu's, 1975). Middlemas (1979) associates this with both the failure of the established political parties to convey popular demands to governments and the relative stability of British politics during much of the twentieth century.

Each political party will accord certain interest groups more influence than others, and work with and through them to ensure that the state functions are performed satisfactorily, both for the interest groups and for the segments of the electorate to whom the party will have to appeal again in a few years. Clearly, given the economic, and in some cases ideological, power of some of the corporate interest groups, it is in the interests of those controlling the state apparatus to collaborate with them, since the alternative is conflict that might be to everybody's disadvantage. If the state doesn't collaborate with the major economic interest groups in contemporary society, for example, the consequences may well be that the latter withdraw their investment from the state's territory, with obvious implications for economic prosperity, social welfare, and the popularity of the political parties concerned.

Where interest groups have it within their power to create crises of various types, so too they create crises for those in charge of the state apparatus. If the crisis largely affects the profitability of investment it is a rationality crisis, which can be tackled by policies that promote accumulation more vigorously. If it largely affects the welfare of individuals it is a legitimation crisis. Several interest groups can stimulate a rationality crisis; investors withdrawing capital, for example, and trade unionists stimulating threats to profitability. Those operating the state have to try and keep both sides content; they may fail, or they may seek to neutralise the impact of one side (the British Labour Party through nationalisation of major industries, for example; the Conservative Party by methods of reducing the power of trades unions). In the end, it is probably the interests of capital that will prevail. But such interests must not be given too many concessions, or this may impact on the provision of welfare and other services and lead to a legitimation crisis, so the state has to balance the two. Where it fails on both, a motivation crisis comes about, with the decline of consensus and the sort of transition from democracy to dictatorship and back again discussed earlier (p.148).

The types of state action

If what the state does is exercise power in order to sustain the mode of production, how does it act? As argued here, the political parties and bureaucracies involved in the operation of the state apparatus bring to their task sets of attitudes which direct their interpretation of the mode of production and the functions of the state. To some extent those attitudes comprise a blueprint for the future, a statement of the form of society that those with power wish to see develop. But many actions of politicians and bureaucrats involve not implementing a blueprint but dealing pragmatically with issues and problems as they arise. Their attitudes suggest to them how they should act, but they are rarely able to call on accumulated evidence, in the way that physicians do for example, which indicates: (a) that a problem is typical of a certain category of problems; and (b) that there is a set procedure available for dealing with such a problem. While this may happen lower down in a bureaucracy, at the higher decision-making levels it rarely does.

Why do those in power face 'new' problems regularly, which call on pragmatic decision-making, in the light of experience with previous problems but needing specific rather than generalised responses? In part it is because capitalism is always changing, in order to counter its own in-built tendencies towards self-destruction: as certain activities become less profitable, so others must be sought, and there are no specific rules to tell investors what will be profitable next. They must 'gamble' in the relatively unknown, and in doing so they create new sets of conditions within which the state must perform its functions. The switch from fossil fuels to nuclear power generation, with all the issues which that has raised for governments, could not have been foreseen long in advance, and so the state had to respond pragmatically to the issues of regulating the nuclear industry as it developed. Secondly, the economic systems operating within capitalism are as complex as the physical ones that are the main focus here, and the models of capitalist economies used to predict the impact of particular policies are extremely large in many cases (as the example in Bennett and Chorley, 1978, p.418, shows). Because of the many interactions involved, a large number of which may be non-linear, the consequences of certain explicit actions can often be foreseen only very generally, let alone the consequences of unforeseen actions. Thus new situations are always occurring, which call for new actions.

How then can we characterise state actions? Brian Berry (1972) has produced a very useful classification of planning activities into four types, and this is valuable for the present situation. The types are as follows:

(1) *Normative, goal-oriented: planning for the future.* This is the 'ideal' type, in which the state prepares a blueprint for the future and then devises, implements and monitors policies intended to move the society towards the agreed end.

(2) *Ameliorative problem-solving: planning for the present.* This could be characterised as 'band-aid' action: a problem arises, and an immediate solution is sought, because rapid action is needed. Many of the problems are relatively trivial, and have been experienced before in slightly different situations, so a fund of expertise should be available to draw upon. But that expertise is usually applied to ameliorate the problem only; a traffic bottleneck is removed by a small piece of engineering, for example, which means that sooner or later another bottleneck will appear somewhere else. Many environmental problems are treated in the same way, in part because there is no alternative: a drought in an area will be tackled by importing water to it; nothing can be done to prevent another drought, apart from facilitating the transfer of water.

(3) *Allocative trend-modifying: planning towards the future.* This involves identifying trends within society, and then deciding which to promote and

which to seek to dampen down, if not eliminate. Society is steered in the way in which it seems to be going, which should enable some of the problems along the route to be identified beforehand and prepared for. There is no blueprint, as in the first type, but rather an acceptance of the status quo and a willingness to work with it. Thus, for example, suburbanisation as a trend may have been identified, and the decision taken to accept it as a desirable evolution of urban form and to facilitate it by the provision of better transport networks.

(4) *Exploitative opportunity-seeking: planning with the future.* Unlike the previous category, in this there is little attempt to recognise the problems that might arise from a trend (such as greater traffic requiring better networks) and instead the trend is allowed to continue – as desirable for the present with the future left to take care of itself. Thus, for example, it may be decided that nuclear power generation is cheaper than that involving fossil fuels, and so investment is encouraged; the problem of how to dispose of the waste will only be identified in the future, instead of being foreseen and influencing the decision whether to promote that trend (as would be the case under type 3).

Of these four, therefore, the first and the third involve some degree of preparation for the future, whereas the other two involve waiting for the future. In many liberal democracies, it is the latter that predominate. Why? One basic reason is the nature of the electoral process. Governments are elected for limited lives – rarely more than four years. Thus anything but a relatively short-term future is of little relevance to politicians who want to be re-elected when they next go to the country for approval. Many parties will take blueprints (or at least partial blueprints) for the future to the electorate, and argue that they involve a long-term programme spanning several sessions of the legislature; they then return in a few years time and ask to be re-elected to finish the job. They may be granted their wish, but many governments fall because of evaluations of their current performance, irrespective of longer-term issues. They may be able to convince the electorate (especially if the opposition lacks credibility) that in a first term they have done the unpleasant things, to prepare for benefits next time; but they may not. Evidence from electoral surveys suggests that increasingly people are voting according to their evaluation of the recent and forthcoming performance of the party (or parties) in power, especially with regard to economic policy (see Johnston et al. 1988), so governments must be able to present a favourable image at election time. This suggests to some a political–economic cycle, in which governments use the year or so immediately prior to an election to stimulate the economy and win votes from prosperous constituents, and the years immediately after their victory to restrain the economic growth they have generated and the problems of inflation that it has caused.

According to this argument, therefore, ameliorative problem-solving and exploitative opportunity-seeking are the types of action likely to dominate political agenda. In addition, it has to be realised that many of the problems that governments and bureaucracies face are not soluble. The concept of a solution to a problem implies a question with a right answer.

But many of these problems do not have a right answer, or at least a single right answer; each of the parties involved has its own view of what the right answer is. For these problems, solution is impossible; all that can be achieved is a resolution, a decision that is accepted by all of the parties concerned. The government in moving towards a resolution therefore has to weigh up the arguments of the contestants and propose a resolution. (The government may itself be a contestant, as with proposals from one part of the state apparatus to build a new road, which are evaluated by another part of the apparatus alongside the counter-proposals of interested parties.) In doing this, the power of the interested parties, including their power to affect the government in some way, may be important; a proposal to dump nuclear waste at one of five sites, several of which were in constituencies of government members, including ministers, was dropped by the British government soon before the 1987 general election.

Environmental problems are largely created by human interference with natural systems, interference that is promoted because it is in the interests of some individual(s) or group(s). The resolution, if not solution, of those problems requires them to be placed on the agenda by other interest groups, whose advocacy can then achieve the state action needed to ameliorate, if not eradicate at source, the problem as perceived. Is this consistent with the operation of political agenda as described here?

Environmental pressure groups

Bringing items on to the political agenda is the role of pressure groups, defined by Ball and Millard as 'social aggregates with some level of cohesion and shared aims which attempt to influence the political decision-making process' (1986, pp.33–4)). (This definition is not meant to deny that individuals, working alone, cannot influence the decision-making process, but that in most cases it is necessary for influential individuals to show that they have the backing and commitment of others of like mind.) There is a wide variety of such groups. One way of distinguishing them is into *interest groups*, which promote the views of people defined by their role in society (such as manufacturers, farmers or trades unionists), and *attitude groups*, which comprise people of a like mind, irrespective of social and/or economic background and characteristics, and which have much more open memberships. Most pressure groups concerned with environmental problems are attitude groups. This creates organisational problems, since they have no obvious constituency on whom to draw, and who might be expected to join (it is hard to promote a 'closed shop' around such problems) and they have no obvious resource base on which they can call to finance their activities; they are dependent on what the members are able and prepared to contribute (which will reflect their commitment to the cause) and what they can raise from sympathetic others. In promoting certain causes they are often countered by well organised and well financed interest groups.

The number of environmental issues and problems generated by human interference with natural systems is immense, providing the opportunity for a large number of pressure groups, the existence of which may be counter-productive and whose co-ordination is extremely difficult; the problems of voluntary organisations are often very substantial. In general terms the groups can be classified according to two criteria.

(1) The *focus* of their activity. Here the main difference is between what one might term generalist attitude groups, which promote debate about environmental issues over their full range – Greenpeace, Friends of the Earth and the Sierra Club are examples of this type of organisation – and those which concentrate on one sphere of the environment only, such as the Ramblers' Association in Britain and the National Audubon Society in the United States. Many organisations are neither generalist nor specialist, of course, but cover a number of usually related issues.

(2) The *specificity* of their goals. The difference here is between groups created for a specific purpose, such as opposing the drainage of an area of wetland of a few hectares, and those with a continuing political programme. The former have many of the characteristics of an interest group, because membership is probably concentrated on, though not exclusively confined to, residents of the local area involved and thus will probably have a limited life; once the problem is resolved, the rationale for the group disappears. The latter have longer programmes, and while they may fight particular issues, their *raison d'être* extends beyond the individual cause. The two groups may conflict. For example, a local group may oppose the construction of a new road through its area but is relatively unconcerned if the road is routed elsewhere. Such an interest group (sometimes termed a NIMBY group, the acronym derived from the 'Not In My Back Yard' focus of their protest) may be opposed by an attitude group opposed to new road construction in general.

How do these groups promote their causes? For the NIMBY groups this is often not a problem, since the existence of the proposal that they oppose in itself leads to the establishment of a forum within which their opposition can be expressed and a legal procedure through which their case can be channelled: for example the land use planning system in the United Kingdom. Similarly, to the extent that such proposals call forth their protests, wider attitude groups can use the same fora and procedures. But their existence indicates a recognition by the state that such conflicts will arise and will call for resolution; these procedures do not cater for 'new' problems, for which there is no recognition and no established mechanism for debate. The pressure groups have to agitate to get new problems on to the political agenda (both electoral and corporate), and also high enough on that agenda to elicit responses.

The initial task of those concerned about an environmental problem is creating awareness that a problem exists; only then can means of counter-ing it be discussed. What strategies can they follow to create that awareness? Clearly, lobbying individuals and groups within the state apparatus, both bureaucrats and politicians, is an important activity; in many countries there is a well-established 'lobbying industry' which offers advice and services to those wishing to contact and influence those with power to act, and decide to act accordingly. Whether their action will be effective depends on their power and the receptivity of the government to what is proposed.

As argued earlier, governments, and politicians generally, are particularly receptive to cases brought to them if they believe that there are political benefits to be gained from acting – or political costs to be incurred from not acting. They may be prepared to promote those benefits themselves; for example, if a government is convinced that certain aerosol sprays are destroying some component of the atmospheric system, it may be prepared to promote a 'public education' campaign to support its proposal to reduce the production of such sprays, if not ban them altogether – and it may enlist the assistance of influential individuals in that campaign. But if it is not convinced either by the scientific evidence brought before it or by the weight of the case that action is needed, then the pressure group may have to act further to convince it. This can involve two sorts of action. The first is amassing further evidence to support the case, especially the scientific basis. The second is obtaining public support. To get this, public awareness may have to be built up first, which could involve undertaking 'illegal' acts to attract publicity and media treatment of the cause.

In weighing up the evidence presented to it, a government or one of its agencies will probably receive alternative evidence from other pressure groups, many of them interest groups. Thus, for example, the case that a certain pesticide is leading to the eutrophication of waters in the area where it is applied may be countered both by the manufacturers of the pesticide, who see their profits under attack, and the farmers who apply the pesticide in order to increase the productivity of their land. The case of acid rain production illustrates the problem well (Park, 1987).

Environmental pressure groups face two major difficulties when they seek to present their cases, especially in public fora such as planning and other inquiries. The first is available resources. In many of those inquiries they are opposed by interest groups with very substantial resources – including in some cases agencies of the state itself, which is also, through another agency, evaluating the case. The pressure groups are rarely rich, and are therefore at a considerable disadvantage (in the ability to employ legal counsel, for example), as was demonstrated in a recent study of a major British inquiry (O'Riordan and Kemp, 1988). The second difficulty is that the nature of much of the research on which their cases are based is inconclusive, because of the complexity of the systems being studied and the lack of any possibility of conducting test experiments (would a trial nuclear explosion be allowed to see what the outcome might be under certain climatic conditions!?) Thus when scientific witnesses are 'on the stand', they may have to admit that they are not certain, leaving those sitting in judgment to decide not on a basis of fact but on an assessment of probabilities, albeit expressed by experts (though, of course, the representatives of opposing interest groups may seek to discredit the evidence of those experts, if not the experts themselves). The problems of scientists as witnesses are major ones, especially as many are advocates of a particular cause (Clark, 1982). And in many cases experts with opposing views can be found, so the decision may then rest on the standing and

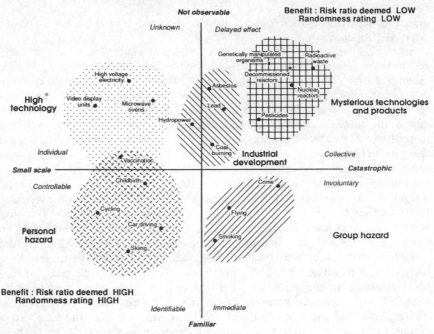

Figure 6.3 A classification of hazards and risks

plausibility of the experts, rather than on the work on which their evidence is based.

It is easier to stimulate interest in, and concern about, some issues than others, as O'Riordan (1987) has argued. He proposes two scales that are relevant to this (Figure 6.3). The first is concerned with familiarity. At one extreme are those potential issues, such as hazards of all varieties, which are immediately identifiable by and familiar to most people. Smoking and skiing are examples of these; they are well-known activities, the dangers which are easily evaluated by individuals for themselves, given a limited amount of information. At the other extreme of the scale are the hazards that are unobservable, whose consequences are not well known, and whose effects are in many cases delayed: asbestos and microwave ovens are cited as examples. The second scale relates to hazard control. At the left-hand extreme are the small-scale hazards that can be controlled by the individual for her- or himself, whereas at the right hand are those whose impact is collective and which cannot be controlled, certainly not by individuals and possibly not be society as a whole. Few hazards come at the extreme left-hand end of the scale (overeating may go there?) because in many, such as riding a bicycle on a public road, however careful the individual is the actions of others can still create hazards over which the individual has no control. At the right-hand end are the 'natural catastrophes', such as earthquakes, against which some collective action can be taken – in the design of buildings for example. Much research on natural hazards, such as floods, has shown that the collective action taken, such as insurance, in effect increases the probability of suffering from the hazard (see Burton et al., 1978).

On the diagram with those two scales as the axes (Figure 6.3), O'Riordan identifies five groups of hazards.

(1) *The personal hazards*, which affect the individual, are largely controllable, either by the individual alone or by the individual and a few others in the vicinity (other car drivers, for example), and involve risks that people can evaluate satisfactorily for themselves without assistance from the state. (This does not, of course, prevent the state from insisting on particular actions to protect individuals against hazards in this category in certain circumstances, such as compulsory hospitalisation for childbirth in some countries.)

(2) *The group hazards*, which again involve relatively familiar situations for which individuals can evaluate the risks and decide whether to participate, such as the risks of flying in commercial aircraft or of eating certain foods. Nevertheless, to the extent that the risks are created by others, such as commercial airlines and foodstuff manufacturers, so the public may demand state action to minimise the risks by insisting on high levels of safety and protection against human error. Similarly, where the activities have spill-over effects, state action may be required to protect innocent potential victims – such as non-smokers who could be affected by the smoking of others nearby, and victims of drivers under the influence of alcohol.

(3) *The high technology hazards*, such as the possible consequences of exposure over long periods to radiation from video-display tubes on office equipment and from microwave ovens, and the believed cancerous consequences of living near to power stations, waste tips, and even under power lines. The impact of such hazards is usually individual, and can be controlled by the individual, in the choice of where to live for example (though some, usually the affluent, have more choice and are better able to afford to live away from hazards than are others). But the nature of the hazard is often poorly understood, in part because its impact is often delayed, perhaps for years. Public information and education is thus needed to mobilise people's concern about the hazards before action can be demanded.

(4) *The industrial development hazards*, which are usually experienced by individuals as members of collectives defined by their co-location, as with the residents of an area affected by pollution from an industrial plant upwind of it, and the lead pollution from car exhausts that may be experienced by those who live alongside major roads. Again, the impact of many of these hazards is poorly understood, in part because they are slow-acting and the cause–effect sequence is not readily observable (if at all).

(5) *The mysterious technologies and products*, which can have mass, catastrophic effects, as with the failure of safety procedures (the nuclear reactor at Chernobyl, for example), but whose sources are very difficult to appreciate for all but the relatively few who are technologically literate. With these it is difficult to promote education about the hazard, especially since understanding it cannot counter the potential mass devastation. Much effort has been advanced in creating a fear of the hazards, therefore, by pressure groups concerned to limit, if not end, their use; the existence of that widespread fear has often provoked state action while other, better

understood, hazards are left unregulated.

Many of these hazards involve human interference with the environment, and others could be placed on the two scales. With some, the activity is not a hazard in itself, but its possible consequence is: ploughing land is not a hazard, but the possible soil erosion that may result is. Many of the activities which lead to environmental degradation are familiar, but their operation may not be observable, either because they are slow-acting or because the impact is felt elsewhere (as with the hole in the ozone layer over the Antarctic apparently caused by the release of CFCs, largely in the northern hemisphere). More importantly, while the actions creating, or at least contributing to, the hazards are individually controllable (we can all stop using aerosol sprays), the impacts of individual use are not limited to those directly involved; it is in the nature of systems that spill-overs occur and there can be many 'innocent victims'. Thus, as argued earlier with regard to the Prisoner's Dilemma (p. 113), it requires collective action to ensure individual control.

So how do pressure groups convince those who control collective action through the state of the need for controls, especially given the time and space delays in the realisation of the impacts of individual action on and in the environment? With the hazards in the top half of Figure 6.3 there is a clear need for education, both of those who will take the action and those (the general public) who will demand it of them. Thus access to education is a major goal of the generalised environmental pressure groups. How do they obtain it? To some extent it is readily available, because scientists and social scientists from the disciplines involved in the identification of the hazards are themselves involved in the education systems, especially at the higher-education level; they can use research findings to influence their students, and thereby slowly influence others through the formal and informal educational channels. But that is often insufficient, and may be both too slow and too fragmented.

Environmental education, by which all are introduced to the science and social science of the environment, is thus vital to the task of the pressure groups. But in this they are opposed by other interest groups, who see such education as potentially damaging and creating a set of attitudes within society at large which might threaten their advancement. So the content and style of education are politically contested, especially since education is one of those public goods which the state provides and/or sponsors in order to promote both accumulation and legitimation of the mode of production. In many countries the content of the educational curriculum is closely prescribed by the state, which therefore has to be convinced of the need for environmental education; this creates a 'Catch-22' situation for the pressure groups involved who may have to seek other means of promoting their arguments. The difficulties they face are illustrated by a 1989 report on environmental education produced by the inspectorate of schools in England and Wales, which argued that pupils should be prepared to counter the 'propaganda' of environmental pressure groups: the headline of the story summarising the report in *The Independent* was 'Pupils 'must know enough to avoid green bias''! (25 January 1989).

Even if the desirability of a policy has been established by an environmental interest group, it still faces many problems in having such a policy implemented and monitored. With regard to implementation, in capitalist societies this frequently involves establishing the costs and evaluating whether these are affordable. As Rees notes, although an economic perspective 'has no monopoly over the truth' (1985, p.259) it is commonly applied to the assessment of proposals, and appraisals are usually based on the goal of achieving economic efficiency. The latter is usually defined according to the Pareto criterion that an allocation of resources is efficient if there is no alternative allocation which simultaneously makes some people better off and no others worse off. The Pareto criterion may be relaxed, however, if nobody was worse off and some were better off, after the latter had compensated the former for any losses that they may have incurred (see Rees, 1985, pp.118–20). Applying such a criterion entails the expression of all values in monetary units, so that a benefit:cost analysis can be undertaken. This can produce some bizarre consequences if taken to its logical conclusions (as Adams, 1970, 1974, has illustrated), and raises crucial issues with regard to the valuation of certain 'goods' that are not marketed (as with clean air and attractive landscapes) as well as the incorporation of spill-over effects in time and space (some of which, as illustrated in Chapter 2, may be slow in developing and long-lasting in their impacts).

The application of benefit:cost analysis and other techniques of economic evaluation raises important political issues for those promoting pro-environmental viewpoints. To some of them, the issues are not economic at all, but moral. Sagoff (1988), for example, presents a strong argument 'Why political questions are not all economic' and attacks those who argue that environmental problems can be solved through market mechanisms (his particular target is the economist Allen Kneese, the author of several influential texts on the subject: e.g. Kneese, 1964; Kneese and Bower, 1968). For Sagoff, issues such as environmental protection are not issues for which the calculus of the market-place is appropriate:

> They involve matters of knowledge, wisdom, morality, and taste that admit of better or worse, right or wrong, true or false – and these concepts differ from that of economic optimality. Surely environmental questions – the protection of wilderness, habitats, water, land, and air as well as policy toward environmental safety and health – involve moral and aesthetic principles and not just economic ones. (1988, p.45)

As we have seen, those in control of the state can and do impose policies which reflect moral and aesthetic concerns and they can commit those subject to the state's sovereignty to pay for such policies. But if they are to do so they must be convinced of the desirability of such policies, of their 'rightness' in moral terms, and they must be able to convince those who will bear the costs that the burden is both necessary and not intolerable. In particular, in capitalist states governments must both be convinced that the economic base will not be substantially eroded and be able to convince those who operate the economic base accordingly. It is not an easy task –

and the policies that are implemented reflect very much on the persuasive powers of those involved. For environmental groups this undoubtedly involves developing popular support for their actions, thereby indicating to politicians that electoral success may be conditional on accepting the arguments. And achieving such popular support may require substantial media campaigns and support, as Lowe and Goyder (1983) conclude from their analysis of the British situation.

Influence in Non-Democratic Societies

How about the non-democratic societies? How might environmental pressure groups influence what happens there? Clearly, in the absence of a democratic process, there is no opportunity for them to seek either to influence the government through the electorate or to stand as candidates themselves. Thus the only option open to them is to seek to put pressure on those in charge of the state apparatus by other means.

Pressure groups associated with environmental concerns are by no means absent from the advanced communist/socialist states, especially those of Eastern Europe. Even more so than in the core countries of the liberal democratic world, the individuals involved in such groups are drawn from the more affluent members of society, especially those with a professional interest in the environment. Their concern for environmental degradation may stem directly from their scientific work, and may be assisted by their contacts with similar scientists in other parts of the world, both as individuals and through the literature; their affluence means that they are less demanding of more material advancement, and are prepared to put other goals first (though this is probably less important than it is in the capitalist countries). What they may lack is access to the local media and the ability to mobilise the population to their cause, although certain of the media are becoming more available to them now, notably the press, and there is less repression of 'underground literature'.

These organisations of committed environmentalists in the advanced communist/socialist countries are operating in contexts where there is very serious environmental degradation; some of the worst effects of acid rain in the world can be found in parts of Czechoslovakia, for example, and some Polish analysts argue that parts of their country are ecologically 'dead'. Scientists who recognise the problems, and perceive a need for alternative policies if the environmental base for rapid industrialisation is to be sustained, are all part of the state apparatus, working for the most part in the academies of science and the universities. Their influence is thus through those bodies and the scientific advice that they give to the higher echelons of the party and the administration. (Some of them may be senior party members also.) But their advice is competing against that of others whose goal is to increase both production and productivity; quantitative measures of economic growth are important indicators of welfare to the senior bureaucrats, and many have lost their positions in a number of the countries because of failure to deliver the targeted volume of production.

Despite these difficulties faced by those committed to environmental policies, several of the countries concerned have set up offices intended to monitor the condition of the environment, and have supported the growth of relevant research institutes within the academies. But by being incorporated within the state apparatus, such institutions frequently find it difficult to promote their cause very far. They are competing with other, generally stronger, parts of the state apparatus for resources and standing, and though they may make important gains in particular circumstances, it is clear that their role does not have a very high priority in most; their actions have been described by Gustafson as 'not pressure-group politics, but the politics of waiting for the open window' (1981, p.51).

To some extent, the opening of windows through which environmentalists in advanced communist/socialist countries can advance their cause depends on the pressure brought to bear on their governments by the governments of other countries, both unilaterally and through multilateral international agencies. The Chernobyl incident of summer 1986, for example, allowed many Eastern and Western European governments to bring pressure on the government of the Soviet Union and to demonstrate to it the ecological truth that natural environmental systems are no respecters of international boundaries. In effect, the pressure that can be brought to bear is akin to that described earlier in the Chicken/Assurance game scenarios. If the authorities in the people's democracies can be led to value the public good of, say, pollution control sufficiently to contribute to it if others do, then their active participation in the development of international policies, and their willingness to allow monitoring of the implementation of such policies, might lead to altered attitudes, to the ultimate benefit of all. Of course, as the recent Law of the Sea problems illustrate, along with those on the use of space presented by Laver (see p.138), states will decline to participate in international collaboration: if they see major benefits from free-riding on the collaboration of others; if they are not convinced of the need for the collaboration in the general public good; or if there are no effective sanctions to stop them benefiting from free-riding.

With regard to the non-democratic countries of the periphery of the world economy, the difficulties of promoting pro-environmental policies are even greater, because the parlous economic state of many makes it difficult for them to trade off possible economic benefits (and the assistance with legitimation and social consensus that these might bring) against protection of the environment, which reduces, if not removes, the value of some of their natural resources. Further, in such countries the mobilisation of opinion in favour of policies that can be interpreted as anti-economic growth is difficult, because of the small size of the educated, affluent population who might both appreciate and be sympathetic to the arguments; there are also problems of opposition to the autocratic rule in many of the countries. This is not to deny the existence of powerful, and sometimes successful, pressure groups within those countries, and the occasional sympathetic reception that political leaders give to environmental causes, but only to note the structural difficulties that are faced. Given that many children in such countries are starving to death every year, it is difficult for governments to promote policies that seem to be reducing the food output, or at least not actively increasing it; arguments that such policies are conserving the environment for the ultimate good of all are hard to sustain when the alternative is death tomorrow for close relatives of those who are not convinced.

Again, some of the best hopes for promoting environmental policies in such countries lie outside them. One way is through inter-governmental links in which advice and assistance with tackling environmental degradation is accompanied by short-term aid to circumvent the shortfall in food. Unfortunately, the advice given often includes the case for rapid promotion of birth control in order to reduce the pressure on the land, a case that may be resisted because it is seen as a way of promoting the interests of those already powerful countries by containing the growth of others that might compete with them in a restructured world economy; to the extent that numbers are equated to power, so restraint may be resisted. The second way is to influence not the governments of the peripheral states, who may be relatively powerless to act, but the agencies that are 'developing' the resources through much of the Third World. Many of those agencies are either multinational corporations whose headquarters are in one of the core countries or are inter-government agencies, such as the International Bank for Reconstruction and Development. If their actions can be shown, via the media, to the population in the core as degrading the environment of the periphery in order to increase the profits of core companies, pressure might be brought upon them to change their practices in order to conserve rather than rape nature in other parts of the earth. As is so often the case with such issues, however, the conflict then becomes one between the powerful economic interest groups and the much less powerful attitude groups. The latter can seek to influence the former by attacking their profits – i.e. by promoting the boycott of goods produced in 'unacceptable' ways – but few boycotts organised on an international basis have been successful for long periods of time, as other efforts to achieve political goals through interruptions to trade have shown.

Successes

The arguments presented in this chapter suggest that the state may not be very receptive to environmental causes, for a variety of reasons linked to its basic functions, particularly that concerned with the promotion of accumulation. And yet much environmental legislation has been passed, and continues to be passed, in many states, especially those in the core of the world economy. There is little doubt that a great deal of that legislation is of the ameliorative problem-solving type, and no state has what can be called a blueprint for living in relative equilibrium with the environment. But many environmental policies have been adopted. It is not the purpose of this book to review them in any detail, but rather to outline the reasons why they have, as part of a process of understanding how collective action has been determined. This outline is in two parts. The first looks at the ability of the state to act; the second looks at the conditions within which it acts.

Collective power and individual freedom

Control of individual and corporate action within the environment in order to promote the general good involves, in many cases, the removal of the rights of individuals and other bodies to use their property as they wish. The operation of capitalism is based on the institution of private property, and the rights of individuals to do what they wish with that property. Thus if the state is to restrict those rights, it will be eroding one of the foundations of the mode of production that it exists to defend and promote. On what grounds does it do that?

The placing of collective interests by the state above those of the individual involves what is known to some as the 'police power', the ability to act in ways that limit individual freedoms in order to promote the general good: it is defined in *Congressional Quarterly's Guide to the U.S. Supreme Court* as 'the authority of the state to govern its citizens, its land and its resources, and to restrict individual freedom to protect or promote the public good . . .' (Witt, 1979, p.358).

This is operated in a large variety of ways, as in the restrictions on the freedom to drive as one wishes by the imposition of laws determining what side of the road you must occupy, making it a crime to drive with more than a minimum level of alcohol in the blood and at more than a certain speed, and so forth. Such laws restrict the freedoms of individuals, but are accepted by society because such restrictions benefit society as a whole; everybody is safer on the roads as a consequence of those restraints.

Can the general principles underlying the above example be applied to the use and disposal of land? In answering this question it is important to note that land is somewhat different from most other forms of private property (see Laver, 1986, p.360). In capitalist societies, commodities have two values: their use value is a measure of their utility, and is thus a valuation based on their importance to consumers, or their ability to satisfy a need; their exchange value is a measure of their relative use value, and is thus an evaluation of the utility of one commodity relative to that of another. The relationship between the use and exchange value of commodities varies considerably, depending on how much people are prepared to pay for something in order to be able to use it. In this context, as Harvey (1973) makes clear, land is something of a special case; compared to most commodities it is immobile, is necessary to all (because it is the source of food and other commodities), is infrequently traded, is permanent and relatively indestructible, and once bought is then usable for long periods of time and so is relatively expensive (most commodities are purchased either for immediate consumption or for use over at most a few years), and can be used in a variety of ways. As such, it has not only high use value but also very high exchange value, because in buying it you are buying the right to use it ad infinitum, and thus reap its use values for ever. Thus if the state is to restrain the use of land for the public good, it is undertaking a major erosion of the rights of private property – to use and to exchange it freely.

The justification for state actions which constitute such erosion varies from country to country, according to the nature of the local political system. In the United States, for example, the Constitution protects private property rights, with the following statement in the Fourteenth Amendment (ratified in 1868):

> No State shall make or enforce any law which shall abridge the privileges or immunities of citizens of the United States; nor shall any State deprive any person of life, liberty, or property, without due process of law . . .

In other words, the state can only act to restrict individuals' use of their property if what it does can be legally justified, and the courts exist to provide protection against any illegal restraints of individual freedom by the state apparatus.

A key case which illustrates the justification of the 'police power' is provided by a 1926 judgment of the United States Supreme Court, which upheld the validity of land use zoning by local government. The case concerned the village of Euclid, in the suburbs of Cleveland, Ohio, where the municipal council proposed a zoning scheme. One of the landowners, Ambler Realty Company, had recently assembled several blocks of land which it intended to develop for industrial use, and which it valued at $10,000 per acre. Most of that land was zoned for residential use, however, which Ambler argued reduced its value to $2500 per acre. Thus the company claimed that it had been deprived of its property rights, without due process, and was set to lose several hundred thousand dollars as a consequence. The Supreme Court found in favour of the municipality in its judgment. The zoning plan had been passed by a properly elected municipal council, 'presumably representing a majority of the inhabitants and voicing their will', and was acting on their behalf 'so that the public welfare may be secure'. Thus the justification accepted by the court, and providing the basis on which all zoning is deemed constitutional in the United States, was that it was a democratic act undertaken for the general good, and thus a proper exercise of the police power. Further cases established that a zoning plan had to be clearly framed as promoting the public good, in order to justify a serious invasion of property, and was not to be an 'arbitrary whim'; people affected by zoning decisions could thus contest whether the zoning was an arbitrary whim, but if they failed to prove that it was, then they could not claim compensation for an act undertaken for the public good. It is, of course, for the state to define and defend what is in the public good, so the defence of zoning is that it creates a pattern of land use that is generally beneficial, even if the exchange value of some people's land is depressed as a consequence. (For fuller details, see Johnston, 1984.)

The police power has been used in a variety of other ways to promote environmental policies since the Euclid decision, and in general the power has gone unchallenged, even though its particular use may not have. For example, the 1970 Water Quality Improvement Act, which controls water pollution, begins with the declaration that it is enacted in

> connection with the exercise of jurisdiction over the waterways of the
> Nation and in consequence of the benefits resulting to the public health
> and welfare by the prevention and control of water pollution . . .

and the 1967 Air Quality Act has as its primary purpose 'to promote health
and welfare and the productive capacity of [the] population . . .'. In these
terms, the police power is justified not only in the context of the legitimation functions of the state but also with respect to the promotion of
accumulation; an Act limiting air pollution increases people's health, and
makes them a better workforce as a consequence.

The United Kingdom lacks a written constitution and a bill of rights;
parliament is sovereign, so its definition of the public welfare, and hence
justification of the use of the police power, holds. The main challenges are
through the electoral system, which can return a government pledged to
rescind an Act that it argues is an unjustified infringement of individual
freedom. Should the British state choose to exercise the police power over
the use of land, with the support of parliament in so doing, then this is
entirely justified: and it has been done on many occasions.

Elsewhere, the police power over the use of land may be somewhat irrelevant, since the land is owned by the state in any case. Common land
rapidly disappeared in most of Western Europe in recent centuries, as
rights of individual use were granted, exemplified by the more than 5000
Acts of Parliament in Great Britain which permitted the enclosure of
common lands. But in some other parts of the world, including much of
the western half of the United States, the land has remained in state hands
so its use is determined by what the state deems to be the public good –
which may involve the state as the land user itself, but more likely involves
it leasing the land to individuals, with clear constraints on what they can
and cannot do with it. That use may, of course, be governed by the desire
for profit alone, or it may include restraints introduced to protect the land
from abuse and the creation of degradation – as happened in New Zealand
after clear evidence that sheep farming in much of the state-owned High
Country was leading to rapid soil erosion. In advanced communist/socialist
states, of course, much of the land is state-owned, and it is possible for land
use policies to be promoted for the public good irrespective of any
individual desire for gain but, as argued earlier, the demand for increased
material welfare in those societies puts great pressure on the state to
increase the productivity of land, with the inherent dangers of degradation
that this can bring.

Land is a common resource in some societies and not in others. Air and
water are in general common resources, so that state action to control their
use is more readily promoted without facing the issues of invading
individual property. There are, of course, issues of where the boundaries
of private and public property lie. Is the air within someone's home private
property, so that they can pollute it and therefore, through the movement
of air, pollute the air outside? And how far below the surface of the earth
do individual property rights extend, an important issue with regard to the

exploitation of both mineral and water resources? Different states have taken different attitudes to these boundary issues, as illustrated by Wescoat's (1985) analysis of Colorado water law and State Court decisions.

The promotion of the public good through environmental legislation

Even where land is treated as private property, the exercise of individual freedom to use (and abuse) it is constrained by the police power; the use of land is thus contingent on state definitions of the wider public interest. If the state recognises that it has such power, then how and why does it choose to exercise it?

Most restrictions on individual freedoms by the state have been introduced as the result of agitation by interest and pressure groups, for legislation or similar action, as described above. Restrictions have been justified as promoting the general welfare, in many cases by appealing to the morality of the action proposed; with environmental causes, part of the justification is ensuring that the environment can sustain life in the future, and thus leaving it in a condition in which we would like to receive it. (This argument characterises John Rawls's, 1971, natural theory of justice.) The state has to be convinced: (a) that the proposed action would have general support, and thus would not contribute toward a legitimation crisis; and (b) that it would not seriously damage accumulation, and thus lead towards a rationality crisis. The latter may be the more difficult to argue, since in many cases a proposal will either increase the costs of production or reduce the potential productivity of land. But with many pieces of environmental legislation, as long as all are subject to them and the costs are equally shared, the benefits to profit-seekers may be substantial too; as the quotation from the US Air Quality Act showed, anti-pollution legislation can be justified in terms of producing a healthier workforce, which should be more productive. Thus much environmental legislation can be justified in terms that in effect imply solving the Prisoner's Dilemma. The main problem, and an increasing one in recent decades, is that environmental legislation in one state alone may affect the competitiveness of its producers relative to those in states with fewer, or no, restrictions, and may make it difficult for the state to attract external investment. For this reason it is difficult to insist on strict constraints in many of the countries of the periphery of the world economy.

The history of environmental legislation is therefore a history of struggle, to convince the state of the desirability, if not necessity, of exercising the police power to control the use of both land, as an item of personal property, and the 'commons', such as air and water. That it has indeed been a struggle is made clear in the title of Sidney Plotkin's book *Keep Out: The Struggle for Land Use Control*, which he introduces as follows:

> Domination and resistance form the central themes of this book, which is an examination of some of the high-level controls of capitalist society and of the ability of human beings to say no. (1987, p.xi)

The issue he discusses is whether local communities can continue to operate exclusionary zoning, by zoning unwanted uses out of their territory through the land use planning power vested in municipalities in most states, or whether those policies can be over ridden by a federal agency set up to further the goals of capitalist enterprises (in this case the oil industry). Similarly, Hays (1987) reviewed the struggles of environmentalists, and their achievements, notably the 1969 National Environmental Policy Act which extended the evaluation of major federal projects beyond the traditional parameters of benefit:cost analysis to incorporate the 'unquantifiable' (see also Garner and O'Riordan, 1982, on the difference between the technical procedure of environmental impact assessment and the wider process of environmental assessment). As Hays notes, those successes generated opposition:

> opposition that was continuous, increasingly vocal and determined, accelerating throughout the 1970s, and rising to a peak in the early 1980s. A coherent anti-environmental movement emerged with an over-riding goal of restraining environmental political influence . . . . Environmentalists presented a serious challenge to agriculture, labour and business, which turned on them with alarm. Although these groups made opportunistic adjustments to environmental objectives, their overall political strategy was one of maximum feasible resistance and minimum feasible retreat. (1987, pp.287–8)

The successes came about because of the demands of affluent Americans; they were countered by the pessimistic managers of the economy who argued that the world could not be made as healthy, clean, safe and beautiful as those people wanted; they would have to settle for less (1987, p.542). Thus the contemporary struggle within American capitalism is not, as Marx predicted, between the proletariat and the bourgeoisie, but between sections of the latter and:

> the growing mass middle class, [which] in seeking to shape a newer world revolving around its values and conceptions about the good life, gave expression to precisely the rising standard of living the managerial and technical leadership professed to extol. (p.542)

The issue, it seems, is the legitimacy of the case made by the latter, of the claims of the 'technical intelligentsia' against those of the 'humanistic intelligentsia' (p.162), and their relative success in the political fora.

In Britain very similar conclusions can be drawn. Sheail's (1976, 1981) outline of the introduction of various pieces of environmental legislation illustrates the importance of 'well-connected' pressure groups, whose members appear to come from the same backgrounds as those described by Hays; according to Lowe and Goyder the growth of such groups:

> derives from intrinsic changes in public consciousness and is not simply a result of encouragement by political elites and the media attention given to environmental issues . . . . Many of the groups springing up questioned the direction of society and tended to view individual environmental problems as having a common cause in economic population growth. (1983, p.181)

For those people, relative affluence and security, and the absence in many cases of any direct link between their work and the production of goods, provided the context within which concern for the environment could be stimulated. For those not so fortunate, and whose daily survival depended on jobs in the production of goods, the ecological movement was less attractive, as it also was to those whose wealth derived directly from the profitability of production. And the state was left in the middle, facing potential rationality and legitimacy crises if it accepted the environmental case too readily, and yet increasingly convinced by the scientific evidence. Thus the struggle continues, between the momentum of the dominant mode of production on the one hand and the claims that it is destroying the earth on the other.

Chapter 7

Alternative Futures

Dark green thinking offers a radical, visionary and fundamentalist challenge to the prevailing economic and political world order. At its most ambitious, green politics sees itself as a global life-saver, an urgent response to fast-approaching ecological collapse. It demands a wholly new ethic in which violent, plundering humankind abandons its destructive ways, recognizes its dependence on Plant Earth and starts living on a more equal footing with the rest of nature. (Jonathon Porrit and David Winner, *The Coming of the Greens*, 1988, p.11)

According to Falk (1972), writing in the early 1970s before environmental issues had reached the prominence of academic analysis, media coverage and position on the political agenda that they now occupy, there are two ways forward from recognition of the environmental carrying capacity constraints so clearly enunciated by Catton (see p.7 above). Each takes four decades to achieve. The first is the pathway to *degenerative strife*, proceeding from the politics of despair in the 1970s through the politics of desperation and then of catastrophe in the next two decades to the era of annihilation from the year 2000 on. The alternative is the pathway to *progressive egalitarianism and justice*, proceeding from a decade of awareness in the 1970s through decades of mobilisation and transformation in the next twenty years and achieving an era of world harmony after AD 2000. Whether the former scenario of despair or the latter scenario of hope will prevail it is perhaps too early to judge. At the transition from the 1980s to the 1990s we should already have a mobilised world ready to move into a decade of transformation: in terms of the economic organisation of capitalism this has almost certainly come about (see Lash and Urry, 1987, for example), but it is doubtful whether that transformation incorporates the relationships between the environment on the one hand and capitalism and advanced communism/socialism on the other. The material quoted at the beginning of Chapter 1 suggests that, in Great Britain at least, we are entering the decade of the politics of catastrophe, having just passed through the years of desperation. Is it too late to anticipate that the scenario of hope is achievable? And if not, how can it be achieved?

The answer to the first question rests in the science of the environment and is outside the scope of the present book, which assumes that it is not too late – if it is, then I have wasted my time writing the book and you have similarly wasted yours reading it!! (Perhaps a note in the Preface should have directed readers to this page first.) And so we turn to the second. From his review of the literature, O'Riordan (1981a, p.302ff.) identifies four proposals for major institutional reform, all based on the argument (advanced by, among others, Pirages and Ehrlich, 1974) that 'the present system of liberal–pluralist politics cannot be sustained' (p.302): special interest groups tend to undermine resolute government, which uses short-term expediency to override long-term commitments; political leaders prevaricate in the face of conflicting proposals and contradictory evidence; the authority of legislatures is eroded by the ability of special interest groups to evade regulation; citizens are weak when confronted with the power of the neo-corporate state, and lack information necessary to counter that power; and 'pluralism is predicated upon compromise, but the fear of scarcity encourages confrontation and irresolution. In such circumstances only the powerful are satisfied' (p.302). In other words, the liberal–democratic state is largely oriented to the resolution of problems, but the potential environmental catastrophe facing the earth requires a solution that it cannot deliver (see p.169).

If the people do not rule in any case (the neo-corporatist argument) and politicians do not serve electorates; if

> Voters are neither concerned nor humane, they are alienated, frustrated, and confused, and are often forced to elect politicians from a group of candidates not of their choosing. Urbanisation, bureaucratic centralisation, mobility, and the dominance of technology, combined with the monotony and impersonalisation of most occupations, breed a collective disinterest in the affairs of others, an almost inhuman lack of compassion for the weaker in distress. (O'Riordan, 1981a, pp.302–3)

then there is clearly a need for a revolution in the organisation of human society. The four outcomes of such a revolution are categorised by O'Riordan as follows.

(1) *A new global order*, in which the current state system is dissolved and replaced by a single, global organisation. Its proponents, according to O'Riordan

> appear to believe that global order can be achieved by transferring the funds currently deployed as military expenditures to the institutions of peace and goodwill, through the recognition of mutual dependence between rich and poor nations, and the wise realisation that life-support systems can only be protected through a coercive common government. (p.303)

They are what Frankel (1987) terms eco-pacifists. Whether the goal is achievable depends on global recognition that the tragedy of the commons is upon us, that we are playing Prisoner's Dilemma games when we should be playing Assurance. This also begs the question of whether ecological equilibrium is achievable within a capitalist mode of production, or even an advanced communist/socialist one built on the goal of increasing material welfare, whatever the nature of the state.

(2) *Centralised authoritarianism*, in which all the problems of liberal democracy are replaced by a totalitarian state which sees the promotion of global ecological equilibrium as its predominant mission.

(3) *The authoritarian commune*, which according to Heilbroner (1974) involves blending the religious orientation and military-style discipline characteristic of a monastery with the policies attempted in China in recent decades. If all people are guaranteed the basic minima of life, live in communal social systems where all are cared for by kin and friends, and economic organisation is based on collectivisation and regional self-sufficiency, then the dynamo of capitalism will be removed, the drive to material possessions that characterises some advanced communist/socialist systems will not replace it, and harmony with the environment will be achieved.

(4) *The anarchist solution*, which goes further than the previous one because it promotes a society without a state, let alone an authoritarian one.

But how are any of these solutions to be attained? Are they not just utopian idealism? With the second and the third, for example, it is necessary for the state in the liberal democracies to be taken over by those promoting an authoritarian mode of government that is 'pro-environment', and that can legitimise its actions. (In the short term at least it would need to sustain itself through coercion, because the policies it would advance would be against the interests of many powerful groups in capitalist society. In the long term, through emancipatory education – as opposed to brain washing: see Johnston, 1988 – it might promote an ideology that would sustain its rule without the backing of a major coercive element.) In the other countries of the world, where liberal democracy is not practised at the present time, it would be necessary for those in power to adopt a totally new range of policies and goals from those they pursue now, which again would put them in conflict with the special interests (both inside and outside the state's territory) on whose support they depend. The third – anarchist – solution would require people to distance themselves from capitalism or advanced communism/socialism and establish separate communities, independent of those still operating the dominant modes of production. Whether this could be done, given the existence of the institution of private property in most states and the collective ownership of land in the others, is very dubious, except with very marginal land (see Johnston, 1986a) or a mass rejection of the dominant modes of production. And with the first solution, there is the need either for those in power in all states to be persuaded to yield their sovereignty, and eventually their existence, voluntarily or for those running some (probably affluent and powerful) states to impose a new global order on all others.

The likelihood of any of these eventualities emerging from the current world order is, I believe, remote. It may be that one or more of them could be created *de novo* after a major global ecological catastrophe which destroyed both the modes of production and the pattern of state power; those who survived would promote a new blueprint, of a society that would never get itself in such a condition again. Such a means to a desirable end is not only defeatist, however, but also implies letting many people (perhaps the great majority of the current population) die during that catastrophe. Furthermore, it may well be that the earth cannot be recovered for human occupancy after such a catastrophe; do we want to take that chance?

If, then, the four scenarios painted by those who want a new type of social order are probably unattainable, what ways forward are there? To answer that question, the final section of this book looks at the limits of political and economic freedom within the contemporary world.

Achievable Equilibrium

Can we continue with the present dominant mode of production in the world economy, with advanced communism/socialism also offering a mode of social and economic organisation in which the achievement of high material consumption levels is a major goal? In the latter countries it appears that such levels are increasingly demanded by the populations concerned, as the state there 'opens up' the possibility of debate about future scenarios. So can that mode of production substantially reduce, if not entirely eliminate, activities that degrade the earth's environment? If not, what is the way forward – through the state, and greater regulation at both national and international level, or through modification of consumption patterns?

Green politics

As we saw in Chapter 6, one possible way of promoting new attitudes towards the environment is via 'green politics', either through specifically created 'green parties' or by 'converting' existing parties (which can include those that govern in the advanced communist/socialist states as well as the capitalist). Neither, it seems, has been particularly successful as a general strategy, although local successes (in time as well as space) have been recorded; proponents of 'green' views are not especially enamoured with 'green politics' at present (as Porrit and Winner, 1988, indicate).

Green politics is associated in many minds with left-wing ideas on a wide range of other issues – as illustrated by a quotation from a leader writer of *The Daily Telegraph*: 'for most Conservatives the word "green" conjures up the most disagreeable images. Legions of eccentric, muesli-crunching peace fanatics in open-toed sandals are hardly the stuff of which Conservative Party majorities are made' (Porrit and Winner, 1988, p.81). The reason for that image is, as Pepper (1985) argues, that most environmentalists, like most socialists, are seeking not modifications to capitalism but radical social change:

> For the socialist, too, seeks radical social change and the liberation of the masses from the tyranny of material want, from capitalist economic

'laws' and from the inter-human and human-to-nature relationships which are predicated by the capitalist mode of production. Furthermore, following Marx, he [sic] believes that such change is *possible*, and that human societies have freedom of will to shape themselves – to 'make their own history' according to their own desires . . . the socialist argues that there is nothing inevitable, 'natural' or predetermined about capitalism, neither should any ultimate limits set by nature be invoked to suggest that there are constraints against achieving a truly socialist future . . . a socialist society is not thought to be so free in relation to nature that it can dominate, exploit and destroy it for its own immediate gain (a crude materialist interpretation of Marx which has been applied in the Soviet Union to such disastrous effect) . . . a socialist society's relationship to nature will be more of a balanced and mutually reciprocal one [than capitalism's]. (1985, p.15)

Such an argument clearly suggests an alliance, if not integration, of green and socialist politics, promoting a realistic 'Red Green' political and social scenario, rather than the 'Green Green' favoured by those Pepper identifies as environmental idealists. Further, whereas the 'Green Green' case is largely supported by middle-class elites in affluent countries, the 'Red Green' arguments would mobilise working-class support too, since that class favours radical economic and social change. (Cotgrove's, 1982, surveys clearly distinguish the middle-class 'nature conservationists', who also support economic individualism, from the left-wing oriented 'environmentalists'.)

But is the 'Red Green' alliance feasible; can socialist and green politicians unite in a common cause of a more just, equitable and environmentally stable society? In Great Britain, many of those committed to the green cause have decided that the Labour Party is not currently a viable ally. Pepper (1986) has analysed this situation and argued that Labour and green should unite in common cause because both base their analysis of contemporary society on the destructive nature of capitalism. The problems with Labour are three, he suggests: its current concern with what he terms 'clientism', negotiating with a range of special interest groups for their electoral support; the continued commitment of the party to policies that will promote economic growth; and the power in the party of the trades unions which, despite the claims of some leaders to the contrary, are really only interested in the share-out of the profits from capitalism. So why support Labour if you are committed to green policies? Because, Pepper argues, Labour is more likely to achieve a socialist future (in the long term) than any other party in Britain, and:

the labour movement has that breadth of vision which can set green policies in the contest of broader social and political policies, therefore, in the long run, making them appeal beyond a middle-class clique. (1986, p.132)

Labour, he suggests, is waiting for the greens to jump on to its long-rolling bandwagon. Pepper wrote after the 1983 general election, and before that of 1987. After the latter, Porrit and Winner wrote that 'Even at the most superficial level, green politics was a complete irrelevance to the Labour party at that time' (1988, p.63), 'The message for Greens intent on taking their politics into the heartland of socialism is surely clear: there is a long, long way to go' (p.71).

Nor were Porrit and Winner impressed with the other parties. (Their comments about the Conservative Party include the admission that 'It is only fair to say, of course, that it is a damn sight harder in government that it is in opposition', (p.79). They don't analyse why this is so, however; why the state is constrained by the mode of production and the interest groups which benefit most from it.) Our discussions in Chapter 6 indicate why this has come about. The political agenda in Britain, and many other liberal–democratic countries, in recent decades has been dominated by economic issues, and in societies based on materialism it is materialist issues that are almost certain to dominate. And yet, as has been argued here, the production and reproduction of those materialist-based societies is founded on particular attitudes towards, and consequences for, the physical environment.

Further, those societies are also founded, at all spatial scales, on gross inequalities in material standards of life – in the commonly used shorthand, they are founded on class conflict. This raises a major issue for the nature of liberal–democratic politics: should those seeking to promote the relative interests on the 'exploited classes' do so within the context of capitalism – promoting a different way of running it – or should they advocate radical social and economic change? Most have chosen the former way, and although they have achieved substantial social change have done so from firmly within the materialist framework. Similarly for the countries outside the affluent core of the world economy, should they seek to rectify their 'exploited' position from within the capitalist framework or without? With few (and usually temporary) exceptions, the answer has been from within. It could well be argued that this is because those wanting to promote radical change are unable, for a variety of reasons, to influence the nature of the political agenda, but that eventually their ideas will prevail. But for those concerned with current environmental problems, the issues are too urgent to wait for that day. The states of the world, individually and together, are currently not the vehicles for achieving the radical social change necessary to ensure environmental survival.

Working within capitalism

If radical change is not to be brought about, at least initially, through the political parties and the state apparatus, how can the environment be protected and its ability to sustain life in the future be enhanced? One argument currently popular in some quarters is to achieve change by working within capitalism, convincing both the consumers and the providers of material goods and services of the threat to the environment posed by many production and consumption processes, stimulating the consumers to demand products that can be provided without major harm to the earth's fragile ecosystems, and persuading the producers of the desirability of catering to those demands. This is a form of 'green consumerism'. If, as many of the traditional models of capitalism argue, producers are merely responders to market signals, then if consumers can be educated to demand certain types of product only then such product lines will succeed and the desired environmental goals will be reached. And even if, as alternative models of capitalism argue, the market is manipulated by the producers, if the producers believe consumers will only buy products they are convinced are 'ecologically sound' then they will orient their activities accordingly.

There is plenty of evidence of such strategies succeeding to some extent, as illustrated in the chapter by Porrit and Winner (1988) on 'Consuming Interests'. Not only are there retail chains that refuse to stock certain lines because of the way in which they are produced, but there are also financial institutions furthering what is known as 'ethical investment': funds are established which will not invest people's savings in what are deemed 'unethical' industries, however potentially profitable they might be – hence tobacco companies and armament producers may be avoided, for example. The success of such campaigns can be illustrated with reference to a booklet produced in early 1989 by Britain's most successful supermarket chain, Sainsbury's, entitled *Sainsbury's Living Today. You and the Environment: It's Your Responsibility Too.* Of its twelve pages the leaflet (which, we are told on the back page, was printed on recycled paper) begins with six that outline some of the major contemporary environmental problems, followed by four headed 'Action by Sainsbury's'. These include the following claims:

(1) For every tree cut down to provide timber for sale in a Sainsbury's store, 'at least four saplings are planted or up to 20 sown and the forest is tended for at least 10 years'.
(2) More than half the new stores built since 1984 have occupied formerly derelict sites, thereby improving urban environments.
(3) All Sainsbury's own-brand aerosols are CFC-free and all new refrigeration equipment in the stores will similarly be CFC-free.
(4) Sainsbury's stock organically grown fruit and vegetables.
(5) None of Sainsbury's own-brand cosmetics are tested on animals.

The leaflet finishes with a list of thirteen actions that all consumers can take, and the firm's slogan: 'Sainsbury's: Helping to Care for the Environment'.

Porrit and Winner recognise the substantial advances that these and similar programmes can achieve, but also indicate the dilemma they pose:

> capitalism itself continues to put Greens in a moral dilemma. If consumption is the name of the game, then at least let it be green. But how does that square with the basic green critique of the consumer-driven economy, in which success is measured by quantitative increases in production and consumption, regardless of its impact on the environment? (1988, p.193)

But the dilemma is much wider. It is not just that success is measured quantitatively as growth, it is that without growth capitalism is unsustainable –

and so, it seems, is the currently available alternative in the socialist countries. Further, such corporate altruism is only sustainable by firms, and by individuals who benefit from ownership (part or total) of those firms, if they are profitable. In the short term it may be that profitability is sustained at a level which allows the corporate altruism to continue, but in the longer term, as Chapters 3 and 4 indicate, a firm that wishes to stand still may find that it falls back, as its competitors increase their productivity and lower their prices. Unless all producers conform, the altruistic are likely to lose in the end; consumers may stay with them in times of plenty, but not in times of relative hardship, and all the evidence suggests that permanent times of plenty are not characteristic of capitalism. Similarly, a state may find it possible to promote some environmental policies (paying farmers not to produce on certain land, or not to use intensive farming methods there) in order to protect the local environment (as in parts of the Broadland in England). But the state can only afford to do that if the society it is running is affluent and profits are being made somewhere (perhaps through the intensification of farming elsewhere, as in the English Fenland); when the squeeze on profitability comes, as analysis of capitalism says it must, and the state's budget is being squeezed too, will it still be able to afford those environmentally desirable policies? (The same can be argued about the apparently altruistic actions of trades unions in blocking certain building projects on environmental grounds – the so-called 'green bans' in Sydney, for example (Short, 1988a, 1988b) – in that they are much less likely to be supported in times of job scarcity than in times of a seller's market for work.)

It may be that education of the consumers can ensure a relatively 'clean' capitalism, but there are substantial barriers to be overcome. The elitism of much of the green movement has been referred to previously in this book. How can the exploited poor of the entire world be mobilised behind 'green consumerism', when many have little if any choice over what they consume? And why should they have to pay more for material prosperity that they have achieved later than people in the countries of the world core, because the latter have now discovered that their prosperity threatens the environment: they have raped the earth and say we have got to pay the price of their crime, is the argument against accepting the advice of the affluent. In any case, how can they be certain that those who invest in production for profit will be true to the environmental ethic? After all, there is considerable evidence at the present time that some firms are responding to 'green consumerism' in the affluent core of the world economy, and especially the affluent suburbia within those countries, while continuing to sell environmentally much more damaging goods elsewhere.

This last issue brings in the state once again. As stressed in the previous chapter, there are many examples where those in control of the state apparatus have accepted arguments regarding environmental problems – whether based on expert advice or responding to popular demands – and implemented policies that ensure environmental improvements; the British Clean Air Act is a case in point. More recently, the campaign for lead-free petrol has been taken up by the British government, which in its budget in March 1989 introduced an increased differential between lead-free and leaded petrol. (Interestingly, the government expected the oil companies to reduce the price of lead-free petrol by 4p per gallon to increase the differential to 10p, but instead the oil companies increased the price of leaded petrol by 4p!) But unless the state is prepared to legislate and then to ensure compliance, which is likely to be both difficult and expensive, there is always the potential for free-riders, who will seek to profit by selling damaging products more cheaply than the less damaging which cost their competitors more to produce.

The success of environmental policies within capitalism, whether of the 'green consumerism' type or others, depends not only on legislation and regulation but also on the discovery of alternative ways of making profits. Thus a state may enforce compliance with certain environmentally desirable policies, but a likely consequence is that investors will then seek alternative, more profitable ways of 'serving' markets. States could require that such new products be subject to environmental audits before their launch, but these raise many logistic and other problems. The apparent destruction of the ozone layer by CFC gases was not foreseen when they were introduced – indeed at that time they were considered very safe and desirable. It could be argued that more investment in scientific research could overcome that problem; that as we become more knowledgeable so we are better prepared to evaluate problems before they even begin. But, as Chapter 2 indicated, the complexity of environmental systems is so great that such an ability is very distant – if indeed it is ever achievable. The implication is that 'green consumerism' will be yet another example of the ameliorative problem-solving that is typical of capitalist societies (see p.169): we respond to the problems we have created, rather than foresee the problems we might create, so that for every problem that we solve at least one new one appears.

This situation is probably inherent to capitalist society in the complex environmental system of the earth, but it is almost certainly advanced by recent political developments in Britain and many other countries. As a response to the economic recession of the 1970s and early 1980s, many states are promoting economic restructuring and recovery through greater liberation of market forces rather than their regulation, as illustrated by the proposals to privatise the water industry in Britain and make the profit motive central to its operations (see p.98). There is much political rhetoric about environmental protection, and willingness to tackle clearly identified problems such as those of CFC gases. But this is very much in the style of ameliorative problem-solving and suggests the absence of any blueprint for an environmentally less damaging future; we will merely respond to the problems we create, despite the evidence that those problems apparently increase in scale and threaten the future of the earth even more.

Finally, is science the answer? Can we develop an understanding of nature that will allow us to promote a form of 'progress' which limits its damage to the environment as far as possible? Possibly, but all the evidence currently available suggests that we won't. Basic scientific research is mostly done in institutions of higher education, but these are being pressed to become more 'commercial' in their attitudes and activities, oriented to serving the interests of capitalism before those of 'knowledge for its own sake'. It is unlikely that scientists will easily get contracts from capitalists to find solutions to environmental problems whose implementation would threaten those capitalists' profits; they are more likely to win support for research that promises profitable returns, as in the burgeoning discipline of biotechnology.

Sustainable development

Is the present population, and the level of material standards that some have achieved and many more wish to emulate, sustainable by the earth's environment? Given the definition of development widely accepted, based on growth in production of commodities for profitable sale, is 'sustainable development' possible, or must we redefine development in order to survive? This is a question addressed by Redclift, whose political economy perspective leads him to identify the production of poverty in the contemporary Third World, and the associated environmental problems, with the dominant mode of production. His case study of Mexico led to the conclusion that:

> The environmental crisis in rural Mexico exhibited two faces: one of them the poverty of neglected rain-fed regions, the other the commercial success, but economic dependency, of the irrigated regions. A policy which addressed rural poverty could only succeed by making fundamental changes in Mexico's structural position which were, ultimately, dependent on its relationship with the international economy, especially the United States. (1984, p.99)

In other words, the production of environmental problems in the world periphery is very much a function of the structuring and operation of the world economy as a whole (see also O'Connor, 1989, who links ecological crises to core–periphery structures at all spatial scales). So is it possible to solve those problems, and produce sustainable relationships with the environment, without a restructuring of the world economy? Redclift's answer is that it is not, that improving agricultural technology in the periphery produces the opposite effect:

> The challenge, then, is not to seek to protect the natural environment from man [sic], but to alter the global economy in which our appetites press on the 'outer limits' of resources. This can only be done by altering the entitlements of the poor in the South [the periphery] so that the environmental discourse becomes a development discourse. (p.130)

Redclift has followed up this conclusion by analysing the proposals of others who argue that sustainable development is possible, that it is

> possible to undertake environmental planning and management in a way that does minimum damage to ecological processes without putting a brake on human aspirations for economic and social improvement. (1987, p.33)

After all, it is argued, many societies in the past have learned to live within the constraints of the environment that they occupied, through the development of what has become known as indigenous knowledge. If that knowledge were harnessed, could it not be used to ensure farming and other practices that were not environmentally destructive – as many demonstration projects indicate is feasible? The problem, as Redclift sees it, is that in such societies:

> Their knowledge is based on the production of use values and the adaptation of their agricultural practices to ecological conditions . . . . The use of indigenous knowledge is linked to the strategies which the culture has devised for coping with risks . . . . The strategies adopted do not necessarily succeed in ensuring adequate livelihoods, but they are designed to reduce the risks to those livelihoods. (1987, pp.153–4)

So can such knowledge be adapted to societies which are based on the production of exchange values (p.181)? Further, Redclift asks, can the traditional cultures which are the repositories of that indigenous knowledge survive in an exchange-value dominated mode of production, with its associated dominant ideology? Can people 'opt out' of capitalism? Can the states within whose territories they are located allow them to, given that most of them are heavily indebted to the capitalist system and require the fruits of production from all of the land and people in order to service that debt and sustain the society as a whole? Redclift concludes not:

> Whether or not development is *necessarily* unsustainable . . . it is clearly unsustainable on current models for many of those whose livelihoods are made in the South, and for reasons that lie outside their control. (1987, p.201)

O'Riordan comes to the same conclusion, arguing that the capitalist and political imperatives characteristic of the Third World 'render sustainable development impossible' (1989, p.41).

The concept of sustainable development is associated by some with the larger issue of whether it is possible to have a 'steady-state economy', defined by Daly as: 'an economy with constant stocks of people and artifacts, maintained at some desired, sufficient levels by low rates of maintenance "throughout"' (1977a, p.17).

This is expanded by indicating that sustaining that society should be designed so that the inputs from the environment are as small as possible (thus minimising environmental depletion), as also should be the disposal of wastes into that environment. The society does not grow, in terms of either its material content or its population numbers. Thus it needs three types of institution (Daly, 1977b): one for stabilising population (the marketing of licences to have children); one for stabilising physical wealth; and one for ensuring an equitable distribution of that physical wealth. Clearly this is a proposal for something very different from the capitalist mode of production with its integral growth dynamo, and thus the issue of whether it is politically feasible (given the place we are starting from and not what might be the case if we were starting afresh with the benefit of knowing what happened in a capitalist society based on exchange values) comes to the forefront.

One part of Daly's case which is widely accepted across the political spectrum in the core of the world economy, and by at least some of the relatively affluent in the periphery, is the necessity of limiting the population of the earth. Just as people have benefited from individual use of their property with little thought for others and for the future, so they have had freedom to use their biological fertility. That is no longer sustainable, it is argued; people must be convinced of the necessity to reduce the population pressure on the earth. As the Duke of Edinburgh put it in his Dimbleby Lecture:

it is up to us as procreators, predators, manipulators, exploiters and consumers to realise that we have to live off the limited land of our planet. We have to learn to accept that any further growth in the human population, any further increase in the exploitation of the Earth's limited natural and mineral resources, and any further degradation of the physical and biological systems of our planet, are bound to cause very serious problems for the generations that we have every reason to believe will come after us. (1989, p.7)

There is no doubt that fewer people, or at least a smaller growth in the number of people, would reduce the immediate pressures on the land. But this would not remove many of the other pressures put on the environment by the general desire for increased material living standards in both of the major current modes of production, nor would it deflect at all from the growth dynamic of capitalism; to some extent, the need to 'mine' the earth for food might be reduced, but the need to 'mine' it for the materials for other saleable commodities might be increased. Breathing space for developing environmental policies it may certainly give (though how much time do we have left?), but no more. And, of course, there remains the issue of inequality. Many of the proposals for 'saving the world's environments' are naively set in a status quo scenario unacceptable to the peoples of the world's periphery; why should they now give up control over their fertility, just as they have yielded control of their property, because a mode of production which they did not create has discovered that it is making a mess of the world?

So how feasible is 'sustainable development' for the world as a whole? O'Riordan identifies four precepts within the overall concept: (1) that it is possible scientifically to 'know' the rates at which resources are renewed, so that their management can be geared to those rates; (2) that renewable resource systems operate homeostatically, so that if we manage them correctly equilibria will be maintained; (3) that the implications of drawing on a resource are constrained to the tight ecosystem of which it is a part; and (4) that using a resource up to the level of renewability is ethically justifiable. He then argues that 'none of these principles is realistic, practicable or justifiable' (1989, p.30). In doing so, he separates the first two precepts, which are statements of the scientific possibility of sustainable utilisation of resources, from the other two, which are concerned with the ethical issues of sustainability. The former is a necessary condition of the latter; if it is right, and sustainable utilisation is feasible, then it becomes a managerial and political goal. But sustainability

is a much broader phenomenon, embracing ethical norms pertaining to the survival of living matter, to the rights of future generations and to institutions responsible for ensuring that such rights are fully taken into account in policies and actions. (p.30)

The argument of Redclift and others is that while sustainable development may be possible in the contemporary Third World, the nature of the capitalist mode of production makes it unattainable. And since the Third World, as argued here, is but one component part of an integrated system of uneven development, if it cannot be achieved there it cannot be achieved globally. Whatever the political rhetoric, as illustrated in Chapter 1, sustainability is not a viable agenda item. As O'Riordan points out, the concept of sustainable utilisation is politically acceptable (because, he says, it is 'safely ambiguous', 1989, p.30) but the concept of sustainability is not (it is 'politically treacherous since it challenges the status quo'). And that, very largely, is the whole argument of the present book in a nutshell; the creation of environmental problems is a product of the dominant mode of production in the world today, and the solution of those problems is difficult because the only institutions within which the necessary collective action could be mobilised exist to promote the interests of that mode of production.

Conclusions?

As indicated at the outset, this book was not written to present a blueprint for the future but rather to indicate the gaps in understanding that many of the blueprints on offer contain. I have sought to show that understanding the nature of environmental problems and how they might be solved requires much more than a scientific appreciation of environmental processes. It demands an understanding of how societies work, and how collective action within those societies is both organised and constrained. Only with that understanding is it possible to discuss how change might be achieved. Thus in conclusion I can do no better than agree with Cotgrove (1982, p.120) that the dominant ideology of world society is cornucopian, with a strong belief in human ability to dominate nature, through science, technology and their application via the market-place, and with the necessary support of the state. Whether that vision is correct is probably best not put to the test, since if it fails it may be too late to design an alternative. But it is very difficult to promote a sustainable alternative within that dominant ideology.

Bibliography

Abel, N.O.J. et al (1985) 'The problems and possibilities of communal land management in Ngwaketse District – a case study', Summary report, International Livestock Centre for Africa.

Abler, R.F., Adams, J.S. and Gould, P.R. (1971) *Spatial Organisation*. Prentice-Hall, Englewood Cliffs, NJ.

Adams, J.G.U. (1970) 'Westminster: the fourth London airport', *Area*, 2: 1–9.

Adams, J.G.U. (1974) '. . . and how much for your grandmother?', *Environment and Planning*, 6: 619–26.

Alford, R.R. and Friedland, R. (1985) *Powers of Theory*. Cambridge University Press, Cambridge.

Allen, B.J. and Crittenden, R.F. (1987) 'Degradation and a pre-capitalist political economy: the case of the New Guinea highlands', in P. Blaikie and H. Brookfield, *Land Degradation and Society*. Methuen, London, pp.145–56.

Archer, J.C. and Taylor, P.J. (1981) *Section and Party*. John Wiley, Chichester, Sussex.

Aubert, J.-F. (1978) 'Switzerland', in D. Butler and A. Ranney (eds) *Referendums*. American Enterprise Institute, Washington, pp.39–66.

Ball, A.R. and Millard, F. (1986) *Pressure Politics in Industrial Societies*. Macmillan, London.

Barlow, J. (1988a) 'A note on biotechnology and the food production chain', *International Journal of Urban and Regional Research*, 12: 229–46.

Barlow, J. (1988b) 'The politics of land into the 1990s', *Policy and Politics*, 16: 111–21.

Bayliss-Smith, T.P. and Feachem, R.G. (eds) (1977) *Subsistence and Survival: Rural Ecology in the Pacific*. Academic Press, London.

Bennett, R.J. and Chorley, R.J. (1978) *Environmental Systems: Philosophy, Analysis and Control*. Methuen, London.

Berg, E. (1978) 'Democracy and self-determination', in P. Birnbaum, J. Lively and G. Parry (eds) *Democracy, Consensus and Social Contract*. Sage Publications, London, pp.149–72.

Berry, B.J.L. (1972) *The Human Consequences of Urbanization*. Macmillan, New York.

Binder, P. (1977) *Treasure Islands*. Blond and Briggs, London.

Blaikie, P. (1985) *The Political Economy of Soil Erosion in Developing Countries*. Longman, London.

Blaikie, P. (1989) 'Natural resource use', in R.J. Johnston and P.J. Taylor (eds) *A World in Crisis?* (2nd edn). Basil Blackwell, Oxford, pp.125–50.

Blaikie, P. and Brookfield, H. (1987a) 'Approaches to the study of land degradation', in P. Blaikie and H. Brookfield, *Land Degradation and Society*. Methuen, London, pp.27–48.

Blaikie, P. and Brookfield, H. (1987b) 'Questions from history in the Mediterranean and Western Europe', in P. Blaikie and H. Brookfield, *Land Degradation and Society*. Methuen, London, pp.122–42.

Blaikie, P. and Brookfield, H. (1987c) 'Common property resources and degradation worldwide', in P. Blaikie and H. Brookfield, *Land Degradation and Society*.

Methuen, London, pp.186–95.

Blaikie, P. and Brookfield, H. (1987d) 'Socialism and the environment', in P. Blaikie and H. Brookfield, *Land Degradation and Society*. Methuen, London, pp.208–13.

Bloch, M. (1961) *Feudal Society*. Routledge and Kegan Paul, London.

Bogdanor, V. and Butler, D. (eds) (1983) *Democracy and Elections*. Cambridge University Press, Cambridge.

Bollen, K.A. (1983) 'World system position, dependency and democracy: the cross-national evidence', *American Sociological Review*, 48: 458–79.

Bradley, P.N. and Carter, S.E. (1989) 'Food production and distribution – and hunger', in R.J. Johnston and P.J. Taylor (eds) *A World in Crisis?* (2nd edn). Basil Blackwell, Oxford, pp.101–24.

Brams, S.J. (1975) *Game Theory and Politics*. The Free Press, New York.

Brotherton, D.I. (1986) 'Party political approaches to rural conservation in Britain', *Environment and Planning A*, 18: 151–60.

Burton, I., Kates, R.W. and White, G.F. (1978) *The Environment as Hazard*. Oxford University Press, New York.

Butler, D. (1960) 'The paradox of party difference', *The American Behavioral Scientist*, 3: 3–5.

Butler, D., Penniman, H.R. and Ranney, A. (eds) (1981) *Democracy at the Polls*. American Enterprise Institute, Washington.

Butlin, R.A. and Dodgshon, R.A. (eds) (1989) *An Historical Geography of England and Wales* (2nd edn). Academic Press, London.

Carroll, J.E. (1986) 'Water resources management as an issue in environmental diplomacy', *Natural Resources Journal*, 26: 207–20.

Catton, W.R. (1978) 'Carrying capacity, overshoot, and the quality of life', in J.M. Yinger and S.J. Cutler (eds) *Major Social Issues: A Multidisciplinary View*. The Free Press, New York, pp.233–49.

Catton, W.R. (1983) 'Social and behavioral aspects of the carrying capacity of natural environments', in I. Altman and J.F. Wohlwill (eds) *Behavior and the Natural Environment*, Volume 6. Plenum Press, New York, pp.269–306.

Catton, W.R. (1985) 'On the dire destiny of human lemmings', in M. Tobias (ed.) *Deep Ecology*. Avant Books, San Diego, pp.74–89.

Catton, W.R. (1987) 'The world's most polymorphic species: carrying capacity transgressed two ways', *BioScience*, 37: 413–19.

Catton, W.R. and Dunlap, R.E. (1980) 'A new ecological paradigm for post-exuberant sociology', *American Behavioral Scientist*, 24: 15–47.

Catton, W.R., Lenski, G. and Buttel, F.H. (1986) 'To what degree is a social system dependent on its resource base?', in J.F. Short (ed.) *The Social Fabric: Dimensions and Issues*. Sage Publications, Beverly Hills, pp.165–86.

Cawson, A. (1987a) 'Corporatism', in V. Bogdanor (ed.) *The Blackwell Encyclopaedia of Political Institutions*. Basil Blackwell, Oxford, pp.154–6.

Cawson, A. (1987b) 'Corporatism', in D. Miller, J. Coleman, W. Connolly and A. Ryan (eds) *The Blackwell Encyclopaedia of Political Thought*. Basil Blackwell, Oxford, pp.104–6.

Chandler, T.J. (1965) *The Climate of London*. Hutchinson, London.

Chisholm, M. (1962) *Rural Settlement and Land Use*. Hutchinson, London.

Chorley, R.J., Beckinsale, R.P. and Dunn, A.J. (1973) *The History of the Study of Landforms: Volume III The Life of William Morris Davis*. Methuen, London.

Chorley, R.J. and Kennedy, B.A. (1971) *Physical Geography: a Systems Approach*. Prentice-Kall, Englewood Cliffs, NJ.

Clark, A.H. (1949) *The Invasion of New Zealand by People, Plants and Animals*.

Rutgers University Press, New Brunswick, NJ.

Clark, G.L. (1982) 'Instrumental reason and policy analysis', in D.T. Herbert and R.J. Johnston (eds) *Geography and the Urban Environment*, Vol. 5. John Wiley, Chichester, Sussex, pp.41–62.

Clark, G.L. and Dear, M.J. (1984) *State Apparatus*. Allen and Unwin, Boston, MA.

Clingan, T.A. (1986) 'The United States and the Law of the Sea Conference', in G. Pontecorvo (ed.) *The New Order of the Oceans*. Columbia University Press, New York, pp.219–37.

Cooke, R.U. (1984) *Geomorphological Hazards in Los Angeles*. Allen and Unwin, London.

Cooke, R.U. and Reeves, R.W. (1976) *Arroyos and Environmental Change in the American South-West*. Clarendon Press, Oxford.

Cotsgrove, S. (1982) *Catastrophe or Cornucopia: the Environment and the Future*. John Wiley, Chichester.

Goulter, P. (1975) *Social Mobilization and Liberal Democracy*. Lexington Books, Lexington, Mass.

Council on Environmental Quality (1982) *The Global 2000 Report for the President*. Penguin Books, London.

Crocombe, R.G. (1972) 'Land tenure in the South Pacific', in R.G. Ward (ed.) *Man in the Pacific Islands*. Clarendon Press, Oxford, pp.219–51.

Crosby, A.W. (1986) *Ecological Imperialism: the Biological Expansion of Europe, 900–1900*. Cambridge University Press, Cambridge.

Crosland, C.A.R. (1956) *The Future of Socialism*. Jonathan Cape, London.

Cumberland, K.B. (1947) *Soil Erosion in New Zealand*. Whitcombe and Tombs, Christchurch.

Curry, L. (1962) 'Climatic change as a random series', *Annals of the Association of American Geographers*, 52: 21–31.

Dahl, R.A. (1978) 'Democracy as polyarchy', in R.D. Gastil (ed.) *Freedom in the World*. G.K. Hall, Boston, MA, pp.134–46.

Daly, H.E. (1977a) *Steady-State Economics*. W.H. Freeman, San Francisco.

Daly, H.E. (1977b) 'The steady-state economy: what, why and how', in D.C. Pirages (ed.) *The Sustainable Society*. Praeger, New York, pp.107–30.

Desai, M. (1983) 'Capitalism', in T. Bottomore, L. Harris, V.G. Kiernan and R. Miliband (eds) *A Dictionary of Marxist Thought*. Basil Blackwell, Oxford, pp.64–7.

Douglas, I. (1983) *The Urban Environment*. Edward Arnold, London.

Douglas, I. (1986) 'The unity of geography is obvious . . .' , *Transactions, Institute of British Geographers*, NS 11: 459–63.

Downs, A. (1957) *An Economic Theory of Democracy*. Harper and Row, New York.

Dryzek, J.A. (1987) *Rational Ecology*. Basil Blackwell, Oxford.

Dubs, M. (1986) 'Minerals of the deep sea: myth and reality', in G. Pontecorvo (ed.) *The New Order of the Oceans*. Columbia University Press, New York, pp.85–124.

Dufournaud, C. and Harrington, J. (1989) 'Temporal and spatial distribution of benefits and costs of basin schemes', *Environment and Planning A*, 22.

Duke of Edinburgh (1989) 'Living off the land', *The Listener*, 121 (issue no. 3104): 4–7.

Dunleavy, P. and Husbands, C.T. (1985) *British Democracy at the Crossroads*. Allen and Unwin, London.

Dunleavy, P. and O'Leary, B. (1987) *Theories of the State*. Macmillan, London.

Eyles, J. and Lee, R. (1982) 'Human geography in explanation', *Transactions, Institute of British Geographers*, NS 7: 117–22.

Falk, R.A. (1972) *This Endangered Planet*. Vintage Books, New York.
Ferejohn, J.A. (1974) *Pork-Barrel Politics*. Stanford University Press, Stanford, CA.
Fernie, J. and Pitkethly, A.S. (1985) *Resources: Environment and Policy*. Harper and Row, London.
Finley, N.I. (1983) 'Slavery', in T. Bottomore, L. Harris, V.G. Kiernan and R. Miliband (eds) *A Dictionary of Marxist Thought*. Basil Blackwell, Oxford, pp.440–1.
Frankel, B. (1987) *The Post-Industrial Utopians*. Polity Press, Cambridge.
Gardiner, V. (1990) 'Pollution of air, land, rivers and coasts', in R.J. Johnston and V. Gardiner (eds) *The Changing Geography of the United Kingdom* (2nd edn). Routledge, London.
Garner, J.F. and O'Riordan, T. (1982) 'Environmental impact at a time of financial restraint', *The Geographical Journal*, 148: 343–61.
Glacken, C.J. (1967) *Traces on the Rhodian Shore*. University of California Press, Berkeley.
Gleick, J. (1988) *Chaos: Making a New Science*. Cardinal Books, London.
Glick, T.C. (1987) 'History and philosophy of geography', *Progress in Human Geography*, 11: 405–16.
Goudie, A.S. (1986a) *The Human Impact on the Natural Environment* (2nd edn). Basil Blackwell, Oxford.
Goudie, A.S. (1986b) 'The integration of human and physical geography', *Transactions, Institute of British Geographers*, NS 11: 454–8.
Gould, P.C. (1988) *Early Green Politics*. Harvester Press, Brighton, Sussex.
Gould, P.R. (1963) 'Man against his environment: a game theoretic framework', *Annals of the Association of American Geographers*, 53: 290–7.
Gouldner, A. (1979) *The Future of Intellectuals and the Rise of the New Middle Class*. Macmillan, London.
Gregory, D. (1980) 'The ideology of control', *Tijdschrift voor Economische en Sociale Geografie*, 71, 327–42.
Gregory, K.J. (1985) *The Nature of Physical Geography*. Edward Arnold, London.
Griffiths, M.J. and Johnston, R.J. (1990) 'What's in a place?'
Grove, J.M. (1988) *The Little Ice Age*. Methuen, London.
Gudgin, G. and Taylor, P.J. (1980) *Seats, Votes and the Spatial Organisation of Elections*. Pion, London.
Gustafson, T. (1981) *Reform in Soviet Politics*. Cambridge University Press, Cambridge.
Haines-Young, R.H. and Petch, J.R. (1985) *Physical Geography: its Nature and Methods*. Harper and Row, London.
Hall, P. (1988) *Cities of Tomorrow*. Basil Blackwell, Oxford.
Hardin, G. (1968) 'The tragedy of the commons: The population problem has no technical solution; it requires a fundamental extension in morality', *Science*, 162: 1243–8.
Hardin, G. (1974) 'Living on a lifeboat', *Bioscience*, 24: 561–8.
Hare, F.K., Kates, R.W. and Warren, A. (1977) 'The making of deserts: climate, ecology and society', *Economic Geography*, 53: 332–46.
Harrop, M. and Miller, W.L. (1987) *Elections and Voters*. Macmillan, London.
Harvey, D. (1973) *Social Justice and the City*. Edward Arnold, London.
Harvey, D. (1974) 'Population, resources, and the ideology of science', *Economic Geography*, 50: 256–77.
Harvey, D. (1982) *The Limits to Capital*. Basil Blackwell, Oxford.
Harvey, D. (1985a) *The Urbanization of Capital*. Basil Blackwell, Oxford.
Harvey, D. (1985b) 'The geopolitics of capitalism', in D. Gregory and J. Urry (eds)

Social Relations and Spatial Structures. Macmillan, London, pp.128–63.

Hay, P.R. and Haward, M.G. (1988) 'Comparative green politics: beyond the European context?' *Political Studies*, 36: 433–48.

Hays, S.P. (1987) *Beauty, Health and Permanence: Environmental Politics in the United States, 1955-1985*. Cambridge University Press, Cambridge.

Hechter, M. (1975) *Internal Colonialism*. Routledge and Kegan Paul, London.

Hechter, M. and Brustein, W. (1980) 'Regional modes of production and patterns of state formation in Western Europe', *American Journal of Sociology*, 85: 1061–94.

Heilbroner, R.L. (1974) *An Inquiry into the Human Prospect*. Harper and Row, New York.

Hilton, R.H. (1983) 'Feudal society', in T. Bottomore, L. Harris, V.G. Kiernan and R. Miliband (eds) *A Dictionary of Marxist Thought*. Basil Blackwell, Oxford, pp.166–71.

Hirsch, F. (1977) *Social Limits to Growth*. Routledge and Kegan Paul, London.

Hobbes, T. (1968) *Leviathan*. Penguin Books, London.

Hodge, D. and Staeheli, L.A. (1989) 'Social transformation and changing urban electoral behaviour', in R.J. Johnston, F.M. Shelley and P.J. Taylor (eds) *Developments in Electoral Geography*. Routledge, London.

Huggett, R.J. (1980) *Systems Analysis in Geography*. Clarendon Press, Oxford.

Hulme, M. (1989) 'Is environmental degradation causing drought in the Sahel?' *Geography*, 74: 38–46.

Ionescu, G. (1975) *Centripetal Politics*. Hart-Davies, London.

Johnston, R.J. (1979a) *Political, Electoral and Spatial Systems*. Oxford University Press, Oxford.

Johnston, R.J. (1979b) *Geography and Geographers: Anglo-American Human Geography since 1945*. Edward Arnold, London.

Johnston, R.J. (1980a) *The Geography of Federal Spending in the United States of America* . John Wiley, Chichester, Sussex.

Johnston, R.J. (1980b) 'On the nature of explanation in human geography', *Transactions, Institute of British Geographers*, NS 5: 402–12.

Johnston, R.J. (1982a) *Geography and the State*. Macmillan, London.

Johnston, R.J. (1982b) 'On the nature of human geography', *Transactions, Institute of British Geographers*, NS 7: 123–5.

Johnston, R.J. (1982c) 'Political geography and political power', in M.J. Holler (ed) *Power, Voting and Voting Power*. Physica-Verlag, Vienna, pp.289–306.

Johnston, R.J. (1983) 'Resource analysis, resource management and the integration of physical and human geography', *Progress in Physical Geography*, 7: 127–46.

Johnston, R.J. (1984) *Residential Segregation, the State and Constitutional Conflict in American Urban Areas*. Academic Press, London.

Johnston, R.J. (1986a) *On Human Geography*. Basil Blackwell, Oxford.

Johnston, R.J. (1986b) 'The state, the region and the division of labor', in A.J. Scott and M. Storper (eds) *Production, Work, Territory*. Allen Unwin, Boston, MA, pp.265–80.

Johnston, R.J. (1986c) 'Four fixations and the unity of geography', *Transactions, Institute of British Geographers*, NS 11: 449–53.

Johnston, R.J. (1988) 'There's a place for us', *New Zealand Geographer*, 44: 8–13.

Johnston, R.J. (1989) 'The individual in the world-economy', in R.J. Johnston and P.J. Taylor (eds) *A World in Crisis?* (2nd edn). Basil Blackwell, Oxford, pp.200–28.

Johnston, R.J. and Honey, R.D. (1988) 'Political geography of contemporary events X: the 1987 general election in New Zealand', *Political Geography Quarterly*, 7: 363–9.

Johnston, R.J., O'Loughlin, J. and Taylor, P.J. (1987) 'The geography of violence and premature death', in R. Vayrynen (ed) *The Quest for Peace*. Sage Publications, London, pp.241–59.

Johnston, R.J. and Pattie, C.J. (1989) 'A nation dividing? Economic well-being, voter response and the changing electoral geography of Great Britain', *Parliamentary Affairs*, 42: 37–57.

Johnston, R.J., Pattie, C.J. and Allsopp, J.G. (1988) *A Nation Dividing?*. Longman, London.

Jones, D.K.C. (1983) 'Environments of concern', *Transactions, Institute of British Geographers*, NS 8: 429–57.

Jones, D.K.C. (1990) 'Human occupance and the physical environment', in R.J. Johnston and V. Gardiner (eds) *The Changing Geography of the United Kingdom* (2nd edn). Routledge, London.

Kennedy, P.M. (1988) *The Rise and Fall of the Great Powers*. Unwin Hyman, London.

Kneese, A.V. (1964) *The Economics of Regional Water Quality*. Johns Hopkins University Press, Baltimore, MD.

Kneese, A.V. and Bower, B.T. (1968) *Managing Water Quality*. Johns Hopkins University Press, Baltimore, MD.

Kolakowski, L. (1978) *Main Currents of Marxist Thought* (3 vols). Oxford University Press, Oxford.

Komarov, B. (1981) *The Destruction of Nature in the Soviet Union*. Pluto Press, London.

Lamprey, H. (1978) 'The integrated project on arid lands', *Nature and Resources*, 14: 2–11.

Landsberg, H.H. (1981) *The Urban Climate*. Academic Press, New York.

Lash, S. and Urry, J. (1987) *The End of Organized Capitalism*. Polity Press, Cambridge.

Laver, M. (1981) *The Politics of Private Desires*. Penguin Books, London.

Laver, M. (1984) 'The politics of inner space: tragedies of three commons', *European Journal of Political Research*, 12: 59–71.

Laver, M. (1986) 'Public, private and common in outer space', *Political Studies*, 34: 359–73.

Lawson, S. (1988) 'Fiji's communal electoral system', *Politics*, 23 (2): 35–47.

Lee, E.C. (1978) 'California', in D. Butler and A. Ranney (eds) *Referendums*. American Enterprise Institute, Washington, pp.87–122.

le Marquand, D. (1986) 'Pre-conditions to cooperation in Canada – U.S. boundary waters', *Natural Resources Journal*, 26: 221–42.

Lipset, S.M. and Rokkan, S.E. (1967) 'Cleavage structures, party systems and voter alignments: an introduction', in S.M. Lipset and S.E. Rokkan (eds) *Party Systems and Voter Alignments*. The Free Press, New York, pp.3–64.

Lloyd, W.F. (1833) *Two Lectures on the Checks to Population*. Oxford University Press, Oxford.

Lorens, E.N. (1963) 'Deterministic non-periodic flow', *Journal of the Atmospheric Sciences*, 20: 130–41.

Lovelock, J. (1988) *The Ages of Gaia: a Biography of Our Living Earth*. Oxford University Press, New York.

Lowe, P. and Goyder, J. (1983) *Environmental Groups in Politics*. Allen and Unwin, London.

Lowenthal, D. (ed.) (1965) *George Perkins Marsh: Man and Nature*. Harvard University Press, Cambridge MA.

McCaskill, L. (1969) *Molesworth*. A.H. and A.W. Reed, Wellington.

McCaskill, L. (1973) *Hold this Land: a History of Soil Conservation in New Zealand*. A.H. and A.W. Reed, Wellington.

Macpherson, C.B. (1968) 'Introduction' to T. Hobbes, *Leviathan*. Penguin Books, London, pp.9–63.

Mann, M. (1984) 'The autonomous power of the state', *European Journal of Sociology*, 25: 185–213.

Mann, M. (1986) *The Sources of Social Power*. Cambridge University Press, Cambridge.

Markusen, A. (1985) *Profit Cycles, Oligopoly and Regional Development*. MIT Press, Cambridge, MA.

Marx, K. (1977) *Capital* (Vol. 1). Lawrence and Wishart, London.

May, R.J. (1976) 'Simple mathematical models with very complicated dynamics', *Nature*, 261: 459–67.

Meadows, D.H., Meadows, D.L., Randers, J. and Behrens, W.W. (1972) *The Limits to Growth*. Universe Books, New York.

Meinig, D.W. (1962) *On the Margins of the Good Earth*. Rand McNally, Chicago.

Middlemass, K. (1979) *Politics in Industrial Society*. André Deutsch, London.

Mikesell, M.W. (1969) 'The deforestation of Mount Lebanon', *Geographical Review*, 59: 1–28.

Milner, C. (1972) 'The use of computer simulation in conservation management', in J.N.R. Jeffers (ed.) *Mathematical Models in Ecology*. Basil Blackwell, Oxford, pp.249–75.

More, R.J. (1967) 'Hydrological models and geography', in R.J. Chorley and P. Haggett (eds) *Models in Geography*. Methuen, London, pp.145–85.

O'Connor, J. (1972) *The Fiscal Crisis of the State*. St Martin's Press, New York.

O'Connor, J. (1989) 'Uneven and combined development and ecological crisis', *Race and Class*, 30 (3): 1–11.

Odell, P.R. (1989) 'Draining the world of energy', in R.J. Johnston and P.J. Taylor (eds) *A World in Crisis?* (2nd edn). Basil Blackwell, Oxford, pp.79–100.

O'Loughlin, J, and Parker, A.J. (1989) 'Tradition contra change: the political geography of Irish referenda', in R.J. Johnston, F.M. Shelley and P.J. Taylor (eds) *Developments in Electoral Geography*. Routledge, London.

Olson, M. (1965) *The Logic of Collective Action*. Harvard University Press, Cambridge, MA.

Openshaw, S., Steadman, P. and Greene, O. (1983) *Domesday*. Basil Blackwell, Oxford.

O'Riordan, T. (1981a) *Environmentalism*. Pion, London.

O'Riordan, T. (1981b) 'Environmentalism and education', *Journal of Geography in Higher Education*, 5: 3–18.

O'Riordan, T. (1987) 'The public and nuclear matters', in N. Geary (ed.) *Nuclear Technology International*. Sterling Publications, London, pp.257–63.

O'Riordan, T. (1989) 'The politics of sustainability', in R.K. Turner (ed.) *Sustainable Environmental Development*. Belhaven Press, London, pp.29–50.

O'Riordan, T. and Kemp, R. (1988) *Sizewell B: Anatomy of an Inquiry*. Macmillan, London.

O'Sullivan, N. (1988) 'The political theory of neo-corporatism', in A. Cox and N. O'Sullivan (eds) *The Corporate State*. Edward Elgar, London, pp.3–26.

Owens, S. (1986) 'Environmental politics in Britain: new paradigm or placebo?' *Area*, 18: 195–201.

Packard, V. (1961) *The Waste Makers*. Longman, London.

Pahl, R.E. (1985) *Divisions of Labour*. Basil Blackwell, Oxford.

Papadakis, E. (1988) 'Social movements, self-limiting radicalism and the Green

Party in West Germany', *Sociology*, 22: 433–54.

Park, C.C. (1987) *Acid Rain: Rhetoric and Reality*. Methuen, London.

Peet, J.R. (1969) 'The spatial expansion of commercial agriculture in the nineteenth century', *Economic Geography*, 45: 283–301.

Pepper, D. (1984) *The Roots of Modern Environmentalism*. Croom Helm, London.

Pepper, D. (1985) 'Determinism, idealism and the politics of environmentalism – a viewpoint', *International Journal of Environmental Studies*, 26: 11–19.

Pepper, D. (1986) 'Radical environmentalism and the labour movement', in J. Weston (ed.) *Red and Green: the New Politics of the Environment*. Pluto Press, London, pp.115–39.

Perry, A.H. (1981) *Environmental Hazards in the British Isles*. Allen and Unwin, London.

Pirages, D.C. and Ehrlich, P.R. (1974) *Ark II: Social Response to Environmental Imperatives*. W.H. Freeman, San Francisco.

Plotkin, S. (1987) *Keep Out: the Struggle for Land Use Control*. University of California Press, Berkeley.

Polanyi, K. (1971) *Primitive, Archaic and Modern Economies: Essays of Karl Polyanyi* (edited by G. Dalton). Beacon Press, Boston, MA.

Porritt, J. and Winner, D. (1988) *The Coming of the Greens*. Collins Fontana, London.

Postan, M.M. (1973) *Essays on Medieval Agriculture and General Problems of the Medieval Economy*. Cambridge University Press, Cambridge.

Powell, J.M. (1970) *The Public Lands of Australia Felix*. Oxford University Press, Melbourne.

Powell, J.M. (1977) *Mirrors of the New World*. Dawson, Folkestone, Kent.

Prescott, J.R.V. (1985) *The Maritime Political Boundaries of the World*. Methuen, London

Rae, D.W. (1971) *The Political Consequences of Electoral Laws*. Yale University Press, New Haven, CT.

Ranney, A. (1978) 'United States of America', in D. Butler and A. Ranney (eds) *Referendums*. American Enterprise Institute, Washington, pp.67–86.

Rawls, J. (1971) *A Theory of Justice*. Harvard University Press, Cambridge, MA.

Redclift, M. (1984) *Development and the Environmental Crisis*. Methuen, London.

Redclift, M. (1987) *Sustainable Development: Exploring the Contradictions*. Methuen, London.

Rees, J. (1985) *Natural Resources: Allocation, Economics and Policy*. Methuen, London.

Roberts, R.S., Ufkes, F., and Shelley, F.M. (1989) 'Populism and agrarian ideology: the 1982 Nebraska corporate farming referendum', in R.J. Johnston, F.M. Shelley and P.J. Taylor, (eds) *Developments in Electoral Geography*. Routledge, London.

Rostow, W.W. (1971) *The Stages of Economic Growth*. Cambridge University Press, Cambridge.

Rudig, W. and Lowe, P. (1986) 'The 'withered' greening of British politics: a study of the Ecology Party', *Political Studies*, 34: 262–84.

Rykiel, E.J. and Kuenzel, N.T. (1971) 'Analog computer models of 'The wolves of Isle Royale', in B.C. Patten (ed.) *Systems Analysis and Simulation in Ecology*, Vol. 1. Academic Press, London, pp.513–41.

Sack, R.D. (1983) 'Human territoriality: a theory', *Annals of the Association of American Geographers*, 73: 55–74.

Sagoff, M. (1988) *The Economy of the Earth: Philosophy, Law and the Environment*. Cambridge University Press, Cambridge.

Sarlvik, B. and Crewe, I. (1983) *Decade of Dealignment*. Cambridge University Press, Cambridge.

Schachter, O. (1986) 'Concepts and realities in the new Law of the Sea', in G. Pontecorvo (ed.) *The New Order of the Oceans*. Columbia University Press, New York, pp.29–59.

Schumacher, E.F. (1973) *Small is Beautiful*. Harper Torchbooks, New York.

Scott, A.J. (1988) *Metropolis*. University of California Press, Los Angeles.

Sewell, W.R.D. and Utton, A.E. (1986) 'Getting to yes in United States – Canadian water disputes', *Natural Resources Journal*, 26: 213–20.

Shaw, B.D. (1981) 'Climate, environment and history: the case of Roman North Africa', in T.M.L. Wigley, M.J. Ingram and G. Farmer (eds) *Climate and History*. Cambridge University Press, Cambridge, pp.379–403.

Sheail, J. (1976) *Nature in Trust*. Blackie, Glasgow.

Sheail, J. (1981) *Rural Conservation in Inter-War Britain*. Clarendon Press, Oxford.

Short, J.R. (1988a) 'Construction workers and the city 1. Analysis', *Environment and Planning A*, 20: 719–32.

Short, J.R. (1988b) 'Construction workers and the city 2. An interview with Jack Mundey', *Environment and Planning A*, 20: 733–40.

Simon, J.L. and Kahn, H. 1984: *The Resourceful Earth – a Response to Global 2000*. Basil Blackwell, Oxford.

Smil, V. (1987) 'Land degradation in China', in P. Blaikie and H. Brookfield, *Land Degradation and Society*. Methuen, London, pp.214–22.

Spoehr, A. (1956) 'Cultural differences in the interpretation of natural resources', in W.L. Thomas (ed.) *Man's Role in Changing the Face of the Earth*. University of Chicago Press, Chicago, pp.93–102.

Stoddart, D.R. (1987) 'To claim the high ground', *Transactions, Institute of British Geographers*, NS 12: 327–36.

Swann, J.F. (1966) 'Acclimatisation of animals', *Encyclopaedia of New Zealand* (Vol. 1). Government Printer, Wellington, pp.2–5.

Taylor, M. (1976) *Anarchy and Cooperation*. John Wiley, Chichester, Sussex.

Taylor, M. (1988) *The Possibility of Cooperation*. Cambridge University Press, Cambridge.

Taylor, M. and Ward, H. (1982) 'Chickens, whales and lumpy goods', *Political Studies*, 30: 350–70.

Taylor, P.J. (1989a) *Political Geography* (2nd edn). Longman, London.

Taylor, P.J. (1989b) 'The error of developmentalism', in D. Gregory and R. Walford (eds) *Horizons in Human Geography*. Macmillan, London, pp.303–19.

Taylor, P.J. (1989c) 'Extending the world of electoral geography', in R.J. Johnston, F.M. Shelley and P.J. Taylor (eds) *Developments in Electoral Geography*. Routledge, London.

Taylor, P.J. and Johnston, R.J. (1979) *Geography of Elections*. Penguin Books, London.

Thomas, K. (1984) *Man and the Natural World*. Penguin Books, London.

Thompson, C. (1989) 'The geography of venture capital', *Progress in Human Geography*, 13: 62–98.

Thornes, J.B. (1987) 'Environmental systems', in M.J. Clark, K.J. Gregory and A.M. Gurnell (eds) *Horizons in Physical Geography*. Macmillan, London, pp.27–46.

Thrift, N.J. (1989) 'The geography of international economic disorder', in R.J. Johnston and P.J. Taylor (eds) *A World in Crisis?* (2nd edn). Basil Blackwell, Oxford, pp.16–78.

Todd, E. (1985) *The Explanation of Ideology: Family Structures and Social Systems*.

Basil Blackwell, Oxford.

Todd, E. (1987) *The Cause of Progress: Culture, Authority and Change*. Basil Blackwell, Oxford.

Trudgill, S.T. (1988) *Soil and Vegetation Systems* (2nd edn). Clarendon Press, Oxford.

Urry, J. (1981) *The Anatomy of Capitalist Societies*. Macmillan, London.

Walker, R.A. and Williams, M.J. (1982) 'Water from power: water supply and regional growth in the Santa Clara Valley', *Economic Geography*, 58: 95–119.

Ward, H. (1987) 'The risks of a reputation for toughness', *British Journal of Political Science*, 17: 23–52.

Watts, M. (1983) *Silent Violence*. University of California Press, Berkeley.

Watts, M. (1989) 'The agrarian question in Africa', *Progress in Human Geography*, 13: 1–41.

Weatherford, M.S. (1986) 'Economic determinants of voting', in S. Long (ed.) *Research in Micro-Politics Volume 1*. Greenwood Press, New York, pp.219–69.

Wescoat, J.L. (1985) 'On water conservation and reform of the prior appropriation doctrine in Colorado', *Economic Geography*, 61: 3–24.

Whatmore, S., Munton, R., Little, J. and Marsden, T. (1987a) 'Towards a typology of farm businesses in contemporary British agriculture', *Sociologia Ruralis*, 27: 21–37.

Whatmore, S., Munton, R., Little, J. and Marsden, T. (1987b) 'Interpreting a relational typology of farm businesses in southern England', *Sociologia Ruralis*, 27: 103–22.

Wheatley, P. (1971) *The Pivot of the Four Quarters*. Aldine Press, Chicago.

White, G.F., Kates. R.W. and Warren, A. (1977) 'The making of deserts: climate, ecology and society', *Economic Geography*, 53: 332–46.

Williams, M. (1989) 'Deforestation: past and present', *Progress in Human Geography*, 13.

Williams, W.T. (1963) 'The social study of family farming', *The Geographical Journal*, 129: 63–74.

Wilson, A.G. (1981a) *Geography and the Environment: Systems Analytical Methods*. John Wiley, Chichester, Sussex.

Wilson, A.G. (1981b) *Catastrophe Theory and Bifurcation*. Croom Helm, London.

Wilson, A.G. (1986) 'Bifurcation', in R.J. Johnston, D. Gregory and D.M. Smith (eds) *The Dictionary of Human Geography* (2nd edn). Basil Blackwell, Oxford, pp.31–2.

Witt, E. (1979) *Guide to the U.S. Supreme Court*. Congressional Quarterly Inc., Washington.

Wittfogel, K.A. (1956) 'The hydraulic civilizations', in W.L. Thomas (ed.) *Man's Role in Changing the Face of the Earth*. University of Chicago Press, Chicago, pp.152–64.

Wittfogel, K.A. (1957) *Oriental Despotism*. Yale University Press, New Haven, CT.

Woods, R.I. (1989) 'Malthus, Marx and population crises', R.J. Johnston and P.J. Taylor (eds) *A World in Crisis?* (2nd edn) Basil Blackwell, Oxford, pp.151–74.

Worster, D. (1979) *Dust Bowl*. Oxford University Press, New York.

Index